W9-BPJ-664

William Miller, PhD, MLS
Rita M. Pellen, MLS
Editors

Libraries Within Their Institutions: Creative Collaborations

Libraries Within Their Institutions: Creative Collaborations has been co-published simultaneously as *Resource Sharing & Information Networks*, Volume 17, Numbers 1/2 2004.

Pre-publication REVIEWS, COMMENTARIES, EVALUATIONS . . .

"This is a work for library managers, administrators, and educational leaders interested in developing collaborative initiatives. Miller and Pellen compile a balanced blend of theory and actual applications by library leaders from across the United States. The book provides descriptions of practical campus-wide literacy committees, new space designs for collaborative services, and chapters on program assessment, planning, and evaluation."

Barbara J. Stites, MLS
Executive Director
Southwest Florida Library Network

The Haworth Information Press®
An Imprint of The Haworth Press, Inc.

Libraries
Within Their Institutions:
Creative Collaborations

Libraries Within Their Institutions: Creative Collaborations has been co-published simultaneously as *Resource Sharing & Information Networks*, Volume 17, Numbers 1/2 2004.

Monographic Separates from *Resource Sharing & Information Networks*™

For additional information on these and other Haworth Press titles, including descriptions, tables of contents, reviews, and prices, use the QuickSearch catalog at http://www.HaworthPress.com.

Libraries Within Their Institutions: Creative Collaborations, edited by William Miller and Rita M. Pellen (Vol. 17, No. 1/2, 2004). *A guide to the wide variety of partnerships between academic libraries and other areas within their own institutions.*

Cooperative Efforts of Libraries, edited by William Miller and Rita M. Pellen (Vol. 16, No. 1/2, 2002). *Explores a wide variety of cooperative initiatives at regional, statewide, and international levels.*

Joint-Use Libraries, edited by William Miller and Rita M. Pellen (Vol. 15, No. 1/2, 2001). *Presents nine examples of situations in which libraries of different types share a building.*

Networks and Resource Sharing in the 21st Century: Re-Engineering the Information Landscape, edited by Mary Huston-Somerville and Catherine C. Wilt (Vol. 10, No. 1/2, 1995). *"Enlightening and portends things to come for those who do not step up and embrace the new electronic information technology as an important business tool." (Bimonthly Review of Law Books)*

Impact of Technology on Resource Sharing: Experimentation and Maturity, edited by Thomas C. Wilson (Vol. 8, No. 1, 1993). *"A refreshing expansive view of library resource sharing." (Special Libraries)*

Periodicals Circulation Statistics at a Mid-Sized Academic Library: Implications for Collection Management, edited by John A. Whisler (Vol. 5, No. 1/2, 1990). *Providing an indication of the relative use of journals in an average academic library, this book will help serials and collection development librarians who must decide to which titles their library will subscribe and how those titles will be maintained in their collections.*

The Public Library in the Bibliographic Network, edited by Betty J. Turock (Vol. 3, No. 2, 1987). *Learn the facts about joining a bibliographic network and the effects that participation can have on your public library's operation.*

Coordinating Cooperative Collection Development: A National Perspective, edited by Wilson Luquire (Vol. 2, No. 3/4, 1986). *"A wealth of interesting and useful information, as well as a smattering of knowledge and even wisdom." (Newsletter of Reference and Adult Services Division, American Library Association)*

Experiences of Library Network Administrators: Papers Based on the Symposium "From Our Past: Toward 2000," edited by Wilson Luquire (Vol. 2, No. 1/2, 1985). *Network administrators describe the origin, history, and process of their organizations.*

Library Networking: Current Problems and Future Prospects, edited by Wilson Luquire (Vol. 1, No. 1/2, 1983). *"Compulsive reading. Highly recommended." (Library Review)*

Libraries
Within Their Institutions:
Creative Collaborations

William Miller
Rita M. Pellen
Editors

Libraries Within Their Institutions: Creative Collaborations has been co-published simultaneously as *Resource Sharing & Information Networks*, Volume 17, Numbers 1/2 2004.

The Haworth Information Press®
An Imprint of The Haworth Press, Inc.

New York • London • Victoria (AU)
www.HaworthPress.com

Published by

The Haworth Information Press®, 10 Alice Street, Binghamton, NY 13904-1580 USA

The Haworth Information Press® is an imprint of The Haworth Press, Inc., 10 Alice Street, Binghamtom, NY 13904-1580 USA.

Libraries Within Their Institutions: Creative Collaborations has been co-published simultaneously as *Resource Sharing & Information Networks*™, Volume 17, Numbers 1/2 2004.

Cover design by Lora Wiggins.

Library of Congress Cataloging-in-Publication Data

Libraries within their institutions : creative collaborations / William Miller, Rita M. Pellen, editors.
    p. cm.
    "Co-published simultaneously as Resource sharing & information networks, volume 17, numbers 1/2, 2004."
    Includes bibliographical references and index.
    ISBN-13: 978-0-7890-2719-1 (hc. : alk. paper)
    ISBN-10: 0-7890-2719-4 (hc. : alk. paper)
    ISBN-13: 978-0-7890-2720-7 (pbk. : alk. paper)
    ISBN-10: 0-7890-2720-8 (pbk. : alk. paper)
    1. Libraries and colleges–United States. 2. Libraries and institutions–United States. 3. Academic libraries–Relations with faculty and curriculum–United States. 4. Information literacy–United States. I. Miller, William, 1947- II. Pellen, Rita M. III. Resource sharing & information networks.
Z718 .L49 2005
027.7–dc22
                                                                        2004030052

Indexing, Abstracting & Website/Internet Coverage

This section provides you with a list of major indexing & abstracting services and other tools for bibliographic access. That is to say, each service began covering this periodical during the year noted in the right column. Most Websites which are listed below have indicated that they will either post, disseminate, compile, archive, cite or alert their own Website users with research-based content from this work. (This list is as current as the copyright date of this publication.)

Abstracting, Website/Indexing Coverage . . . . Year When Coverage Began

- *AATA Online: Abstracts of International Conservation Literature (formerly Art & Archeology Technical Abstracts) <http://aata.getty.edu>* 2004

- *Academic Abstracts/CD-ROM* 1995

- *Academic Search: database of 2,000 selected academic serials, updated monthly: EBSCO Publishing* 1996

- *Academic Search Elite (EBSCO)* 1996

- *Academic Search Premier (EBSCO) <http://www.epnet.com/academic/acasearchprem.asp>* 1995

- *ACM Guide to Computer Literature <http://www.acm.org>* 1985

- *Business Source Corporate: coverage of nearly 3,350 quality magazines and journals; designed to meet the diverse information needs of corporations; EBSCO Publishing <http://www.epnet.com/corporate/bsourcecorp.asp>* 1995

- *Cambridge Scientific Abstracts is a leading publisher of scientific information in print journals, online databases, CD-ROM and via the Internet <http://www.csa.com>* 1989

(continued)

(continued)

(continued)

Special Bibliographic Notes related to special journal issues
(separates) and indexing/abstracting:

- indexing/abstracting services in this list will also cover material in any "separate" that is co-published simultaneously with Haworth's special thematic journal issue or DocuSerial. Indexing/abstracting usually covers material at the article/chapter level.
- monographic co-editions are intended for either non-subscribers or libraries which intend to purchase a second copy for their circulating collections.
- monographic co-editions are reported to all jobbers/wholesalers/approval plans. The source journal is listed as the "series" to assist the prevention of duplicate purchasing in the same manner utilized for books-in-series.
- to facilitate user/access services all indexing/abstracting services are encouraged to utilize the co-indexing entry note indicated at the bottom of the first page of each article/chapter/contribution.
- this is intended to assist a library user of any reference tool (whether print, electronic, online, or CD-ROM) to locate the monographic version if the library has purchased this version but not a subscription to the source journal.
- individual articles/chapters in any Haworth publication are also available through the Haworth Document Delivery Service (HDDS).

Libraries
Within Their Institutions:
Creative Collaborations

CONTENTS

ABOUT THE EDITORS

William Miller, PhD, MLS, is Director of Libraries at Florida Atlantic University in Boca Raton. He formerly served as Head of Reference at Michigan State University in East Lansing, and as Associate Dean of Libraries at Bowling Green State University in Ohio. Dr. Miller is past President of the Association of College and Research Libraries, has served as Chair of the *Choice* magazine editorial board, and is a contributing editor of *Library Issues*. He was named Instruction Librarian of the Year in 2004 by the Association of College and Research Libraries Instruction Section.

Rita M. Pellen, MLS, is Associate Director of Libraries at Florida Atlantic University in Boca Raton. She was formerly Assistant Director of Public Services and Head of the Reference Department at Florida Atlantic. In 1993, Ms. Pellen received the Gabor Exemplary Employee Award in recognition for outstanding service to FAU, and in 1997, the "Literati Club Award for Excellence" for the outstanding paper presented in *The Bottom Line*. She has served on committees in LAMA, ACRL, and ALCTS, as well as the Southeast Florida Library Information Network, SEFLIN, a multi-type library cooperative in South Florida. Honor society memberships include Beta Phi Mu and Phi Kappa Phi.

Introduction:
Cooperation Within Institutions

For this volume, we wanted to discover the variety of ways in which libraries cooperate with non-library entities within their own institutions; such cooperation involves work with faculty members, city governments, information technology departments, and research institutes. It is the rare library that exists in a vacuum; most are part of a system, such as a university or a municipality, and all libraries exist in a broader societal context which requires interaction and cooperative activity. In order to best serve those who need them, libraries must cooperate widely with entities other than themselves.

Within academic institutions, it is not surprising that the faculty are the group with which librarians seek cooperation most often. Several articles in this volume highlight those efforts.

Barbara Dewey discusses the concept of the embedded librarian, placing librarians in a variety of other campus settings such as writing centers or teaching excellence centers, as well as in academic departments to enhance support for teaching, learning, and research. Deborah Huerta and Victoria McMillan discuss team-teaching both introductory and advanced courses on scientific writing, which produces a synergy that greatly improves the quality of the writing. Joni Warner and Nancy Seamans focus on collaboration with campus teaching centers as a way to improve instruction, with benefits for both sides.

Alexius Macklin and Michael Fosmire discuss the integration of information literacy into an academic curriculum by cooperating with faculty. They discuss implementing the ACRL core competencies for information literacy directly into course content. Margaret Maurer and Don Wicks discuss cooperation between the School of Library and Information Science and the Libraries

[Haworth co-indexing entry note]: "Introduction: Cooperation Within Libraries." Miller, William. Co-published simultaneously in *Resource Sharing & Information Networks* (The Haworth Information Press, an imprint of The Haworth Press, Inc.) Vol. 17, No. 1/2, 2004, pp. 1-3; and: *Libraries Within Their Institutions: Creative Collaborations* (ed: William Miller, and Rita M. Pellen) The Haworth Information Press, an imprint of The Haworth Press, Inc., 2004, pp. 1-3. Single or multiple copies of this article are available for a fee from The Haworth Document Delivery Service [1-800-HAWORTH, 9:00 a.m. - 5:00 p.m. (EST). E-mail address: docdelivery@haworthpress.com].

http://www.haworthpress.com/web/RSIN
Digital Object Identifier: 10.1300/J121v17n01_01

at Kent State, in the area of collection management. This is, again, a symbiotic relationship in which the school provides enhanced course work while the Libraries provide the practical experience students crave.

Melissa Moore discusses the need to take a long-term perspective on librarian-faculty cooperation, which she says should be built on deep personal relationships. Jordana Shane discusses the creation of a campus-wide information literacy initiative as an opportunity to "travel across literal and figurative boundaries, going wherever necessary to get the job done," and she discusses the qualities necessary for successful implementation of such a cooperative program. Trudi Jacobson and Carol Germain discuss the impact of a campus-wide information literacy committee in helping faculty to meet accrediting agency requirements and design their courses to enhance instruction.

Faculty members, however, are by no means the only group with which librarians cooperate within their institutions. Academic librarians, Juliet Boisselle, Susan Fliss, Lori Mestre, and Fred Zinn discuss a Mellon Foundation-funded workshop entitled "Talking Toward Techno-Pedagogy," which involved not only librarians and faculty, but also students and instructional technologists at ten small colleges and larger institutions. The workshops were designed to help infuse technology and information literacy into the curricula. The result has been much-increased collaboration between faculty, librarians, IT staff, staff of teaching excellence centers, and students.

Jill McKinstry discusses a partnership at the University of Washington with the Office of Undergraduate Education, and Computing & Communications, to turn the undergraduate library into a "collaboratory" and a facility focused on fluency in all areas of information technology and information literacy. Joan Lippincott discusses the creation of collaborative facilities based in libraries but in concert with other entities; these would include information commons, teaching and learning centers, and multi-media studios.

Gail McMillan discusses cooperative efforts among the library, graduate school, computer services department, and technology department at Virginia Tech to preserve electronic theses and dissertations. Andrew Adaryukov discusses a cooperative digitization project involving an academic department, a statewide digitization project, and work with donors. Christie Flynn, Debra Gilchrist, and Lynn Olson discuss using assessment as a tool for collaboration. They comment that "writing outcomes, developing assessment methods for instruction, services, and facilities, and analyzing assessment results are all partnership activities, calling on our ability to work together . . . throughout the institution."

Our previous volume, *Joint-Use Libraries* (New York: The Haworth, Press, Inc., 2001) explored the general topic of institutions cooperating with each other to create libraries jointly; most of these involve universities cooperating with community colleges, public libraries cooperating with academic institutions, public libraries cooperating with K-12 schools, and a variety of tripartite arrangements, also. That volume featured an article on the new joint library run by San José State University and the City of San José. In this volume, we feature an article on the technological aspects required to establish that joint-use library. Richard Woods writes about the choice of an online system for the new, merged library, and about co-managing IT staffing and services, including the challenges of working with the bureaucracies of a university and a municipality.

It is a tribute to librarians everywhere that they so often reach out to work with others within their overall institutions. In a forthcoming companion volume, we will also explore cooperative efforts of libraries with entities outside of their immediate institutions. These efforts, taken as a whole, illustrate the remarkable range of cooperative endeavor which derives, ultimately, from the service orientation that characterizes our profession, and marks it as significantly different from so many others.

William Miller
Director of Libraries
Florida Atlantic University

The Embedded Librarian:
Strategic Campus Collaborations

Barbara I. Dewey

SUMMARY. Librarians play a central role in advancing colleges' and universities' strategic priorities through constant collaboration. Embedding oneself at as many venues as possible will ensure that library staff, collections, and services are more fully integrated into all aspects of campus life. Participation by librarians helps the campus move forward because of their uniquely broad perspective and general point of view. *[Article copies available for a fee from The Haworth Document Delivery Service: 1-800-HAWORTH. E-mail address: <docdelivery@haworthpress.com> Website: <http://www.HaworthPress.com> © 2004 by The Haworth Press, Inc. All rights reserved.]*

KEYWORDS. Bibliographic instruction/college and university students, college and university libraries/relations with faculty and curriculum, embedded librarian, library collaboration

INTRODUCTION

The metaphor of "embedded librarian" is inspired by the recent phenomenon of embedding journalists into various military sectors during the Iraq war

Barbara I. Dewey is Dean of Libraries, University of Tennessee, Knoxville, TN 37996 (E-mail: bdewey@utk.edu).

[Haworth co-indexing entry note]: "The Embedded Librarian: Strategic Campus Collaborations." Dewey, Barbara I. Co-published simultaneously in *Resource Sharing & Information Networks* (The Haworth Information Press, an imprint of The Haworth Press, Inc.) Vol. 17, No. 1/2, 2004, pp. 5-17; and: *Libraries Within Their Institutions: Creative Collaborations* (ed: William Miller, and Rita M. Pellen) The Haworth Information Press, an imprint of The Haworth Press, Inc., 2004, pp. 5-17. Single or multiple copies of this article are available for a fee from The Haworth Document Delivery Service [1-800-HAWORTH, 9:00 a.m. - 5:00 p.m. (EST). E-mail address: docdelivery@haworthpress.com].

http://www.haworthpress.com/web/RSIN
© 2004 by The Haworth Press, Inc. All rights reserved.
Digital Object Identifier: 10.1300/J121v17n01_02

and its aftermath. The concept of embedding implies a more comprehensive integration of one group with another to the extent that the group seeking to integrate is experiencing and observing, as nearly as possible, the daily life of the primary group. Embedding requires more direct and purposeful interaction than acting in parallel with another person, group, or activity. Overt purposefulness makes embedding an appropriate definition of the most comprehensive collaborations for librarians in the higher education community.

This paper focuses on the imperative for academic librarians to become embedded in the priorities of teaching, learning, and research in truly relevant ways. Embedding as an effective mode of collaboration will be explored through examples relating to the physical and virtual environment. An analysis of current approaches and next steps for the future will be addressed, with the goal of providing food for thought as librarians assess programs and activities in terms of positive collaboration and effectiveness.

LIBRARIANS AND COLLABORATIVE CAMPUS SPACES

Is the library as a physical space relevant to the embedded librarian concept? Traditionally, we assumed that people will come to the library as a distinct and identifiable space. Rules of engagement for the library as a location imply the need for students and faculty to enter and use the facility under the librarian's terms. Interestingly, this was not always the case historically. Libraries originally sprung up in academic departments, often built by individual book-loving faculty. In this context the library was embedded in the department, created by faculty, and operated on their own terms, typically until it became too large for the department or the faculty member to operate effectively. The emerging research library, an integration of individual or departmental collections, was custodial, static, and passive in nature. However, things are changing rapidly in today's campus libraries. Many of these changes are related to the impact of information technology. Innovative and exciting collaborations account for a major part of the library's transition from passive to active, reactive to proactive, staid to lively, and singular to social.

Collaborative facilities bring new energy and relevance to the academic library. In a world where 73% of college students use the Internet more than the library according to a recent Pew study,[1] new library spaces are dramatically increasing numbers of visitors. They come for research, creative activities, cultural events, social opportunities, and refreshment. Wilson notes:

> Libraries often represent the largest footprint on university and college campuses. When space is scarce and expensive, it is difficult to justify

responsibly facilities that are not fully utilized. Creative minds have called for collaboration in space management. Wise souls talk in terms of stewardship rather than ownership of space.[2]

Collaborating to design and operate new spaces provides an atmosphere of mutual excitement, support, and commitment for the projects.

Spaces for creative activity are not new to libraries. Students and faculty have been inspired for decades by contemplative study and reading to write a considerable portion of the world's scholarship. New spaces now in place or in the planning phase are intended to enable creation of new forms of scholarship using text, images, audio, and visual materials. Examples of these spaces include University of Tennessee's Studio,[3] University of Alabama's Sanford Media Resource and Design Center,[4] University of Iowa's Information Arcade,[5] and Washington University's Arc Library Technology Center.[6] These spaces are planned in collaboration with faculty, students, and information technologists. The emerging New Media Commons at the University of California, Berkeley is part of a new collaboration of seven academic departments called the Center for New Media and illustrates the importance of shared objectives, planning, resource development, and staffing.[7]

Creative spaces can be comprehensive or quite specialized to particular disciplines and activities. For example, Washington University's Nancy Spirtas Kranzberg Illustrated Book Studio is a partnership between the University Libraries and the School of Art. The studio is dedicated to the study of the book, authorship, and publishing. Though the center is currently in a library facility, it may move to the new Fox Arts Center, underscoring the fact that new collaborative services and spaces may be embedded in locations other than the library but still have a strong library connection.[8] The spaces have become so pervasive over the last decade that a new international organization, New Media Consortium (NMC), emerged in 1993 to deal with training, research and development, and other issues related to new media facilities, many of them in libraries.[9] The collaborative nature of these spaces is reflected in staffing models, which emphasize individual expertise requiring different skill sets from a variety of disciplines.

Innovative service-oriented spaces are also emerging through strategic collaborations. The University of Tennessee Libraries recently opened the satellite Writing Center operated by the English Department to assist students with writing projects. It is a perfect match for students because a major part of writing contains information-seeking activities. Librarians stand ready to provide assistance with students' research while English graduate students provide help with the writing itself.[10] The University of California, Berkeley's Student Learning Center features a satellite service in the Undergraduate Library for writing and career development including joint publicity and crossing training with staff to improve referrals between student and library services.[11] A number of libraries around the country have a center related to teaching excellence located in the library. The University of Iowa's Center for Teaching's library location brings more business to its doors and enhances collaboration with librarians and faculty.[12]

Initiatives to enhance teaching and learning include development of innovative classrooms, specialized labs, auditoriums, and other teaching support spaces featuring central participation by librarians. Embedding librarians brings the learning process in closer proximity to the scholarship on which the disciplines are based and to those that service it–librarians. The concept of collaborative research, teaching, and study space continues to morph into major campus facilities. The University of Georgia's Student Learning Center, one of the newest comprehensive centers, was built in partnership with the Libraries, Enterprise Information Services, and the Office of Instructional Support and Development, and blends a variety of faculty and student-centered instructional, study, and social spaces in an appealing and innovative design.[13] Other facilities including University of Michigan's Media Union[14] and the University of Southern California's Leavey Library[15] are notable examples of collaborative, multi-use learning spaces. Intensive interaction between librarians, faculty, and students is occurring in exciting ways in these newly emerging facilities. Leavey Library's Center for Scholarly Technology's roster of activities, including joint conferences, lecture series, faculty training programs for application of technology to the classroom or for research, team development of critical thinking course components, and joint grants for research and development projects, demonstrates the end results of collaboration.[16]

EMBEDDED IN RESEARCH

Integration with scholarly resources is a given for academic research. Research accomplished in partnership with librarians who are subject experts in the appropriate discipline occurs more on an informal basis where librarians are acknowledged as being key to the project or publication's success. Increasing research partnerships in a more formal sense, where librarians are directly contributing to the outcome, requires a deeper level of embeddedness than casual contact. It requires a sophisticated knowledge of faculty research and an ability to determine how one's own expertise, both as a librarian and as subject expert, can contribute. Other research partnerships focus on joint federal or foundation grants where a library partnership can be very beneficial to all partners. Additionally, libraries as sources of information on grant venues provide an important collaboration avenue.

Collaboration with research centers and institutes is another important avenue for fruitful partnerships. Librarians are in the business of research support but, on most campuses, have little direct contact with research centers. A strategic effort to make consistent contact with specialized research centers ensures that researchers have the most thorough and current information resources and accompanying expertise to support their work. The University of Tennessee's Howard H. Baker Center for Public Policy has a strong partnership with the University Libraries. In particular, the Center and the Libraries are jointly seeking papers of prominent Tennessee political figures, leveraging the expertise of both entities.[17] The ability for librarians to demonstrate how library collections and services directly support research should be publicized as a way to strengthen research programs throughout the campus.

THE NEW ACADEMIC SALON

Libraries are filled with art, literature, and scholarship that define and describe the world's culture. Cultural events are becoming an important extension of the traditional preservation of culture role that librarians have embraced for centuries. The University of Tennessee[18] and North Carolina State University have writer-in-residence programs including readings and other related events occurring in the library. The Tennessee program is a collaboration with the English Department's Creative Program and often features student writers in its events. How appropriate to have authors reading in the place where their creations are housed for current and future audiences. The library as cultural center offers many other opportunities to work with departments of Music, Art, Architecture, and others to schedule exhibitions, concerts, and other activities. These activities bring more and different audiences into the library and provide yet another way to develop enduring bonds with departments around campus.

Library coffee shops are another venue for readings, concerts, and other cultural events. Additionally, the interaction between faculty and students in these relaxing, often salon-like spaces is an important aspect of the library watering hole. Coffee shops provide an important social space for all to enjoy. They are the new "salon" of universities, encouraging discussion, interaction, and human comforts of refreshment.

THE PERVASIVE CAMPUS LIBRARIAN

Librarians are in a unique position to become involved in core activities and initiatives throughout the university. The fact that we are generalists and devoted to all disciplines and all sectors of the academic user community gives us a special insight on ways to advance the university and achieve its mission. However, in order to be productive and effective throughout the campus, librarians must strategically and energetically seek and accept leadership roles. Central administrators may not automatically consider that a librarian should be tapped or invited to participate on campus-wide projects. Thus, librarians must take it upon themselves to establish an acute sense of important campus agendas and propose involvement including reasons why their perspective is important. A proactive approach is essential in getting one or more seats at the right tables rather than waiting to be asked.

Potential venues for the embedded campus librarian are numerous. Successful participation requires that librarians' work in these various venues be for the benefit of the institution rather than focused solely on library matters. Involvement in campus strategic planning is a very important place to start and holds many benefits for library involvement. Since the campus strategic plan is an important general roadmap for the institution, it provides an outstanding opportunity for integration of key library-related initiatives to be woven into the document such as robust access to collections, information literacy integrated throughout the curriculum, recruitment/retention and attention to diversity, and strong support for teaching, learning, and research.

Campus governance is another very important place for librarian involvement, if at all possible. Active participation on the campus Faculty Senate, Faculty Senate Committees, and campus advisory groups brings a greater understanding by faculty of librarians and what they have to offer. Librarians have a much greater say in the direction of the campus and can inform others, in particular, about issues where we have deep knowledge and expertise including intellectual and academic freedom, copyright, and scholarly communication, to name a few. Of course, involvement, at least in an ex officio capacity, of librarians on faculty senate library committees is obvious. However, our presence on research councils, information technology committees, teaching councils, diversity committees, curriculum committees, and many others is also an avenue for very significant contributions.

A thorough understanding of the institution's administrative structure and its key players provides a guide to priority contacts and other venues for involvement. The chief academic officer and his/her staff are obvious targets for extensive contact and involvement. Others include the chief financial officer, the chief operations officer, the chief student affairs officer, and the campus official for equity and diversity. At many institutions, some of these high-level administrators have steering or advisory committees which provide an opportunity to participate in critically important decision making for the campus and, therefore, the library.

Several kinds of administrative officers are often overlooked by librarians for beneficial collaboration. Individuals in charge of institutional research and assessment, for example, can be excellent partners for a wide variety of library projects requiring data. In turn, they benefit from interaction with librarians through heightened awareness of resources important to their work and through a partnership that is closer to the academic side of the university. Often they are isolated from colleges and departments and, when approached, are delighted to have their expertise recognized. Partnerships with institutional research can also insure that appropriate library data are gathered and analyzed correctly for institutional and broader comparative purposes. The outcome for the library might be a fairer salary comparison, a chance to weigh in on campus peer selection, and a contact person for internal database usage.

Central administrators, along with the chief academic officer, make critical funding and policy decisions affecting the library. It might be time to ensure that they have regular contact and, in fact, dedicated support from the library for their work. In turn, they will have more in-depth knowledge of the library and its importance to the campus. Heightened visibility of the library in these arenas should pay off when the time comes for resource allocations.

Academic departments are obvious collaborators with the library. The question on many campuses becomes how to leverage collaboration in the most effective way for librarians to gain sufficient entrée into teaching, learning, and research. Berkeley's librarians spearheaded the Mellon Faculty Institute for Undergraduate Research, which enabled 13 faculty to incorporate research assignments into undergraduate courses to teach students how to use digital and print library resources effectively. Participants were drawn from the humanities, social sciences, engineering, and biology. Patricia Iannuzzi, chair of the Mellon steering committee, noted that "the library has evolved from being a repository of material to an educational partner."[19]

The subject or departmental librarian model is a common approach for making contact with departments. Another method is to encourage each department to have a faculty representative to liaise with the library. The most effective collaborations are multi-dimensional, addressing more than just collection development. Integration of information literacy skills into individual departmental curriculum, research consultation, and partnerships in research and teaching should also be part of the library liaison with departments.

A major driver in the success of the departmental collaboration is whether the library has a proactive or passive approach. More libraries are considering a model in which subject or departmental librarians are housed, or at least regularly visit, the department and, like teaching faculty, have office or consultation hours right in the department. The University of Alabama has assigned a reference librarian to the Department of Criminal Justice where he spends time in an office assigned to him by the departmental chair, offering assistance to undergraduates, graduate students, and faculty. The University of Illinois at Urbana/Champaign negotiates joint faculty appointments with academic departments. Benefits of close departmental collaboration include a greater understanding and, therefore, a greater ability to address current research and teaching needs. Arizona State University Libraries is participating with two collaborative initiatives. The Information Infusion Initiative of the College of Liberal Arts and Sciences is designed to infuse information technology and information literacy across the curriculum. Initially, implementation is in three areas: (1) Humanities and Social Sciences, (2) Geography and Geological Sciences, and (3) the Learning Communities. A committee of faculty and a librarian are working on practical websites addressing information literacy in these academic areas.[20] The Learning Communities initative provides an alternative to the general education courses for entering freshmen where courses from different disciplines are integrated around a single topic and are team-taught by faculty and supported by a librarian. Learning Communities' library activities include orientation, instructional sessions, research consultations, librarian participation on class trips, and faculty meetings. The librarian is a dedicated contact person for faculty and students, making it easier for them to take advantage of specialized expertise.[21] The library has a broader base of support from departments whose members know that they are gaining maximum benefit, not only from the collections, but also from the expertise brought specifically for their department.

LIBRARIANS AND TEACHING

To be truly integrated throughout the teaching and learning activities of our campuses is the core of being a truly embedded librarian. It can happen within the departmental model and through other means. Curriculum development and the integration of information literacy and library user education broadly in the campus curriculum can only be achieved through direct and concerted involvement by librarians in developing overarching goals for the educated graduate of that particular institution. For example, the University of Tennessee recently established new general education requirements for all undergraduate students. Ensuring that librarians were on the appropriate committees resulted in written and oral skill requirements that include ability to:

- Acquire information by conducting independent research, both in a conventional library setting and through the use of rapidly developing electronic technologies
- Evaluate the reliability, accuracy, and logical soundness of the information
- Use the information that they have acquired.[22]

Attention to collegiate curriculum reform, such as the reform of undergraduate engineering or business curriculum, can result in the integration of appropriate information-seeking and analysis skills into appropriate courses. Partnership with librarians might mean that faculty use tools or other components achieving the agreed-upon learning objectives themselves rather than relying on the traditional in-class library instruction.

RELATIONSHIP WITH STUDENTS

Librarians are in constant contact with a portion of the student population on a daily basis. Consistent contact with student government leaders and an awareness of how students are organized and represented throughout the campus can lead to a greater integration and understanding of their needs, wants, and concerns. Regular meetings with student government leadership are a must. Often these meetings can uncover and address concerns and needs from the students' perspectives before they become critical. Broadening the base of student input can be achieved by establishing student advisory committees for the library with representation from various departments and/or colleges. Gaining access to student groups, Greek organizations, and dorm governance could uncover innovative ways to reach students in more effective and age-appropriate ways. Although becoming "embedded" with students is pretty unrealistic for librarians as well as faculty and administrators, a variety of partnerships and opportunities for dialogue can result in mutual respect and trust, with more productive usage of valuable library resources and expertise by our core user group being the end result. From these partnerships stem innovative ways of "getting to" students through such programs as North Carolina State University Libraries' Peer Research Advisors' Program, where outstanding undergraduates from underrepresented groups are trained to assist their student colleagues with research skills.[23]

EMBEDDED IN FUNDRAISING

Resource developments consisting of robust fundraising and grants programs are critical for colleges and universities to be competitive and successful institutions. Libraries support all areas of the institution and, in the embedded model, should be well integrated into campus development efforts and priorities. Positioning the library as a key component of campus fundraising efforts requires both in-depth knowledge of the campus development structure and its players, as well as an ability to educate and convince key decision makers on the potential success of raising funds for library programs and initiatives. Successful fundraising requires high visibility, and effective embedding strategies with campus public relations offices are essential to ensure press releases and features about the library in major publications. Partnership activities mentioned throughout this article are great subjects for such publicity. Collaboration with athletic departments can also result in fundraising and high visibility for the library, particularly on campuses with high profile sports programs. Oklahoma's football coach is working with University of Oklahoma Libraries to raise a $1 million endowment. Coaches at Penn State, University of South Carolina, and Texas Tech are also partners in library fundraising because of personal interest and the concerted efforts of library directors at these institutions to encourage their participation.

INFLUENCING CAMPUS VIRTUAL SPACE

Embedding the library into the university's virtual space is as important as the physical collaborations mentioned earlier. The campus website is now *the* gateway into the university. The library must be highly visible and well integrated into campus virtual space. A study of the homepages of CIC institutions in 1999 revealed that 33% of these major research libraries were not on their institution's homepage.[24] By 2004, only one institution omitted libraries on its homepage. Easily locating the library's website directly from the university's homepage is fundamental to its successful virtual integration. Homepage positioning is only the beginning. Library web links should occur from as many campus sites as possible including from College, academic departments, and research centers' homepages.

Positioning the library web link effectively requires close collaboration with campus administrators responsible for web development, deans, department heads, research directors, and others. One efficient way of saturating campus virtual space with library presence is to ensure its position on the campus portal. This approach is particularly effective when the portal contains a standard set of links that are supposed to appear on every campus unit's webpage.

A discipline-based approach includes links on academic department web-pages to relevant subject guides, electronic resources, and customized services. The service links can include direct access to the appropriate subject librarian, to interlibrary loan, and to other services. These links enable the faculty or students to easily find resources and services specifically relevant to their discipline. Another approach to discipline-based integration is a "my library" capability where the student, faculty member, or administrator creates a personal library webpage containing frequently used sites and services.

Embedding the library into the teaching and learning mission of the university can be accomplished through positioning links within a campus online curriculum system such as WebCT and Blackboard. Creative approaches with faculty provide ways to directly integrate library resources such as databases, electronic reserve readings, images, and other relevant materials into the faculty member's course webpage. Additionally, links to virtual reference services such as Tennessee's AskUs.Now[25] or the Association of Southeastern Research Libraries (ASERL)'s Ask-A-Librarian provide students with direct, and sometimes immediate, access to a librarian for expert assistance.[26] Additionally, links to web-based tutorials developed by librarians to address certain class needs related to research and information seeking embed library expertise into courses. Tutorials such as Iowa's have a self-testing capability to ensure that students have properly internalized the appropriate concepts.

FACULTY, STUDENTS, ADMINISTRATORS, AND LIBRARIANS AS CO-CREATORS

Today's embedded librarians play a major leadership role in pushing an academic co-creator model for scholarship and scholarly communication where students, faculty, and librarians are all co-creators of the research and learning process. The development of media labs, mentioned earlier, can be the physical "face" of co-creation. New developments include services such as: hosting scholarly websites, as with University of Iowa's Bailiwick where "academic passions can be realized in HTML as highly specialized and creative web pages";[27] facilitating creation and dissemination of Blogs, as with the University of Minnesota's UThink service;[28] and self-archiving electronic publishing systems. The development of institutional repositories is providing a major impetus for the development of a digital architecture that provides a relatively easy way for faculty and students to add their scholarship, databases, or other scholarly resources for others to use. Librarians, successfully embedded in the process are at the forefront of campus institutional repository development. Ohio State's Knowledge Bank,[29] MIT's DSpace,[30] and Virginia's Central Digital Repository[31] are examples.

The emerging capability for knowledge creation locally provides more opportunities for collaboration between librarians, faculty, and administrators. Although the impetus for local electronic publishing of journals, monographs, and other born-digital resources is, in part, the skyrocketing cost of commercial scholarly publishing, the end result expands the universe of scholarship. New kinds of electronic and multimedia publications often serve rapidly expanding multidisciplinary scholarship. Local electronic publishing programs include application of peer review or its equivalent, copyright systems, and marketing. Librarians working with faculty should be developing the infrastructure for a successful publishing and dissemination effort. Campus-wide collaborations such as University of Tennessee's Scholarly Communications Committee embed librarians into all aspects of the knowledge creation, service, and dissemination process. Our presence ensures the pursuit of open access and broader notions about acceptable forms of scholarship in the academy.

The embedded librarian, who is truly integrated into the academic, administrative, athletic, cultural, research, teaching, and learning arenas of the university, provides quality and depth to the total campus experience. Extensive integration of scholarly resources, and expertise on how to locate and apply them, also leverages the major investment universities make in supporting the library. The power of embedding goes further than the library because it informs and improves the mission of the university for excellence in teaching and research. Core values of diversity and the value of interdisciplinarity are reinforced and often championed by librarians. Recognition of the power of embedding, integrating, and collaborating leads to amazing innovations in the academy that would not exist without the influence and leadership of librarians.

NOTES

1. Jones, Steve et al. *The Internet Goes to College: How Students Are Living in the Future with Today's Technology.* Washington, DC: Pew Internet & American Life Project, 2002. p. 12 <www.pewinternet.org/reports/pdfs/PIP_College_Report.pdf>.

2. Wilson, Lizabeth A. "Collaborate or Die: Designing Library Space," *ARL: A Bimonthly Report on Research Library Issues and Actions from ARL, CNI, and SPARC.* V. 222 (June 2002).

3. University of Tennessee. The Studio <http://www.lib.utk.edu/mediacenter/studio/index.html>.

4. University of Alabama. Sanford Media Resource and Design Center <http://www.lib.ua.edu/randd/>.

5. University of Iowa. Information Arcade <http://www.lib.uiowa.edu/arcade/>.

6. Washington University. Arc Library Technology Center <http://library.wustl.edu/units/arc/>.

7. University of California, Berkeley. Center for New Media <http://art.berkeley.edu/niemeyer/stories/cnm-emerging.htm>.

8. Washington University. Nancy Spirtas Kranzberg Illustrated Book Studio <http://em-dash.org/bookstudio/indexFlash.html>.

9. New Media Consortium <www.nmc.org>.

10. University of Tennessee. Department of English. Writing Center <http://web.utk.edu/~english/writing.php>.

11. University of California. Berkeley. Student Learning Center <http://slc.berkeley.edu/>.

12. University of Iowa Center for Teaching <http://www.uiowa.edu/~centeach/>.

13. University of Georgia. Student Learning Center <http://slc.uga.edu/facility.html>.

14. University of Michigan. Media Union <http://www.ummu.umich.edu/>.

15. University of Southern California. Leavey Library <http://www.usc.edu/isd/locations/undergrad/leavey/>.

16. University of Southern California. Leavey Library. Center for Scholarly Technology <http://www.usc.edu/isd/locations/cst/tls/opportunities/curricular_design.html>.

17. University of Tennessee. Howard H. Baker, Jr. Center for Public Policy <http://bakercenter.utk.edu/>.

18. Harris, Steven. "Writers in the Library: Literary Programming on a Shoestring," *College & Research Libraries News* 63 (6) (June 2002) <http://www.ala.org/ala/acrl/acrlpubs/crlnews/backissues2002/june/writerslibrary.htm>.

19. Edelstein, Wendy. "Improving Undergraduate Research Skills," *Berkeleyan.* January 21, 2004 <www.berkeley.edu/news/berkeleyan/2004/01/04_mellon.shtml>.

20. Arizona State University. Information Literacy Website <http://cli.la.asu.edu/it/learncomm>.

21. Arizona State University. College of Arts and Sciences. Learning Communities <http:clasdean.la.asu.edu/lcsite/learning.html>.

22. University of Tennessee. Undergraduate Catalog, 2004-2005 <http://diglib.lib.utk.edu/dlc/catalog/images/u/2004/u_gereq.pdf>.

23. North Carolina State University. Peer Research Advisors Program <http://www.lib.ncsu.edu/risd/pra/>.

24. Dewey, Barbara I. "In Search of Services: A Study of CIC Library Web-based Services," *Information Technology and Libraries* (June 1999), v. 18: 84-91.

25. University of Tennessee. AskUs.Now <http://www.lib.utk.edu/refs/askusnow/>.

26. Association of Southeastern Research Libraries. Ask-A-Librarian <http://www.ask-a-librarian.org/>.

27. University of Iowa. Bailiwick Server <http://bailiwick.lib.uiowa.edu/>.

28. University of Minnesota. UThink: Blogs at the University Libraries <http://blog.lib.umn.edu/>.

29. Ohio State University. Knowledge Bank <http://www.lib.ohio-state.edu/KBinfo/>.

30. MIT. DSpace <https://dspace.mit.edu/index.jsp>.

31. University of Virginia Central Digital Repository <http://www.lib.virginia.edu/digital/resndev/repository.html>.

Reflections on Collaborative Teaching of Science Information Literacy and Science Writing: Plans, Processes and Pratfalls

Deborah Huerta
Victoria McMillan

SUMMARY. Examines the philosophy behind development of two team-taught courses in scientific writing: one for first-year students, the second for advanced students preparing for graduate and professional careers in science. Using student self-evaluations, course evaluations, and anecdotal evidence, chronicles some strengths and weaknesses of our ten-year experience with collaborative instruction and elaborates on both successful and unsuccessful pedagogies. *[Article copies available for a fee from The Haworth Document Delivery Service: 1-800-HAWORTH. E-mail address: <docdelivery@haworthpress.com> Website: <http://www.HaworthPress.com> © 2004 by The Haworth Press, Inc. All rights reserved.]*

Deborah Huerta is Associate Professor, University Libraries, and Head, George R. Cooley Science Library (E-mail: dhuerta@mail.colgate.edu), and Victoria McMillan is Research Associate in Biology, and Associate Professor of Scientific Writing (E-mail: vmcmillan@mail.colgate.edu), both at Colgate University, Hamilton, NY 13346.

[Haworth co-indexing entry note]: "Reflections on Collaborative Teaching of Science Information Literacy and Science Writing: Plans, Processes and Pratfalls." Huerta, Deborah, and Victoria McMillan. Co-published simultaneously in *Resource Sharing & Information Networks* (The Haworth Information Press, an imprint of The Haworth Press, Inc.) Vol. 17, No. 1/2, 2004, pp. 19-28; and: *Libraries Within Their Institutions: Creative Collaborations* (ed: William Miller, and Rita M. Pellen) The Haworth Information Press, an imprint of The Haworth Press, Inc., 2004, pp. 19-28. Single or multiple copies of this article are available for a fee from The Haworth Document Delivery Service [1-800-HAWORTH, 9:00 a.m. - 5:00 p.m. (EST). E-mail address: docdelivery@haworthpress.com].

http://www.haworthpress.com/web/RSIN
© 2004 by The Haworth Press, Inc. All rights reserved.
Digital Object Identifier: 10.1300/J121v17n01_03

KEYWORDS. Composition instruction, faculty collaboration, information literacy, science writing, team-teaching, undergraduate education, pedagogy

INTRODUCTION

For more than ten years at Colgate University we have co-instructed science library research/writing courses for undergraduates (Huerta and McMillan 2000). Academic librarians at Colgate are encouraged to provide, indeed solicit, opportunities to instruct students. In our case, one of us, Victoria, is a biologist and scientific writing instructor, while Deborah is a science librarian. For several years, Victoria invited Deborah to provide an introduction to library resources for students in her biology and health classes. These sessions, although useful to students, were too brief to explore the deep connections between research and the writing process. With the support of the Interdisciplinary Writing Department, the Biology Department, and the University Libraries, we developed two levels of scientific writing courses reflecting what we perceived as the true needs of undergraduates.

Our entry-level course, taught as a First-Year Seminar, attempts to bridge the gap between high school and college library research/writing expectations (Ercegovac 2003). The upper-level course, cross-listed as a 400-level biology or composition class, is designed to prepare science majors for research and writing in professional and graduate schools.

Our collaboration grew out of our conviction that a fusion of composition and science expertise and librarianship might demystify the obstacles to effective research and writing in the sciences (Farber 1999; Winner 1998). We hoped to model the interrelationship between research and writing by team-teaching each class together (Krest and Carle 1999; Rader 2004). This model might provide insight for students into vital and reiterative connections among the nature of scientific questions, scientific literature, and scientific writing (Elmborg 2003; McMillan 2001).

Our expectations for both courses were to help students become their own writing critics so that they might rethink the questions they were posing and achieve clarity when communicating their thoughts. To do so, we believed we should emphasize both product and process. In an increasingly murky digital world, we wanted our students to make distinctions between scholarly and non-scholarly sources as well as science secondary and primary sources (Raspa and Ward 2000). We hoped to provide guidance for effective and efficient information retrieval. In addition, we wished to introduce the variety of conventions used in science communication, along with the major theme that scientists write in different formats for certain audiences, using many documentation styles (McMillan and Huerta 2002). We also felt they needed to understand that these purposes and processes are interrelated and constitute lineages of intellectual heritage transcending time and geopolitical boundaries.

Pedagogical commonalities exist in both courses to address consistent problems most students encounter when faced with science research and writing assignments. For example, many students, whether they are first-year students or seniors, and despite our enthusiastic exhortations to select a review paper topic of great personal interest, have difficulty selecting a subject. Many students start with the first thought that occurs to them, choosing topics that are much too broad, such as dinosaurs or hurricanes. Others select ideas that will lead them into vastly complicated topics such as origins of the moon or, in the case of first-year students, areas such as biochemistry or molecular genetics. Still others attempt to bypass science altogether or select topics of questionable scientific merit; for example, we have vetoed ethics of stem cell research and parapsychology as acceptable topics for scientific reviews.

Distinctions between primary and secondary sources mystify students (Janick-Buckner 1997; Muench 2000). Many beginning students automatically assume that all journal articles are primary sources. Some even perceive their own review papers as primary sources. The generic category *books* holds particular authority for many students who fail to understand that, in science, books are generally secondary sources. For even some of our advanced students, refining search strategies for primary sources and use of even the most basic library services, such as interlibrary loan, appear to be hitherto undiscovered.

Grammatical issues and wordiness, although worse at the entry-level, haunt upper-level students as well. Common problems include comma splices, sentence fragments, subject/verb agreement, and misuse of words such as *data*, *significant*, *affect/effect*, and *its/it's*. Also problematic are documentation issues such as citing the source where the information was encountered rather than locating the original source. Students also remain confused about what to cite, when to cite it, or why to cite it. Finally, mastering the tone of scientific discourse remains elusive despite our best efforts.

Yet, virtually all of our Student Evaluation of Teaching (SET) forms are positive. In addition, student self-assessments written as a final piece in both courses are glowing and replete with convictions of learning achieved. These claims leave us stunned, for the students appear to have received much more than we believe they could have conceivably obtained.

PLANS AND PRATFALLS

Our reasons for doubt seem obvious. Students in both tiers, both knowingly and unconsciously, sabotage us. Their ways are various. The first major obstacle is choosing a topic for a lengthy scientific review paper. We have tried an over-arching theme for the course with a scholarly monograph as a text (Serpell 1996). We have suggested large categories that might be of interest. We have made lists of successful topics selected by previous students. We have always returned to urging them to pick a topic about which they care deeply.

Nonetheless, they sabotage the assignment, and themselves, with respect to topic selection, particularly in the introductory course. Having not done preliminary work to ascertain whether their choice of subject is sufficiently captivating to engage them for a semester, they lose interest and blame the topic. It does not surprise us that, in their Writer's Profile, an essay requiring them to analyze their own writing process, only 15% of 183 students even mentioned topic selection (i.e., "being interested in my topic") as a factor affecting their writing success. Perhaps the most discouraging comment came from one student who wrote, "In reality I do not find any topics appealing to me, regardless of what they are." Although such students are fortunately in the minority, their resistance to the research and writing process remains one of our most difficult pedagogical challenges.

In addition, they often fail to comprehend any disjuncture between use of appropriate science scholarly databases and Google (or "webbing" as one student put it), using search engines as one might have used an encyclopedia in the pre-digital age. They cling to books to avoid journal articles and, in contradictory fashion, display impatience with scholarly overview sources while proclaiming the virtue of inappropriate web sites. After their major research and writing assignment, a scientific review paper, we ask them to recycle their subject through smaller pieces such as a magazine or newspaper article (Guyer 1998; Mysliwiec, Shibley, Jr., and Dunbar 2003). However, they evade the intent of these assignments by disregarding audience. They resort to skimming their primary sources rather than close reading for comprehension and analysis (Kuldell 2003).

Vocabulary issues abound, even though only 9% of 183 students initially identified vocabulary as a concern in their Writer's Profiles. Refusing to develop the necessary background knowledge, students complain they cannot engage with the material because they cannot understand the scientific language of their references. For example, we have had students who simply could not cope with the vocabulary or the ideas involved in genetically modified foods, coral reef death, or butterfly migration although they themselves had selected the topics as interesting. We tend to view such discomfort in the learning process as growth potential, but it is often not viewed similarly by the students. Of course, some of these problems are developmental, particularly for first-year students, who have had little previous exposure to scholarly sources. Such students view such sources (and topics) as simply boring or interesting, hard or easy, good or bad, etc. They also have trouble distinguishing between differences in spoken language and written language, and tend to ignore the models (sample professional papers) we provide as guides for different types of writing assignments.

Procrastination is also a problem for most of our students, even though few (e.g., 9% out of 183) have ever identified this issue as a problem in their writing. At both levels, students are also highly resistant to revision. This problem remains even though we schedule frequent peer-review workshops and provide extensive feedback on early drafts. Despite pointed, productive suggestions from both of us, most students are loathe to cut or change a single word, at least until they receive their first portfolio grade. Moreover, like instructors in other disciplines, we have had our share of plagiarism problems, despite our close attention to the student research and writing process every step of the way.

Needless to say, by the end of each semester, having struggled with the obstacles outlined above, we are barely holding each other up and wondering why we wrestle with these courses year after year. Every semester now has a predictable cycle, a recognizable rhythm. When we think we have finally debugged the course, the same problems occur or there are new wrinkles. We start with great optimism and are in despair by mid-semester.

PROCESSES AND PEDAGOGY

How do we address these perennial problems? Therein lies the strength of our collaboration. We work so closely together, as well as with each student, that we can fairly accurately prescribe remedies from our different perspectives (Stein and Lamb 1998). We try to turn potential disasters into success by attempting to reach students at their own level and then guide their individual growth. In courses such as ours, where the actual subject matter is created by the students, sharing the responsibility with another committed instructor is crucial.

In general, we structure both courses around student portfolios of accumulated assignments, peer workshops, and individual conferences (Slater 1997). The portfolios are turned in at mid-semester and at the end of the semester. They include bibliographies, partial drafts of papers, revisions, and completed papers. We both make comments on all drafts throughout the semester and together assign grades to the portfolios. We also confer extensively about the efforts of individual students, often noting strengths or deficiencies from the perspectives of our own professions.

The peer workshops are opportunities to read student drafts of portions of writing assignments (Koprowski 1997). Students have workshop schedules well in advance, in addition to a code of deportment for the workshops. For example, all students are expected to critique the presenter's work constructively and to sign the draft before returning it; hence, no comment is ever anonymous. They are also expected to provide oral feedback during class about passages that are unclear or wordy and make specific suggestions for improvement.

We schedule at least two individual conferences with each student and both of us. These meetings provide students with the opportunity to express concerns privately and we, in turn, offer individual suggestions for improvement.

We have experimented with problem-based learning and group activities (Duch, Groh, and Allen 2001; Herreid 1997; Rangachari 1995). For example, with the entry-level class we use an abstract assignment to teach how to read a primary journal article and how to write a concise summary of it (Cremmins 1996; Foos 1987). As preparation, we give students a research article missing its title, keywords and abstract. We ask them to read closely each section of the article: introduction, materials and methods, results, discussion (Day 1998). In their own words, they must suggest a sentence or two that captures the authors' major points in each section. Collectively the class constructs an abstract on the blackboard, along with a title and keywords. We then compare their piece with the original. Next, the students are assigned to groups; each group receives a different article that is missing its abstract. They are to convene outside of class and reconstruct the missing parts and present the group's effort at the next class. To their surprise, often the students' title, abstract, and keywords more closely and clearly summarize the paper than do those of the authors.

Another assignment designed to ensure close reading and attention to keywords and subject headings is to have students index their own review paper. This assignment is not a simple word count and analysis; it requires that students also identify embedded concepts in their own writing that are not named but reflect themes in their pieces. The exercise promotes awareness of concepts used in organizing and accessing scientific literature. It also requires a thorough rereading of their work with an eye to editing for clarity and coherence.

In addition, we ask entry-level students to read their review paper draft and identify the topic sentence in each paragraph, as well as transitions within and between paragraphs (Hairston 1997). Usually, their first individual conference is built around this "paragraph analysis" assignment. At this conference, some students, still confused, may ask us which sentence in a particular paragraph is the topic sentence. We reply that *they* are the authors and if they do not know what the topic sentence is, how will the reader? Along with establishing coherence and clarity in their drafts, this exercise reminds students that they are not simply writing in a vacuum, but instead to a specific group of readers. If students can identify and establish a relationship with their audience, the writing process can be demystified and they will communicate their ideas more clearly.

With the advanced class, we use both a working bibliography initial research assignment followed by an annotated bibliography of primary research articles. In the annotations, students are to summarize key research objectives in each paper and state why the article supports the goals for their own review. Students often complain about the amount of time this assignment takes. However, many realize that, if they do the assignment thoughtfully, they have created a detailed outline or master plan for their paper.

We give the advanced students great flexibility in choosing their review paper, beginning with their topic. Some students are working on data analysis in a lab and welcome the opportunity to do a literature review in conjunction with their laboratory work. Others pursue a subject they hope to study in graduate school. Many students simply wish to learn more about a scientific topic that interests them personally.

We require that advanced students select a scholarly journal that might be interested (fictitiously) in publishing their review paper. Often the process of journal selection is closely tied to their initial literature research. As the students draft their review, they must follow the journal's Instructions for Authors and include those instructions, for our reference, in their portfolio. Like the beginning students, the advanced students then must redirect their writing for a magazine audience. For first-year students the model we provide is *Discover*. Advanced students may have a choice of magazine venues. Some select *Discover*, while others choose *Scientific American*, *Natural History*, or other popular science magazines.

We offer various options to the advanced-level students for a final piece of writing. Over the years these have included a poster presentation, a grant proposal, a scientific vitae and cover letter for their dream research job, a book review for *Nature* or *Science*, a feature article for *Science Times*, an essay on the life of a scientist, or some other project they can convince us is worth doing.

In both courses, students write a final self-assessment of their efforts throughout the course. In this essay, they are to showcase their triumphs and concerns and write about their passage through both research and writing.

These essays are generally open and honest. They describe student doubts, fears, dislikes, and challenges. They are usually very praiseworthy, with comments such as "when I graduate this is the only course I'll take with me," or "if only I had had this course sooner," or "I'm telling all my friends to take this course," or "this course should be required." We have had students who have actually gone on to jobs abstracting and those who have gone on to publish as scientists. We have had students who say they have been transformed by the course.

This collaboration has also transformed both of us and the ways that we teach. We understand the agonies students suffer in general as they write, as well as their individual challenges and dilemmas. Before we embarked upon this collaboration, we perceived only segments of the research and writing process. Librarians tend to work with students at the beginning of a research paper, but have little contact after initial forays into the literature. Composition instructors may see students when they are already in trouble with their writing. As collaborators, we are privy to the entire learning process from start to finish. We are not simply teaching a set of skills. We know the writing process is a vast reiterative undertaking in which research and writing are integral (Isbell 1995); as students learn more about a subject, their questions and inquiries change. If they come to an impasse, they must return to the literature and probe it more thoroughly.

We have seen beginning students gain confidence and comprehension of process. We have seen confidence emerge from knowing how literature is organized and accessed, how inquiries can be structured and refined, and how papers can be written in stages and revised to reflect students' best efforts. We believe that students can successfully overcome the procrastination habit and, in doing so, avoid plagiarism or work that is not their best writing. We know many students do eventually grasp the concept of writing to a particular audience. We also know that, despite fear of criticism, students can learn to trust suggestions from their peers and from us.

CONCLUSIONS

Writing is hard work, and for us, the teaching of writing is made easier by team-teaching. Each of us brings different insights to students' problems and different ways to help them learn. Many students have never had so much attention paid to their writing. Without exception, students who have commented in SET forms on this collaboration have been extremely positive. For example, one student wrote, "I think that the fact that there were two instructors made all the difference. Not only were there great suggestions to be made, but we received two opinions on every piece of work we submitted. I think that this is an invaluable resource to have." Another commented, "I think by having two professors every important aspect was taught. Also we as students had two forms of feedback. The professors effectively balanced their teachings so that the course was fun and interesting. I think having two professors was the greatest asset to the class."

Despite our predictable dismay as each semester unfolds, in the end both SET forms and student self-assessments suggest that most students are, in fact, learning much of what we had hoped to teach them. We remain confused about this apparent disjunction between what we feel we are *not* teaching them successfully and what they themselves feel they are taking away from the course; however, clearly we are doing something right most of the time, even in the case of highly resistant students. Perhaps it is the act of collaboration itself–the joint presence at every class of two committed instructors–that makes the critical difference. Two instructors, two dedicated readers, add a certain gravitas to the task that focuses student attention on the importance of their work–from topic selection to the research process, to paragraph selection and even the placement of every comma. Neither of us feels that we could teach these classes alone. Our continuing collaboration remains as engaging and productive for us as it is, apparently, for our students.

REFERENCES

Cremmins, E. T. 1996. *The art of abstracting.* 2nd ed. Arlington, VA: Information Resources Press.

Day, R. A. 1998. *How to Write & Publish a Scientific Paper.* 5th ed. Phoenix, AZ: Oryx.

Duch, B. J., Groh, S. E. and D. E. Allen. 2001. *The power of problem-based learning: a practical "how to" for teaching undergraduate courses in any discipline.* Sterling, VA: Stylus.

Elmborg, J. K. 2003. Information literacy and writing across the curriculum; sharing the vision. *Reference Services Review* 31:68-80.

Ercegovac, Z. 2003. Bridging the knowledge gap between secondary and higher education. *College & Research Libraries* 64:75-85.

Farber, E. 1999. Faculty-librarian cooperation: a personal retrospective. *Reference Services Review* 27:229-34.

Foos, K. M. 1987. Abstracts can enhance writing skills. *Journal of College Science Teaching* 16:254-5.

Guyer, R. L. 1998. Spread the word: writing science to be read. *Asha* 40:34-7.

Hairston, M. C. 1998. *Successful Writing.* New York: W. W. Norton.

Herreid, C. F. 1997. What is a case? *Journal of College Science Teaching* 27:92-4.

Huerta, D., and V. E. McMillan. 2000. Collaborative instruction by writing and library faculty: a two-tiered approach to the teaching of scientific writing. *Issues in Science and Technology Librarianship*, no. 28 (Fall), http://www.istl.org/00-fall/article1. html. (accessed May 19, 2004).

Isbell, D. 1995. Teaching writing and research as inseparable: a faculty-librarian teaching team. *Reference Services Review* 23 (Winter):51-62.

Janick-Buckner, D. 1997. Getting undergraduates to critically read and discuss primary literature. *Journal of College Science Teaching* 27:29-32.

Koprowski, J. L. 1997. Sharpening the craft of scientific writing: a peer-review strategy to improve student writing. *Journal of College Science Teaching* 27:133-5.

Krest, M. and D. O. Carle. 1999. Teaching scientific writing: a model for integrating research, writing & critical thinking. *American Biology Teacher* 61:223-7.

Kuldell, N. 2003. Read like a scientist to write like a scientist: using authentic literature in the classroom. *Journal of College Science Teaching* 33:32-5.

McMillan, V. E. 2001. *Writing papers in the biological sciences.* 3rd. ed. Boston: Bedford/St.Martin's.

McMillan, V. E. and D. Huerta. 2002. Eye on audience: adaptive strategies for teaching writing. *Journal of College Science Teaching* 32:241-5.

Muench, S. B. 2000. Choosing primary literature in biology to achieve specific educational goals. *Journal of College Science Teaching* 29:255-60.

Mysliwiec, T. H., Shibley, Jr., I. and M. E. Dunbar. 2003. Using newspapers to facilitate learning. *Journal of College Science Teaching* 33:24-28.

Rader, H. B. 2004. Building faculty-librarian partnerships to prepare students for information fluency. *College & Research Libraries News* 65:74-6, 80, 83.

Rangachari, P. K.1995. Active learning: in context. *Advances in Physiology Education* 13:S75-S80.

Raspa, D. and D. Ward, eds. 2000. *The collaborative imperative: Librarians and faculty working together in the information university.* Chicago: Association of College and Research Libraries.

Serpell, J. 1996. *In the company of animals: a study of human-animal relationships.* New York: Cambridge University Press.

Slater, T. F. 1997. The effectiveness of portfolio assessments in science. *Journal of College Science Teaching* 26:315-8.

Stein, L. L. and J. M. Lamb. 1998. Not just another BI: faculty-librarian collaboration to guide students through the research process. *Research Strategies* 16:29-39.

Winner, M. C. 1998. Librarians as partners in the classroom. *Reference Services Review* 26:25-30.

Teaching Centers, Libraries, and Benefits to Both

Joni E. Warner
Nancy H. Seamans

SUMMARY. Campus teaching centers dedicated to improving instruction are commonplace today in academe. This article presents ways in which libraries and teaching centers have developed partnerships and identifies benefits for both entities. Specific examples are drawn from the authors' two institutions, including a review of the ways that relationships were developed and how both the teaching center and the library have benefited. Additionally, the authors suggest ways in which other institutions might develop these kinds of relationships or expand those that already exist, and identify other campus units that may provide valuable partnerships for academic librarians. *[Article copies available for a fee from The Haworth Document Delivery Service: 1-800-HAWORTH. E-mail address: <docdelivery@haworthpress.com> Website: <http://www.HaworthPress.com> © 2004 by The Haworth Press, Inc. All rights reserved.]*

Joni E. Warner is Coordinator, Instructional Services, University of Notre Dame, 222B Hesburgh Library, Notre Dame, IN 46556-5629 (E-mail: Joni.E.Warner.29@nd.edu).

Nancy H. Seamans is Director, Instruction & Reference Department, University Libraries (0434), Virginia Tech, Blacksburg, VA 24061-0434 (E-mail: nseamans@vt.edu).

[Haworth co-indexing entry note]: "Teaching Centers, Libraries, and Benefits to Both." Warner, Joni E., and Nancy H. Seamans. Co-published simultaneously in *Resource Sharing & Information Networks* (The Haworth Information Press, an imprint of The Haworth Press, Inc.) Vol. 17, No. 1/2, 2004, pp. 29-42; and: *Libraries Within Their Institutions: Creative Collaborations* (ed: William Miller, and Rita M. Pellen) The Haworth Information Press, an imprint of The Haworth Press, Inc., 2004, pp. 29-42. Single or multiple copies of this article are available for a fee from The Haworth Document Delivery Service [1-800-HAWORTH, 9:00 a.m. - 5:00 p.m. (EST). E-mail address: docdelivery@haworthpress.com].

http://www.haworthpress.com/web/RSIN
© 2004 by The Haworth Press, Inc. All rights reserved.
Digital Object Identifier: 10.1300/J121v17n01_04

KEYWORDS. Collaboration, teaching excellence, teaching centers, Notre Dame, Virginia Tech, library instruction

Teaching librarians have been part of the academic community for more than 100 years. However, the extent of library instructional activities has exploded within the past quarter century. The past twenty-five years have also seen the development of academic teaching centers, designed to support faculty members, in a variety of ways, in developing skills as teachers. Librarians have benefited from the development of these centers, but also have much to contribute to their successes. Case studies of the relationship between librarians and teaching centers at Notre Dame and Virginia Tech suggest how these relationships can be developed, how they might evolve over time, and how other institutions might benefit from such relationships.

BACKGROUND–
THE CAMPUS TEACHING CENTER AND ITS ROLE
IN THE COLLEGE/UNIVERSITY

Founded in 1962, the teaching center at the University of Michigan, Ann Arbor is generally identified as the first such center established in the United States. Throughout the 1970s the number of these centers grew, and today it is commonplace to have some type of teaching center on academic campuses.

Most teaching centers have as their mission the support and advancement of teaching and learning. They accomplish this by offering a range of activities in the areas of instructional development, organizational development, faculty development, educational research, and related programs and projects (Quinlan, 1991). In addition, a teaching center provides support to the college and university community through the following "essential events":

- Conducting faculty and graduate assistant orientation;
- Assisting faculty in enhancing their teaching skills;
- Sponsoring and coordinating workshops for teaching enhancement;
- Supporting production and utilization of multimedia in the classroom;
- Publishing a newsletter to promote the center's goals and activities (Bakutes, 1994).

Teaching centers have a variety of designations, including such names as teaching and learning center, center for excellence, center for teaching and learning, center for advancement of teaching, instructional development center, and faculty development center. They are often funded via grants from organizations such as the Lilly Endowment or Mellon Foundations. Quinlan comments that centers "have been started and continued as hard-line budget items" and that "[a]n institutional commitment to fund such a center makes a powerful statement about teaching and learning as a campus priority" (Quinlan, 1991). In July 2002, the teaching and learning center at the University of Nebraska–Lincoln, the second oldest center in the country, was eliminated as part of university-wide budget cuts. According to the *Chronicle of Higher Education*, the decision to close the center "sparked outrage among some professors who wonder whether the administration is truly committed to good teaching" (Bartlett, 2002). This response is an indication of the political ramifications of having or not having this kind of center, particularly in a time when institutions, particularly those with a significant research component, are struggling to find a balance between teaching and research.

The size of the institution often determines who will manage a teaching center. Program directors range from faculty members on release time, faculty with reduced teaching loads, or full-time directors. A director, part-time faculty, graduate assistants, and clerical employees staff many programs. Some centers operate on a volunteer basis, while others obtain either university or grant funding to support the center's endeavors. Quinlan indicates that "[t]he success of a program rests on the support it receives (or not) from faculty and administrators" (Quinlan, 1991).

UNIVERSITY OF NOTRE DAME–
KANEB CENTER FOR TEACHING AND LEARNING

In 1994, the Academic Council of the University of Notre Dame, along with other campus entities such as the College of Arts and Letters Committee on the Quality of Undergraduate Education, and the University Task Force on Teaching, recommended the establishment of a campus teaching center. The center was created by a gift from a Notre Dame trustee, John A. Kaneb of Massachusetts, who chaired the governing board's committee on student affairs (University of Notre Dame Public Relations and Information, 1995).

In September 1995, the provost appointed a committee to conduct a search for a director of the center. The search committee consisted of a broad representation of faculty from various departments such as theology and philosophy, engineering, marketing, history, and mathematics, and also the Dean of the First Year of Studies and an associate provost. The Kaneb Center for Teaching and Learning, known on campus as the Kaneb, opened in the fall of

1996 and was staffed by a director, one faculty member, and support staff. The center's mission, as outlined in a September 1995 letter to the campus faculty from the search committee, was "to support the teaching mission of the University by:

- Assisting faculty members to evaluate and improve their teaching performance
- Assisting graduate students to develop teaching skills and to function effectively in their teaching role
- Assisting students in their efforts to become more effective learners" (Kaneb Center Search Committee, 1995).

The programs and workshops offered through the Kaneb emphasize learning environments and teaching practices, and range from using PowerPoint in the classroom to discussions on assessment in the curriculum to summer faculty reading groups. Throughout the years, the programs have been coordinated by the Kaneb and taught by center staff, campus teaching and research faculty, and librarians.

Conversations between the Kaneb and the University Libraries began in late 1996. The director of the Kaneb began discussing how the work of each is connected not only as teaching and learning units, but also as service providers to faculty and teaching assistants. The first collaboration was making available the Kaneb's collection of teaching materials in the University Libraries online catalog system. Although the Kaneb had a Web site which listed its materials, the plan was to be much more efficient by having its material available in the one centralized campus location, the library online catalog.

Staffing changes at both the Kaneb and the University Libraries resulted in several years when collaborations and conversations between the two units were minimal. However, the library and the Kaneb once again became involved with one another's teaching in 2002. University Libraries approached the Kaneb about co-teaching a faculty program to improve use of the Internet. Librarians perceived that many faculty felt overwhelmed by the amount of information available on the University Libraries Web page, and on the Internet at large. After much discussion between the Coordinator of Library Instruction and one of the Kaneb's faculty consultants, it was agreed that, based on feedback from teaching faculty, librarians should co-teach a program offering techniques for the Web, and tips on search strategies and obtaining a better understanding of what is available on the Internet. After much planning, a session titled *Mining the Internet* was co-taught by a librarian and teaching center faculty member. This was the first time a librarian was involved in any type of teaching center program at Notre Dame. It was well-received and is tentatively planned to be taught again.

During the past eight years, the mission of the Kaneb has been reviewed and revised to reflect a parallel alignment with the goals and objectives of the university's teaching mission (University of Notre Dame, The Kaneb Center, 2002). Today, the University of Notre Dame's Kaneb Center for Teaching and Learning staff includes a director who reports to the provost and who is also a part-time mathematics faculty member. Additional staff includes an assistant director, a consultant to faculty, a teaching assistant program coordinator, a faculty learning communities' coordinator, a program and marketing manager, and one clerical support staff.

The Kaneb serves as a catalyst, encouraging campus groups such as the University Libraries and campus computer centers to offer training for faculty. The resulting collaborations ensure quality teaching and learning, and also increase the number of faculty who are not only willing to teach but also to share their vision of teaching and learning. Ultimately, the partnership will create an environment where librarians are more widely recognized and valued by others on campus. As Caspers and Lenn state, "we librarians must define our place as teachers in the educational mission of our institutions" (Caspers and Lenn, 2000).

Librarians as Customers

Part of the University Libraries strategic plan to facilitate Notre Dame's teaching efforts is to educate librarians in the pedagogy of teaching. One of the many outcomes of achieving this goal was partnering with the Kaneb to develop and teach a workshop for librarians. It seemed natural and logical to develop a relationship with the teaching center to educate librarians on the most effective ways of teaching. The Kaneb offered a variety of programs to fit librarians' needs and was willing to review options in addition to the traditional services offered to campus teaching and research faculty. After much discussion with librarians about what they desire to learn and improve most in their teaching, a Kaneb program entitled *How to Get Good Classroom Discussion* was developed.

The program proved beneficial to both the library and the teaching center. The faculty at the teaching center, knowing very little about librarians as teachers, gained a better understanding of the role the librarian plays in the curriculum and as a teacher. Library faculty found simple and effective ways to introduce and generate classroom discussion in library instructional sessions that increased their comfort level in the classroom without feeling embarrassed or nervous. Many librarians commented that they felt ready to begin incorporating some of these suggested activities into their instructional sessions.

A wide variety of workshop topics offered by the Kaneb could be adapted to fit the continuing education needs of the library faculty. Workshops include such topics as *Teaching Well Using Technology*; *Teaching Well*; *Saving Time*; *Using Writing to Enhance Student Learning*; and *Understanding the Notre Dame Student and Student Culture*. These types of programs continue to be offered as a way to foster growth in teaching and learning for the library faculty. Additional educational opportunities for librarians interested in teaching and learning exist through the Kaneb Center. Librarians have been encouraged to become involved in summer reading groups that include book titles such as Parker Palmer's *Courage to Teach*, and to attend campus workshops such as *Teaching University Seminars, Interactive Learning in the Sciences, Active Learning in the Classroom*, and the *4 M's of Teaching*.

Librarians as Participants

The University of Notre Dame participates in the national Carnegie Scholarship of Teaching Program; providing support to faculty who are immersed in teaching is one of the program's objectives. Faculty members are invited to submit an investigative proposal which would address either a teaching challenge within their specific discipline or a substantial or meaningful topic.

In 2000, a Notre Dame librarian and a faculty member for a University Seminar (freshman) course were awarded a research grant through the teaching center. The director of the teaching center encouraged the application after reading an article in a library newsletter about the collaboration between the professor and the librarian.

The grant supported a two-year study of the effect of course-based library instruction on the acquisition of research skills and the development of lifelong learning habits. The study also investigated the extent to which course-based library instruction in the teaching of literature, specifically, a course entitled *Caribbean Voices*, could help students to acquire basic research skills, and whether this could also encourage them to develop the habit of lifelong learning.

Data collected in the first year were used to revise the course for the second year, so that more accurate determinations about the efficacy of teaching practice in the course and the overall usefulness of course-based library instruction could be made. The primary instrument for data collection was a survey that questioned students about their research experiences, and their perceptions of research and of the library at important moments during the class. In order to measure student acquisition of basic research skills, the investigators also examined student work throughout the semester to see whether students master the skills the library modules in the class are designed to teach.

Librarians as Providers

Each year the Kaneb hosts a panel on the campus services available to University Seminar courses. University Seminars are required classes for all first-year students, taught by a variety of full-time teaching and research faculty from different academic disciplines, thus allowing students to pursue their major interests while working on their writing and critical reading skills. The panel discussion participants included personnel from the University Writing Center and the Campus Museum, as well as the Coordinator of Library Instruction. Each unit discussed the services available to the University Seminar instructors to enhance their courses; as a result of this exposure and other marketing efforts, the University Seminar library instruction increased approximately 29 percent in the year 2002-2003.

In the next few years, the Kaneb Center plans to expand programming for the teaching assistants (TAs), and the library plans to be involved in the outreach efforts to this particular group. This program equips TAs for what lies ahead in the Notre Dame classroom and for a possible career in teaching. A variety of programs and orientations for TAs already exists on campus, but they need to be combined in order to establish a place for conversation and reflection on teaching experience. The Kaneb hopes to offer programming for all TAs before the semester begins each year. The library has already begun conversations with a Kaneb liaison about involving librarians in this program. Library personnel look forward to being a part of the pedagogical conversations and collaborations for the TAs, and are confident that librarians can assist them in learning how to incorporate research skills into their coursework.

Benefits to the Library and the Kaneb Center

At Notre Dame, the University Libraries plans to work with the campus teaching center to accomplish many of the goals and action items set forth in the University Libraries Strategic Plan. A few of the goals that include partnering with the Kaneb Center for Teaching and Learning are:

- Increase partnerships and collaborate with teaching faculty to incorporate a library research component into the academic courses
- Gather information to refine/redefine library instruction learning objectives

- Incorporate library instructional services into courses using instructional management courseware
- Develop an internal assessment tool to measure the effectiveness of library instruction

"We must be known as practitioners of pedagogical transformation and reform," states McCormick (2003). By working with the Kaneb, the University Libraries can begin to accomplish many of its goals. By demonstrating and providing instructional training to campus teaching and research faculty, librarians can begin the conversations with various groups about the importance of information literacy skills and the need and desire to incorporate these skills into the curriculum. Notre Dame librarians can open many doors that will help in planning for an assessment tool and redefine learning objectives as collaborative work with the Kaneb staff. The staff provides relevant training on these issues for the entire Notre Dame community. These types of issues are facing all in the academy, not just academic librarians. Therefore, being a part of the conversations on campus is critical. In the end, librarians will be a central part of the teaching and learning process at Notre Dame and will be recognized as teachers, and bring an endless array of possibilities to the academic environment.

During the next academic year, the University Libraries is to assist the Kaneb in accomplishing its goals by delivering programs and workshops to the campus faculty through the Kaneb and also by co-sponsoring a workshop. As McCormick states, "In the same way that we can deepen relationships to individual faculty members by being introduced to them through teaching centers, we can reach out to many members of the teaching faculty at a time through presenting programming" (McCormick, 2003). It is time for librarians to step forward to become leaders and to benefit from the instructional opportunities that await them.

The Kaneb will begin to expand and adapt its programs and workshops in order to meet the needs of the departments and colleges. The library will be there to help it achieve and identify successful practice in teaching. By becoming a part of the Kaneb programming, librarians are placing themselves at the center or heart of the campus teaching culture and may soon be accepted and acknowledged as teachers on campus.

In addition to the expansion of programs and other goals, the Kaneb Center plans to intensify evaluation of teaching, and expand orientation for new faculty and training for TAs in the coming years. These types of programs and instructional situations provide the University Libraries with the unique opportunity to be a leader of the conversations about building a learning community that is the essential support for learning, a community in which we can all be immersed into a student-centered learning environment where the focus is on critical thinking and problem solving. As Rader states, "Academic librarians in the 21st century will continue to be major players in education and should become the center for teaching, learning and research on their campus if they utilize their unique and specialized expertise, think out of the box, reach out to form new partnerships and achieve measurable educational outcomes" (Rader, 2001).

VIRGINIA TECH–
THE CENTER FOR EXCELLENCE
IN UNDERGRADUATE TEACHING

Planning for Virginia Tech's Center for Excellence in Undergraduate Teaching (CEUT) took place during the 1992-93 academic year. A librarian was among those who convened to plan a program to improve teaching, and a librarian was one of twenty people who met regularly throughout that year to plan and, ultimately, recommend creation of a teaching excellence center.

The role envisioned for the University Libraries was as an information broker: "CEUT will work with the Virginia Tech University Libraries as an information broker. We recommend that a library faculty member be available four hours a week in the Center for consultation with instructional faculty providing information on particular teaching problems and assisting in the preparation of subject specific bibliographies or other class instructional materials." Also envisioned was access to the ERIC database through the library's CD-ROM network and a document delivery service that would facilitate access to ERIC resources. The planning document also identifies challenges that the proposed center might address, including "Incorporating *information literacy* into the curriculum" (Virginia Polytechnic Institute and State University, CEUT, 2003).

The Center for Excellence in Undergraduate Teaching was first funded for the 1993-94 academic year, and thus, has just celebrated its tenth anniversary. However, the relationship between the CEUT has not developed in quite the way the planning committee envisioned. A librarian has never held office hours in the Center, but since Virginia Tech's College Librarian program began the same year as CEUT, the idea of library faculty members being available for consultation with instructional faculty was implemented to a broader degree than the planning committee imagined. Librarians have offices in the colleges they support, and thus, are able to provide a distributed level of service that goes well beyond what was imagined when office hours in the Center were proposed. As for incorporating information literacy into the curriculum, there has been much discussion, particularly during the past four years, but as yet there is no formal mechanism for this kind of integration.

Librarians as Customers

There was no strong relationship between the CEUT and the University Libraries for the first few years of the Center's existence, but that changed dramatically when a new library Instruction Department was created at Virginia Tech in 1999. The fifteen people including eleven librarians and four support staff who made up the department were, in effect, charged with becoming teaching librarians and expanding the teaching role of the University Libraries. One component of this was quickly identified as the need to better understand the entire process of instruction, and CEUT was approached and asked to help the librarians in this endeavor. A faculty development consultant with CEUT worked closely with the librarians. She first consulted extensively with the librarians, trying to understand the challenges of doing one-shot instructional sessions and the level of discomfort among many of the librarians teaching large numbers of classes; she then tailored sessions on presentation skills and assessment techniques to the needs of the librarians. These customized sessions, designed as developmental workshops for the library personnel, resulted in an improved understanding by the librarians of teaching methods, the research on teaching, pedagogy in general, better use of technology in teaching, and an overall increased comfort level with teaching.

Librarians as Participants

Librarians also began to participate in other general workshops offered by CEUT, including sessions such as *Critical Thinking*; *Understanding ESL: English As a Second Language*; *Faculty as Skillful Presenters*; *Digital Portfolios and Higher Education*; *Preventing Plagiarism: A Technological Overview*; *Academic Integrity*; and *Re-Imagining Classroom Research*. Several librarians participated in year-long study groups, including one group of ROTC faculty members and a librarian reviewing the issues associated with a common reading experience for all ROTC students, and a group, including a librarian that has investigated course design around themes of "Living in the 21st century" and "Earth sustainability."

Librarians as Providers

As CEUT personnel came to better understand the role of the library in the University's teaching and learning enterprise, they encouraged and supported librarians' design of sessions that would be offered by CEUT. The first workshop, offered in 2000, was entitled *Designing Research Assignments* and taught by a team of four librarians. Subsequently, two additional workshops, *Library Support for Distant Students* and *Critical Thinking and Information Literacy*, have been developed and offered as a regular part of the CEUT workshop schedule.

Benefits to the Library and to CEUT

The most obvious benefit of the relationship between CEUT and the University Libraries is as a resource: the library can call upon the expertise that is gathered by CEUT and can use it to improve library teaching. However, an unexpected benefit has been a subtle shift in the way the librarians are viewed by their colleagues around the university. There is an increased sense of the librarians as peers, colleagues who take seriously their role in the teaching and learning missions of the university and who contribute in ways beyond the traditional role of providing information resources and document delivery services.

The CEUT has benefited from the relationship via the several workshops that have been developed and offered by librarians, but there is more to the relationship than that. At CEUT's 2002 year-end reception, held annually to recognize faculty who have been part of CEUT workshops and activities throughout the previous year, the director of the CEUT singled out the library participants as welcome additions to the CEUT family and talked about the perspective that librarians bring. Reflection on his comments suggests that the view of teaching excellence provided by the library is not centered in a single discipline but is more global and holistic, providing a kind of overview that often helps link teaching faculty from different disciplines and allows them to also see a more university-wide view of teaching endeavors.

The future of the relationship between CEUT and the University Libraries at Virginia Tech seems secure. The opportunity to continue to offer the existing three workshops are available and the librarians' suggestions for new workshops are welcomed.

The success of CEUT for undergraduate teaching excellence has resulted in discussion of how the model can be used to develop teaching skills in Virginia Tech's graduate students who will be the professors of the future. Graduate students are encouraged to participate in existing CEUT offerings, but a new campus initiative is focusing on providing this population with targeted resources and support for their development as graduate teaching assistants, and library personnel have been involved at every step.

Involvement in CEUT appears to have been a catalyst for involvement by librarians in other campus teaching endeavors. During the past five years, librarians have been invited to be part of the program for a summer workshop offered by the University Writing Program, and part of a working group that investigated alternatives to the University's existing writing intensive requirement. A librarian has been a member of the University Core Curriculum Committee, and has played a key role in a campus-wide endeavor to revitalize the core curriculum. Librarians have become part of a faculty liaison program with dorm students and have been invited to dorms to participate in discussions.

RECOMMENDATION FOR OTHERS

The relationship that librarians at both Notre Dame and Virginia Tech have had with their teaching excellence centers suggests that other institutions which have not yet forged this kind of relationship can also reap the benefits. It is critical that library personnel find a way to be at the table when innovations in teaching are being discussed and to be prepared to participate in, and contribute to, the conversations about these innovations.

The process of developing a relationship with an existing center might most readily be accomplished by being both a participant in, and a producer of, workshops and other offerings of such a center. If that kind of relationship proves difficult to establish or to maintain, serving as an information resource for the endeavors of a campus teaching center is a way to stay connected with what is going on and to be seen as a partner in the teaching enterprise. Raspa and Ward suggest that "[f]ive fundamental qualities are required for collaboration: passion, persistence, playfulness, promotion, and project" (Raspa and Ward, 2000). When all of these items are in place, collaboration is attainable. Librarians can readily bring all of these qualities to a relationship with a campus teaching center and use them to create an institutional collaboration that will do much for both the library and the teaching center.

Kalin and Snavely state that "[w]e must become partners in our institutions' instructional mission" (Kalin and Snavely, 2001). For an institution that does not have such a center but is planning one, participation by librarians in the planning process would be instrumental in establishing a relationship from the outset.

Times of campus change and innovation often prove to be times when the library can insert itself into the curriculum, and it is important to be aware of what is occurring so that such opportunities are not missed. A curriculum redesign or the implementation of new components of an existing curriculum, development of new academic programs, or new teaching or assessment initiatives on campus are all opportunities to be more involved with the teaching mission of the institution. Library collaboration with teaching and research faculty is growing, and playing an active role in a curriculum and helping to develop student research and information seeking skills are an integral part of that collaboration.

Involvement with teaching excellence centers may lead to relationships with other entities on campus that have a role in ensuring the academic success of students. The opportunities must be cultivated. Awareness of institutional developments in such areas as student outcomes assessment, critical thinking assessment, and institutional and programmatic assessment may suggest new partnership opportunities. Outreach to a variety of campus communities–residential life programs, athletics, honors program, academic advising personnel–will surely create opportunities for library engagement that are outside of traditional roles.

In any circumstance, an important complement to all of these endeavors is having a library champion, someone from the library who is passionate about teaching excellence or someone from the academy who understands and values the library role in teaching excellence. The efforts of this individual can go a long way toward ensuring that the library is recognized as a campus teaching partner. Another variable is the need for librarians to demonstrate that they are capable of being peers with their teaching faculty colleagues on campus. Much is written in the library literature about the need to collaborate with faculty, but until the culture of the institution recognizes librarians as teaching peers, rather than as supporters of teaching, the role of the library will often be marginalized. Partnerships with teaching excellence centers are but one way to ensure that this kind of marginalizing will not occur.

SELECTED BIBLIOGRAPHY

Bakutes, Arlene Pickett. "An Examination of Faculty Development Centers." *Contemporary Education* 69 (1998): 168-171. In EBSCOhost Academic Search Elite [database online]. Retrieved 12 March 2004.

Bartlett, Thomas. "The Unkindest Cut." *Chronicle of Higher Education* 48 (March 22, 2002): 10-13. In EBSCOhost Academic Search Elite [database online]. Retrieved 8 March 2004.

Caspers, Jean and Lenn, Katy. "The Future of Collaboration Between Librarians and Teaching Faculty," in *The Collaborative Imperative: Librarians and Faculty Working Together in the Information Universe*. Chicago: Association of College and Research Libraries, American Library Association, 2000.

Jacobson, Trudi E. "Partnerships Between Library Instruction Units and Campus Teaching Centers." *Journal of Academic Librarianship* 27, 4 (July 2001): 311-316. In Elsevier ScienceDirect [database online]. Retrieved 21 May 2004.

Kalin, Sally and Snavely, Loanne. "Strategies to Make the Library an Instructional Partner on Campus," in *Library User Education: Powerful Learning, Powerful Partnerships*. Maryland: Scarecrow Press, 2001.

Kaneb Center Search Committee to University of Notre Dame Faculty, *Search Committee Letter to University of Notre Dame Faculty*, 15, September 1995. Notre Dame printed materials PNDP 30-Ka-1, University of Notre Dame Archives.

McCormick, Martha Henn. "Teaching Excellence and the Academic Librarian: Paralleling the Teaching Faculty's Track," in *Expectations of Librarians in the 21st Century*. Connecticut: Greenwood Press, 2003.

Quinlan, Kathleen. "About Teaching & Learning Centers." *AAHE Bulletin* 44 (1991): 11-16.

Rader, Hannelore. "Cooperative Ventures between the University and the Library" in *67th IFLA Council and General Conference*: August 16-25, 2001. http://www.ifla.org.sg/IV/ifla67/papers/081-164e.pdf. Retrieved 26 May 2004.

Raspa, Dick and Ward, Dane. "Listening for Collaboration: Faculty and Librarians Working Together" in *The Collaborative Imperative: Librarians and Faculty Working Together in the Information Universe*. Chicago: Association of College and Research Libraries, American Library Association, 2000.

University of Notre Dame. *The Kaneb Center*. [Updated 2002; retrieved 27 May 2004]. Available from http://kaneb.nd.edu/.

University of Notre Dame Public Relations and Information to University of Notre Dame Faculty and Staff, *Notre Dame News*, 10, May 1995. Found in Notre Dame printed materials PNDP 40-Ka-1, University of Notre Dame Archives.

Virginia Polytechnic Institute and State University. *CEUT: Center for Excellence in Undergraduate Teaching (CEUT History)*. [Updated 2003; retrieved 27 May 2004]. Available from http://www.ceut.vt.edu/text/history/pbs.htm.

A Blueprint for Progress:
Collaborating with Faculty
to Integrate Information Literacy
into the Curriculum at Purdue University

Alexius Smith Macklin
Michael Fosmire

SUMMARY. Students coping with the escalating complexities of available electronic resources often demonstrate undesirable behaviors including the inability to identify information needs, uncertainty about selecting information resources, poor evaluation of information sources, and inappropriate use of information for problem solving. To eliminate these obstacles in higher education, librarians and faculty at Purdue University collaborated to integrate the Association of College and Research Libraries (ACRL) core competencies for information literacy directly into course content. This manuscript describes the development of an overt information-centered curriculum and its impact on student learning. *[Article copies available for a fee from The Haworth Document Delivery Service: 1-800-HAWORTH. E-mail address: <docdelivery@haworthpress.com> Website: <http://www.HaworthPress.com> © 2004 by The Haworth Press, Inc. All rights reserved.]*

Alexius Smith Macklin, MLIS, BA, is User Instruction Librarian (E-mail: alexius@purdue.edu), and Michael Fosmire, MLS, BA, is Head, Physical Sciences, Engineering and Technology Division (E-mail: fosmire@purdue.edu), both at Purdue University Libraries, 504 West State Street, West Lafayette, IN 47907-2058.

[Haworth co-indexing entry note]: "A Blueprint for Progress: Collaborating with Faculty to Integrate Information Literacy into the Curriculum at Purdue University." Macklin, Alexius Smith, and Michael Fosmire. Co-published simultaneously in *Resource Sharing & Information Networks* (The Haworth Information Press, an imprint of The Haworth Press, Inc.) Vol. 17, No. 1/2, 2004, pp. 43-56; and: *Libraries Within Their Institutions: Creative Collaborations* (ed: William Miller, and Rita M. Pellen) The Haworth Information Press, an imprint of The Haworth Press, Inc., 2004, pp. 43-56. Single or multiple copies of this article are available for a fee from The Haworth Document Delivery Service [1-800-HAWORTH, 9:00 a.m. - 5:00 p.m. (EST). E-mail address: docdelivery@haworthpress.com].

KEYWORDS. Integrated curriculum, problem-based learning (PBL), information literacy, faculty collaboration

INTRODUCTION

There are subtle differences between being information literate and being able to use information technology. Although many students claim a high level of comfort with Web-based information resources, they are frequently accessing an overabundance of information before they actually know what their information need is. This type of search behavior often leads to ineffective or insufficient results, or short-circuiting the research process before it begins (Bruce, 1997). The bigger problem, however, lies in the fundamental user belief that competence with technology and the ability to retrieve information are the same skill sets. In fact, they are not. Information literacy enables a person to master content and extend his or her problem-solving skills, become more self-directed, and assume greater control over learning (Breivik, 1998). Until this higher order thinking is employed, using the technology is simply a matter of psychomotor skills and requires very little critical analysis on the part of the learner.

Information literacy helps individuals recognize when information is needed and maintain the ability to locate, evaluate, and use needed information effectively. The Association of College and Research Libraries (ACRL) defines an information literate person as one who is able to:

• Determine the extent of information needed
• Access the needed information effectively and efficiently
• Evaluate information and its sources critically
• Incorporate selected information into one's knowledge base
• Use information effectively to accomplish a specific purpose
• Understand the economic, legal, and social issues surrounding the use of information and
• Use information ethically and legally

There are many definitions for information literacy and they tend to overlap with the idea of computer literacy and library instruction. While there is a significant relationship between these terms, being information literate is more about the ability to locate, evaluate, and use information to become independent lifelong learners. In its narrowest sense, it includes the practical skills involved in the effective use of information technology and information resources, either print or electronic. Mastering a rapidly changing environment, as well as devising transferable strategies for retrieving information in a variety of formats, is the essential quality of being information literate. To be effective, however, information literacy instruction must be integrated directly into course content when the skills can be applied immediately to accomplish some purpose.

At Purdue University, the development of an information literacy integration project facilitated the selection of resources, the evaluation of data, and the sharing of knowledge and information management tools across disciplines. For the initial program, librarians and faculty used the ACRL information literacy competencies as the foundation for setting learning objectives and anticipated outcomes for participating classes. A hands-on approach provided relevant and interesting, yet complex and fully-developed information problems for the students to practice search strategies and evaluation of sources. In an effort to maintain best practice of information literacy skill development, librarians were closely involved in planning and evaluating student work. They worked collaboratively with faculty as active participants observing students and collecting data on the impact of information skills integration. The results from this project were assessed using qualitative and quantitative measures of students' attitudes about information literacy and the progress of their work throughout the semester.

GETTING STARTED

A semester before planning the pilot phase of this project, a series of professional development workshops on information literacy awareness was organized to recruit faculty partners and support collaboration. As part of the workshops, approximately 50 participants identified the most critical information skills for success in their field. These lists were reviewed by the facilitators and arranged according to where they fit into the ACRL information literacy competencies. Four categories emerged and the skills were ranked in order of application and importance to the group:

1. How information is collected
2. How information is accessed (not just search engines on the Web)
3. How information is evaluated
4. How information is used to solve problems

The facilitators conducted this exercise before introducing the ACRL information literacy competencies. As a result of this activity, they were able to better understand what the faculty believed about the importance of information skill building, create a foundation on which to integrate information skills into the curriculum, and establish a system for collaboration (Smith and LaLopa, 2000). This is referred to as "learning the profession," or understanding from an insider's perspective what is most important to teach (Abell, 1994). Faculty participating in the pilot of the curriculum integration project related to these benchmarks because they, not library professionals, wrote them. Stripped of jargon, this simple tool identified where in the curriculum it was most appropriate to address critical information skills. The responses from the survey (Figure 1) were analyzed and measured against the ACRL competencies to ensure that best practices for information literacy were being used for content development throughout the project.

PILOT PHASE

There were two courses in the pilot program: EAS 109, Earth and Atmospheric Science, and SCI 490, Science and Society. Two faculty members, three teaching assistants, and two librarians (one with content knowledge in science and one with instructional design expertise) worked together to integrate information skills as a required part of course content. The group planned over the summer months and ran the pilot in the fall semester, 2001. Approximately 120 students were enrolled across the two courses. Both of the participating professors incorporated a version of the 50-minute bibliographic instruction session in previous years, so the librarians used those experiences as a starting point for deciding how to fit information skills seamlessly into the syllabus using a new delivery method. An example of the instruction materials designed in collaboration with the faculty is on the topic of global warming:

George W. Bush backed off a campaign promise to regulate CO_2 emissions and has asked for more research on the science of global warming. He requested a report from the National Academy of Sciences and stated that the United States was leaving the Kyoto Protocol because:

- The Academy's report tells us that we do not know how much effect natural fluctuations in climate may have had on warming.
- We do not know how much our climate could or will change in the future.
- We do not know how fast change will occur or even how some of our actions could impact it. For example, our useful efforts to reduce sulfur emissions may have actually increased warming, because sulfate particles reflect sunlight, bouncing it back into space.
- And finally, no one can say with any certainty what constitutes a dangerous level of warming and, therefore, what level must be avoided.

You are a multinational delegation fresh from the Marrakesh 'Seventh Conference of the Parties' (http://www.unfccc.de/cop7/). Your goal is to convince the United States to rejoin the Kyoto Protocol, making the global warming accords that much more powerful. Determine to whom and how you should make your case to have the best chance of succeeding in bringing the U.S. back into the fold.

FIGURE 1. Faculty Survey: Information Literacy Skill Assessment

Faculty members participating in the pilot phase of the curriculum integration project were asked to rank information skills according to importance in their course:

- Very important = 1
- Important = 2
- Somewhat important = 3
- Somewhat unimportant = 4
- Unimportant = 5

Formulate a research question/develop a thesis statement:

1	2	3	4	5

Identify key concepts and terms to describe a topic:

1	2	3	4	5

Use a variety of information sources, such as books, scholarly journals, and the Web.

1	2	3	4	5

Access needed information effectively and efficiently:

1	2	3	4	5

Evaluate resources for credibility and relevance:

1	2	3	4	5

Use information effectively to accomplish a specific purpose (e.g., a research paper):

1	2	3	4	5

Demonstrate an understanding of intellectual property (e.g., plagiarism):

1	2	3	4	5

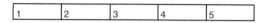

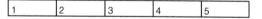

The following learning objectives were developed for consistency among activities in the information literacy curriculum integration project. There are three levels, based on Bloom's (1956) taxonomy, for every skill-building task: *Level 1* = Orientation; *Level 2* = Intermediate; and *Level 3* = Advanced or Higher order thinking.

Level 1: Orientation

After reading various problem scenarios, the students will:

- Develop a question/hypothesis/problem statement by identifying what they already know about the given problem scenario
- Identify keywords for constructing search statements/strategies to test in various search engines

Level 2: Intermediate

By working through problem-solving activities, designed to teach advanced strategies for information retrieval, the students will:

- Construct search statements and test them in a variety of electronic databases
- Conduct peer-review evaluations of the information gathered by classmates
- Revise search terms/strategies to increase quality of information found

Level 3: Advanced

After gathering high-quality information resources, the students will:

- Extract relevant information from resources selected
- Synthesize information from multiple sources
- Present a coherent, documented solution to the problem
- Correctly cite information used

The theoretical framework for this information literacy curriculum integration project is problem-based learning (PBL). This approach to teaching and learning started at McMaster University in 1969 as curriculum reform for medical schools. It is now one of the most advanced instructional methodologies being used across disciplines today (Duch, Gron, and Allen, 2001). This strategy creates learning opportunities out of everyday situations, turning otherwise boring lectures into dynamic learning experiences. The problems are deliberately ill-structured (or open-ended) and are typically based on real-life simulations; they are designed for thoughtful and careful analysis to help improve critical thinking skills by applying the learner's own expertise and experience to data collection, analysis, and formulation of a solution. In this pilot program, group learning was used to facilitate sharing of ideas and insights about the problems and information needs. The faculty reported that interactive relationships between peers, instructors, and librarians led to more sophisticated solutions than when the students worked independently on information retrieval activities. They commented that critical thinking skills were demonstrated primarily in the ways in which the students selected and used information.

NEEDS ASSESSMENT

Central to the design of this information literacy curriculum is a commitment to building a learning environment for improving the technical and information literacy skills of the students enrolled at Purdue University. A task force of librarians, faculty, graduate assistants from the School of Education, and graduate students from the Statistics department coordinated the development and implementation of the needs assessment tool for the first phase of the project. A major initiative of this group was to measure the level of problem-solving, technical competence, and information literacy skills, and to evaluate the information-seeking behaviors of the participants in the pilot. The survey results (Figure 2) indicated that 22 randomly selected, undergraduate students enrolled in both EAS 109 and SCI 490 evaluated their technical and problem-solving skills very high. They evaluated themselves, however, much lower on research skills and team or group work activities.

Additionally, the same students were asked to rank their information literacy skills according to confidence level. In this survey (Figure 3), they reported being self-assured of the value of information but less so about their ability to evaluate it effectively or to use it to solve a problem. The results show 72% of the students surveyed believe that they are information literate. These findings, along with previous studies (Kuhlthau, C., Turock, B., and Belvin, R., 1992; Jonassen D. H. and Henning, P., 1999; and Eager, C. and Oppenheim, C., 1996), demonstrate that inflated confidence levels and familiarity with information technology hinder the effectiveness of typical library instruction sessions. An anonymous author wrote that it is impossible to teach something someone already thinks he knows. In this pilot program, librarians and faculty collaborated to find a strategy for reaching students at a point of need, when information literacy can most efficiently be learned and retained.

Because of students' existing beliefs that they are already information literate, it was necessary to begin the integration of information skill building where they could use the tools they knew. Librarians expected that, given the problem solving activity, students would first turn to their favorite search engines on the World Wide Web for information. Allowing them to work within

FIGURE 2. Analysis of Student Self-Assessment of Research and Technology Skills

	Confident	Average	Undecided
I rate myself as a researcher	.36	.54	.10
I rate myself using information technology	.50	.40	.10
I rate my problem-solving skills	.53	.47	
I rate my ability to work in a group	.40	.40	.20

FIGURE 3. Analysis of Student Self-Assessment of Information Literacy Skills

	Confident	Average	Undecided
I rate my understanding of the value of information	.90		.10
I rate my ability to evaluate information effectively	.59	.10	.31
I rate my ability to construct quality search strategies	.59	.10	.31
I rate myself as information literate	.72	.16	.22

their comfort zone alleviated any concerns about not being knowledgeable regarding the topic or their ability to work in a group. Instead of fearing the unknown, they relied on using a familiar resource to find some background materials and to begin establishing ideas for workable solutions. They were quickly engaged in the project and found useful data to enhance or guide their understanding of the given problem. As information sources on the World Wide Web were exhausted, librarians took the opportunity to introduce additional resources such as indexes to scholarly journal articles. Although many students knew about these databases, few used them. Now, they were open to trying different ways for finding further information on their topics.

This constructivist approach to teaching is based on creating an interest in new resources by building on previous experiences. Once trust was established in the two pilot classrooms, and existing knowledge of information retrieval was validated, students were receptive to learning more. The three steps used to develop this classroom environment are based on the learning theories of David Ausubel (1963). His work states that meaningful learning happens when students consciously and explicitly tie new knowledge to relevant concepts within their own knowledge structure. The pilot project accomplished this through:

- Introducing new concepts by building on what the student already knows.

- Discriminating new conceptual understandings from what is already known by examining similarities and differences (i.e., how scholarly indexes and the World Wide Web are similar/different).
- Using instructional supports (concept maps, worksheets, dialog, peer mentoring) to help integrate new concepts into the student's existing knowledge bank.

CURRICULUM DEVELOPMENT

For the pilot project, librarians and faculty agreed on using instructional supports to help guide the learners through the complicated information retrieval and problem-solving experience. These tools, along with some carefully planned instruction, were the right combination of problem solving, content knowledge, and critical thinking needed to integrate information literacy seamlessly into the curriculum. The instructional supports provided a well-designed method of bridging and linking old information to new concepts and, in this case, new skills. Instructional supports are used to give structure and meaning to learning complex ideas. This is important for open-ended approaches like problem-based learning (PBL), which can be overwhelming especially when students are unfamiliar with the topic or they are not sure where to find relevant information. In this curriculum, four kinds of instructional supports were used to augment the PBL experience including:

- Concept maps
- Worksheets
- Dialog with instructors and librarians
- Peer-to-peer mentoring

Concept maps guide learners to relate existing knowledge to information needs and help instructors observe the problem solving and information retrieval process (Novak, 1998). In both of the pilot courses, once the problem statement was revealed, students were given a K-N-D map (What do I KNOW about this problem already? What do I NEED to know in order to propose a solution? What will I DO to solve the problem?) to work on individually. After spending some time working alone, they came together in small groups to compare maps and decided how to reorganize their collective knowledge to formulate one cohesive plan of action. The preparation work, prior to working in the groups is critical to getting full participation. Rather than basing grades only on group work, individual activities were incorporated into the curriculum to help eliminate social loafing and to evaluate students' performance

(LaLopa, 2000). Similarly, worksheets were used to guide and measure both individual and group contributions to the information retrieval experience. Some of the guiding questions used include:

- What indexes did you use?
- What words did you use in your search?
- How many results did your search retrieve?
- Did you revise your search?
- How did your revised search improve your results?

Planned dialog between instructors and librarians, students and instructors, students and librarians, and students and students were also important instructional supports in this curriculum design. As students engaged in the problem solving and information retrieval process, faculty and librarians circulated around the classroom asking questions of the groups as they worked. Some of questions required the students to describe the journal articles or Web sites they used and why the content was relevant to the given problem. Additionally, some questions related to credibility to ensure that students knew how to check the authority of a source. Throughout the semester, students were encouraged to ask for one-on-one help as needed. Librarians and faculty kept office hours for appointments or drop-in assistance, and all group problem-solving activities took place in computer labs where access to the Internet, including the libraries' catalog and indexes to scholarly journal articles, was possible. This also provided the students with essential time to work on projects as a group, without having to be concerned with schedules and arranging meeting times. Doing these activities within the time allotted for the regularly scheduled class helped students work more effectively in groups and they reported having positive experiences throughout the semester.

IMPACTS

In order to accomplish the first phase goal of assessing the actual technical and information literacy skills of the target group, the following behaviors and phenomena were observed over a period of 15 weeks:

- How information was accessed
- How information was used
- How many different formats of information sources were cited

During instruction, librarians acting as participant observers in the classroom noticed that students accessed the World Wide Web, using their favorite search engine, to find relevant data to support the given information need. Very few used the catalog or scholarly resources as their starting point, even if they demonstrated prior knowledge of these tools. When interviewed by the librarians about their use of the World Wide Web search engine as the primary information retrieval tool, students stated a belief that the search engines they selected were more effective in finding information than the catalog or indexes. They could find information faster and in full-text format, therefore meeting information needs on-demand. When asked if relevance and credibility were more important than finding information on-demand, they unanimously reported no. These responses support observations that students rely on the World Wide Web and are not using scholarly electronic databases for research assignments and projects.

At the end of the 15-week semester, the same 22 students were given two more self-assessments. The first one measured their attitudes about the importance of information literacy. The second asked them to evaluate their information skills after participating in this experimental curriculum integration project. This second self-assessment tool was a more detailed version of the one used prior to instruction. It specifically asked the students to evaluate themselves on the same skills that the faculty selected as learning outcomes for the pilot course. The only item that remained the same was the question on their ability to evaluate information sources. In the pre-assessment (Figure 4), 59% of the students reported high confidence in this skill set.

Ironically, the numbers flipped after instruction with only 41% reporting they felt a high level of confidence. This led the faculty and the librarians to question two things: were the students self-reflecting about the process and realizing that they did not know as much as they thought they did, or were more evaluation exercises required for the curriculum? Maybe the answer was both! In the post-assessment (Figure 5), students seemed to rate themselves more closely to their actual achievement on the course assignments. Many gained new insights in problem solving and information retrieval. Some required more guidance throughout the process and produced average work. Overall, the faculty said that the final projects and papers were much better for having integrated these skills directly into the course requirements.

CONCLUSION

After completing the pilot program, the faculty and librarian collaborators determined that one size does not fit all when designing a curriculum for information literacy integration. Often there are several iterations of defining and refining information skills needed for various tasks, and how best to teach

FIGURE 4. Students' Attitudes Toward the Importance of Information Literacy Content

	Very Important	Somewhat Important	Somewhat Unimportant	Very Unimportant	Don't Know
Formulate a research question	10	8	3	1	0
Describe a topic	12	7	1	1	1
Use a variety of resources	16	3	1	1	1
Find needed information	18	4	0	0	0
Evaluate sources	14	6	2	0	0
Cite information	16	4	2	0	0

FIGURE 5. Students' Self-Assessment of Information Literacy Skills at the End of the 15-Week Pilot Program

	Confident	Average	Don't Know
Formulate a research question	11	11	0
Describe a topic	16	5	1
Use a variety of resources	16	6	1
Find needed information	13	9	0
Evaluate sources	9	13	0
Cite information	18	4	0

them when ability and comfort levels differ among members of the class. The approach used in this project incorporated non-traditional models of instruction, as well as some more conventional techniques to help reveal and dispel common misconceptions about what students are able to do with information technology. The basis for establishing working relationships with both faculty and students was awareness. The more faculty participants reflected on their beliefs regarding information skills, the easier it was to collaborate. Additionally, the more students were challenged to test their own skills, the more they realized how much they needed to learn.

This was a time-intensive project. The planning process took three months of weekly, one-hour meetings and about 40 hours of planning, designing, and testing instructional materials. The results, however, are well worth the time invested:

• Faculty members are continuing to use the curriculum independent of librarian involvement in the classroom.

- Librarians are continuing to create learning tools and provide instructional support through on-line course management software.
- Student performance is improved as more relevant, scholarly materials are cited for research papers and projects.
- Word-of-mouth "advertising" from satisfied faculty participants is drawing more partners into the library.

REFERENCES

Abell, A. (1994). *Information Use and Business Success: A Review of Recent Research on Effective Information Delivery.* In M. Feeney, M. Grieves (Eds.), *The Value and Impact of Information,* 233, London: Bowker-Saur.

Ahoa, S. (2000, August). *Hidden Curriculum in Higher Education.* Paper presented at Innovations in Higher Education Conference. Helsinki, Finland. Available online: http://www.utu.fi/RUSE/projekiti/piilopor.htm.

Anderson, T. (2002). *Revealing the Hidden Curriculum of E-Learning. In Distance Education and Distributed Learning.* Eds., C. Vrasidasa and G. Glass. Greenwich, CT: Information Age Publishing.

Association of College and Research Libraries (ACRL). *Information Literacy Competencies for Higher Education.* Available online: http://www.ala.org/ Content/NavigationMenu/ACRL/Standards_and_Guidelines/Information_Literacy_ Competency_Standards_for_Higher_Education.htm.

Ausubel, D. (1963). *The Psychology of Meaningful Verbal Learning: An Introduction to School Learning.* New York: Grune and Stratton.

Bergenhenegouwen, G. (1987). *Hidden Curriculum in the University. Higher Education,* 16 (2), 535-543.

Berger, K. and Hines, R. (1994). *What Does the User Really Want? The Library User Survey Project at Duke University. The Journal of Academic Librarianship,* 20 (2), 306-309.

Bloom, B. S. (1956). *Taxonomy of Educational Objectives: The Classification of Educational Goals, by a Committee of College and University Examiners.* New York: Longmans, Green.

Breivik, P. S. (1998). *Student Learning in the Information Age.* Phoenix, AZ: The Oryx Press.

Bruce, C. (1997). *The Relational Approach: A New Model for Information Literacy. The New Review of Information and Library Research,* 3, 1-22.

Covi, L., and Kling, R. (1996). *Organizational Dimensions of Effective Library Use: Closed Rational and Open Natural Systems Models. Journal of the American Society for Information Science,* 47 (9), 672-689.

Curl, S. (2001). *Subramanyam Revisited: Creating a New Model for Information Literacy Instruction. College & Research Libraries,* 62 (5), 455-64.

Duch, B., Gron, S., and Allen, D. (2001). *The Power of Problem-based Learning: A Practical "How To" for Teaching Undergraduate Courses in Any Discipline.* Sterling, VA: Stylus Publishing.

Eager, C. and Oppenheim, C. (1996). *An Observational Method for Understanding User Needs Studies. Journal of Librarianship and Information Science*, 28 (1), 16-23.

Jonassen D. H. and Henning, P. (May-June, 1999). *Mental Models: Knowledge in the Head and Knowledge in the World. Educational Technology*, 39, 37-42.

Kuhlthau, C., Turock, B., and Belvin, R. (1992). *Facilitating Information Seeking Through Cognitive Models of Search Process.* In the *Proceedings of the 55th Annual Meeting of ASIS*, 70-75.

LaLopa, J. M. (2000). *Work Teams.* In Kavanaugh, R. K. *Hospitality Supervision*, 3rd. Ed. East Lansing, MI: Educational Institute of the American Hotel and Motel Association.

Novak, J. D. (1998). *Learning, Creating, and Using Knowledge: Concept Maps as Facilitative Tools in Schools and Corporations.* Mahwah, NJ: L. Erlbaum Associates.

Payette, S. and Rieger, D. (1998). *Supporting Scholarly Inquiry: Incorporating Users in the Design of the Digital Library Program. Information Processing and Management*, 34 (5), 535-555.

Smith, A. and LaLopa, J. (2000). *Teaching Students to Think: How Problem-based Learning is Revolutionizing the Classroom. Chef Educator Today*, 1 (1), 25-27.

Collaboration in Collection Management:
A Convergence of Education and Practice

Margaret Beecher Maurer
Don A. Wicks

SUMMARY. At Kent State University, Libraries and Media Services (LMS) and the School of Library and Information Science (SLIS) have been working closely in the area of collection management. The article explores the multi-faceted way in which the LMS-SLIS collaboration manifests itself and shows how this collaboration goes beyond what might be expected as the normal relationship between a library school and its resident library. *[Article copies available for a fee from The Haworth Document Delivery Service: 1-800-HAWORTH. E-mail address: <docdelivery@haworthpress.com> Website: <http://www.HaworthPress.com> © 2004 by The Haworth Press, Inc. All rights reserved.]*

KEYWORDS. Collaboration, collection management, technical services, collection development, education for librarianship, library school curriculum, library schools, academic libraries, practical training, assessment, cooperation, education for catalogers

---

Margaret Beecher Maurer, MLS, is Assistant Professor and Cataloging Manager, Kent State University Libraries and Media Services (E-mail: mmaurer@lms.kent.edu), and Don A. Wicks, PhD, is Associate Professor, School of Library and Information Science (E-mail: dwicks@kent.edu), both at Kent State University, P.O. Box 5190, Kent, OH 44242-0001.

[Haworth co-indexing entry note]: "Collaboration in Collection Management: A Convergence of Education and Practice." Maurer, Margaret Beecher, and Don A. Wicks. Co-published simultaneously in *Resource Sharing & Information Networks* (The Haworth Information Press, an imprint of The Haworth Press, Inc.) Vol. 17, No. 1/2, 2004, pp. 57-75; and: *Libraries Within Their Institutions: Creative Collaborations* (ed: William Miller, and Rita M. Pellen) The Haworth Information Press, an imprint of The Haworth Press, Inc., 2004, pp. 57-75. Single or multiple copies of this article are available for a fee from The Haworth Document Delivery Service [1-800-HAWORTH, 9:00 a.m. - 5:00 p.m. (EST). E-mail address: docdelivery@ haworthpress.com].

http://www.haworthpress.com/web/RSIN
© 2004 by The Haworth Press, Inc. All rights reserved.
Digital Object Identifier: 10.1300/J121v17n01_06

INTRODUCTION

Kent State University Libraries and Media Services (LMS)'s Collection Management Division and Kent State University's School of Library and Information Science have been collaborating extensively since 1999. Together they have forged a relationship that benefits both institutions, as well as the University's students. This collaboration was motivated by shared goals. There is a sense of responsibility both on the part of the library in providing a lab for the only library school in the state of Ohio, and on the part of the School towards its students and their need for practical application of what is taught in the classroom, not to mention its desire to contribute to the profession in general and to this library in particular.

This article explores the context that has motivated the Library and the Library School, including national trends and issues in librarianship that are shaping the nature of collection development and technical services work. Some of these include:

- The role and importance of practical education for librarianship.
- The availability of courses in technical services and cataloguing.
- Other forces shaping curriculum development for library schools.
- The impact of temporary student apprentices in the collection management unit.
- The changing nature of technical services work, and
- Economic factors that are impacting staffing patterns in collection management units.

The authors describe the multi-faceted way in which the LMS-SLIS collaboration manifests itself and show how this collaboration goes beyond what might be expected as the normal relationship between a library school and its resident library.

At Kent, the Collection Management Division is comprised of Collection Development, Technical Services, Reserves Services, and Circulation. Collaborative efforts that are discussed in this paper happened in the Collection Development and Technical Services areas of Collection Management. Starting in 1999, and developing from that point, the two entities began to become more interconnected through the employment of graduate student assistants (hourly employees), practicum students, and student volunteers to perform tasks in LMS. In 2000, they began providing tours of their Technical Services area for SLIS classes. Library faculty organized presentations on technical services work starting in 2000 as well, and Library faculty began teaching technical services classes for SLIS in 2003. Three different types of collaborations will be discussed: collaboration through students, curricular collaborations, and research collaborations. A discussion of the context for these events will be provided through a literature review. This will be followed by a presentation of the specifics of the LMS-SLIS collaboration.

LITERATURE REVIEW

The issue of training is most often at the heart of discussion about collaboration between library schools and libraries. How librarians are best trained has been a subject of interest in the literature for more than a century.

The history of library education is briefly presented in Rubin (2000). He reports that prior to the establishment of Dewey's School of Library Economy at Columbia University in 1887, library education took the form of apprenticeships, supplemented by reading the literature which developed in earnest in 1876 with the founding of the *American Library Journal* and the publication of the Bureau of Education's Special Report entitled *Public Libraries in the United States of America.* This Report contained chapters on different types of libraries, how to publicize libraries, explanations of different cataloging schemes, lists of reference books, and other training materials. Dewey's model included practice work and the suggestion of months of work experience after the formal training ended. By 1900, there were four library schools in the United States and by 1919, fifteen. Robinson (1985) examined discussions in *Library Journal* in the 1910s and 1920s and discovered that while some spokespersons were calling for an emphasis on general knowledge, others wanted more practical training and, perhaps, even a return to an apprenticeship-based system of preparation for library careers.

C. C. Williamson, an economist and librarian, issued his famous report on library education in 1923, calling for a two-year program of study, with both theory and application included in the curriculum. Coleman (1989) reflected on Williamson's report and on subsequent studies of preparation for library careers. Williamson, Coleman said, advocated practicum training but lamented the quality of existing practica. Rothsten, Coleman added, wrote in 1968 that the situation had changed little from Williamson's day and that the practicum was of minor importance in American programs compared to its place in British library schools. Grotzinger in 1971 and Palmer in 1973 noticed an increased interest in offering practica as part of the curriculum and Witucke in 1976 found that 95 percent of schools which responded to her survey offered a practicum worth three credits (requiring 91-120 hours). Coleman's updated study found that 55 of 60 schools surveyed included a practicum in the curriculum, with 26 saying it was a requirement for students in the school media concentration and only four requiring it for all students. Coleman concluded that interest was high but that there was a lack of consistency among schools in how practica were administered.

Coe (1989) advocates the practicum for cataloging students, tying its value to eventual job placement for students. Some librarians also see work experience in the library as a recruiting tool. Intner and Hill (1991) advocate such experience for undergraduates who might be led to consider librarianship and, after graduate training, return to the library which gave them their first exposure to library work. Joudrey (2002) offers a thorough review of the literature on the practice versus theory debate and says it is "the single most frequently discussed issue in the recent literature on bibliographic control education" (p. 65).

Futas (1994) adds many other benefits to practical training in her article on the place of the practicum in collection development. She lists benefits to the student, the educator, and the librarian, then summarizes the debate over the pros and cons of such an internship. On the pro side, Futas suggests that collection development is better learned in the context of the library than the isolation of the classroom. The student learns what influences collection decisions and how the processes work, and sees new technology applied in the workplace. The library can get maintenance and evaluation tasks done by providing minimal orientation for the student. Students can contribute by preparing or updating collection policies for the library. On the con side, Futas reminds readers that the student's practicum time may be too limited to allow for adequate knowledge of the workplace and its clientele. The library, also, may end up giving too much in the form of training to make the limited contribution of the student worthwhile. Similarly, there may be too much administrative time required of the faculty member.

These cautions aside, the partnership of libraries and library schools in the education of the student is nonetheless seen by some professional associations as a valuable goal. The Association for Library Collections and Technical Services (ALCTS) in its "Educational Policy Statement" (June 27, 1995) sees a balance of responsibility between the library school and the library. Its statement asks schools to provide a curriculum which stresses basic values, "theory over practice," and "decision making over performance of specific duties." The workplace is expected to provide for the continuing education and training needs, especially of novice librarians. The ALCTS statement also lists standards expected of collections librarians.

Other players in the business of collection development have also weighed in on the side of practical training. Moynahan (1997), a publisher turned cataloger, reviews the history of the practicum in library education, pointing out that many professions (for example, law, medicine, engineering) require some type of out-of-classroom experience as part of the degree process. She then goes on to discuss the value to a collections librarian of a practicum with a publisher. A student could learn intellectual property issues from a different point of view, and could begin the process of networking which is important in acquisitions work.

More recently, Brine and Feather (2002), writing from a British perspective, state that the need for both academic study and practical training is "universally recognized" even if the emphasis placed on one or the other has varied greatly over time and geography. They then discuss the development of standards for information professionals in Great Britain. The standards are meant to assist librarians in charting their own professional development.

These British standards, like those of ALCTS mentioned above, provide a window into what professionals think workers in collections and technical services should know and where the teaching and learning will take place. Brine and Feather, for example, suggest that a student will leave school understanding why a skill is needed and possessing a basic level of ability in the skill. A higher level of ability will be found in the professional's first posting and a full command of the skill with ability to work independently will be true of the experienced professional. The ALCTS statement lists many skills under five subheadings (organization, preserving access, selection and acquisition, management, and research analysis), but offers only the general guidance that the school begins an educational process which the library continues.

Some observers have perceived a decline in the attention given to technical services education in library schools. Saye (2002) concludes that "cataloging will continue its decline in the professional education curriculum" (p. 141), resulting in the need for library staff to assume greater responsibility in training new graduates. Mugridge and Furniss (2002) agree, saying there is a "perceived" lack of hands-on practice in library school and that most librarians will have to "learn about authority control on the job." Hill (2002) traces the history of the teaching of cataloging, seeing a lessening in the number of cataloging courses offered in library schools, particularly in the 1970s and 1980s, then offers the opinion that "library schools have abrogated their responsibility to educate catalogers and technical services managers" (p. 249). She does allow that there are many skills which one would not expect to acquire in library school, among them computer skills, communications skills, management skills, and personnel skills. For these, the library professional must have a willingness and commitment to learn.

If the education of catalogers has declined as these writers say, the prognostications of Wilder (2002) become all the more a concern. Wilder says that retirements from cataloguing departments between 2000 and 2010 will lead to a need to replace one-third of such staff. He adds that this gap is compounded by an accompanying decline in hiring, especially of entry-level librarians.

Very recently, Hill (2004) has suggested that the course load in library school, which was adequate 60 years ago, is insufficient for today's needs. She also laments the small size of library school faculties and the tendency to entrust the teaching of cataloging to adjuncts who are neither trained to teach nor held to the same requirements of research and discovery as full-time faculty. Cataloging has become more complex, adds Hill, because of new formats, new OPAC search capabilities, and ". . . increased expectations for bibliographic control" (p. 12). Libraries will have to carry the burden of continuing training of new hires, and additional training will have to be obtained from associations, vendors, bibliographic networks, regional providers, cooperative projects, and the online continuing education offerings of, yes, library schools. Such ongoing educational opportunities will be necessary, she says, even if library schools provided "fabulous" education for entry-level librarians. This perceived need for training beyond library school is echoed by Harralson (2001). According to Harralson, an MLS from an ALA-accredited library school used to be the only requirement for entry-level professional positions. Increasingly, libraries are preferring, and indeed asking for, one or two years of on-the-job training. This is understandable given the lack of redundancy that is evolving in library staffing patterns.

Intner (2002) has been less critical of library schools, advocating the traditional approach which sees the teaching of theory, background, and history of cataloging operations in the classroom by instructors who can keep up on the research and who do not have to spend their time producing cataloging records, as do the librarians. Initial practice, Intner adds, can be done in the school laboratory where mistakes can be easily corrected, or in small libraries, but only the larger workplaces (primarily, large academic libraries, in her view) can offer the practice needed in working with new and varied materials. She emphasized that time on the job, exposure to sophisticated materials, and the guidance of experienced staff are the only ways to learn advanced cataloging.

Examples of cooperative efforts between school and library can be found in the literature. Genovese (1991) described the work done by library school students at the University of Arizona College of Law Library. Many projects in the cataloging department were going undone, so the library employed library school students, believing that their interest, desire for experience, and basic knowledge of the principles and techniques involved in these projects would serve the institution well. They invested some training time and found that it paid off in quality work and the completion of various cataloging projects.

At Dominican University Graduate School of Library and Information Science, a mentoring program has been established in a cataloging course. Using WebBoard technology, the students can have their work critiqued by interested, experienced professionals. The instructor has observed that theory and applications discussed in class have been enhanced through this collaboration, and that the students also gain opportunities for future networking (Koh, 2002). Where a library may feel it cannot invest time in an internship, some librarians may see this online mentoring approach as a feasible way to add to the students' preparation. The students echoed the value of this approach when they wrote that networking with real-world practitioners verified what was being taught in the classroom and complemented their text-book learning (Aulik et al., 2002). And the mentors said that the experience sharpened their own skills and gave them opportunity to work with resources they may not have been familiar with in their own environments (Harcourt and Neumeister 2002).

Collaboration in collection development has also been reported by Wicks, Bartolo, and Swords (2001). In this case the collaboration was four-fold, involving students in a selections and acquisitions course at Kent State University, librarians, a vendor representative, and faculty across disciplines who serve as departmental representatives in matters concerning the library. The students benefited the library by assisting in the preparation of new collection profiles and the students, in turn, gained insight into that process, the writing of collection policies, and the use of vendor software.

The cooperation of school and library as described in the aforementioned articles was foreseen by Michael Gorman more than twenty years ago. In the first issue of *Technical Services Quarterly* (Fall 1983), Gorman reflected that since Dewey's time library schools have had to face the challenge of balancing the demands of practicality and theory. This challenge would be greater still by 2001, he predicted. Thus, he foresaw the integration of library schools and libraries. "That (more properly speaking) re-integration is," he added, "in my view, the only way in which library education and the practice of librarianship can inform and strengthen each other" and produce well-equipped librarians (p. 70).

A CASE IN POINT:
KENT STATE UNIVERSITY'S LMS AND SLIS

The experience of library science educators and professional librarians, as reflected in the literature just discussed, suggests that there is a need for collaboration between the library school and the library. Librarians at the Kent State University School of Library and Information Science (SLIS) and the KSU Libraries and Media Services (LMS)'s Collection Management Division were motivated to collaborate by several key issues. The primary motivation for the Library School was to improve student learning in the areas of technical services and collection management. The library faculty were motivated by a recognition of their unique position as the library which served the only library school in the state. They postulated that they could contribute to their profession by becoming more of a lab for SLIS and that they could get things accomplished that they did not have the resources to do without student assistance. Both sides could also see an opportunity to contribute to the profession in general and this library in particular.

COLLABORATION THROUGH STUDENT WORKERS

Kent State's Collection Management Division works with three different types of students: graduate student assistants (GSAs), practicum students, and volunteers. GSAs work for an hourly wage and perform a wide variety of needed tasks. Their work tends to be more maintenance-oriented than the work performed by practicum students, because the latter are paying the university to gain an educational experience, while the former are employed by the Library for a wage. Often students move from one status to another, perhaps starting as a practicum student and then becoming a GSA when the opportunity presents itself. Some of the volunteers are former employees who are seeking post-graduate employment and want to retain their cataloging skills as well as gain new experience.

Working with student employees is similar to hiring a long stream of temporary employees. The library benefits from their relatively low cost and from the greater flexibility afforded by students cycling in and out of jobs. Jobs can be re-designed quickly in response to changing conditions even if the same student remains in the position. Of course, the administrative and training costs are much higher than they are for permanent employees, but the lower wages that the students are paid helps to offset this. Also the library must build safeguards into the job design, hiring, training, and separation processes to minimize the costs and maximize the benefits. At Kent State, the Library constantly assesses the situation, the job, and the student's performance, leaving itself open to change as needed.

GRADUATE STUDENT ASSISTANTS

The hiring of GSAs should be treated as professionally as the hiring of other classes of employees in order to benefit in the long term. Fewer hiring mistakes are made, and the library is able to be very strategic about what the GSAs are accomplishing The first step in the process is reassessing the position. Before the library even begins to recruit candidates for its GSA positions, it looks at what the previous student was doing, what it would like to change, and what its needs are. It revises the job description and the job requirements as needed, and only then does it search for a student. It takes the selection and hiring of students very seriously.

Current requirements are that GSAs are enrolled in the KSU SLIS program, are able to work 12-30 hours per week during semesters during normal business hours, and are able to work at least two semesters. For cataloging practica, the preference is for applicants who have a knowledge of cataloging standards, who have completed the cataloging course at SLIS, and who can work between semesters. Specific positions also require certain experience or background such as experience working with serials or with government documents, or a background in music. Generally, the Library prefers students that have some cataloging experience.

Interviews are conducted in a professional manner with all students asked the same questions and with two staff members present for each interview. The students are queried regarding their preferred learning styles, their ability to apply skills from one arena to another, how they handle problems they encounter, their ability to work independently, and what their skill level is with basic office software and computers. A serious effort at this point in the process will prevent the Library from making unnecessary mistakes.

Once a successful candidate is identified the Library must provide the individual with the resources to do the work. The Collection Development area has six student workstations that are used for all student employees, practicum students, and volunteers. During busy semesters the stations must actually be scheduled for half-day blocks. The students are also provided with any other equipment they need, including any software authorizations. For example, a student working with OCLC is given his or her own authorization, which fosters a greater sense of pride and identity than using a generic account would provide.

The educational benefits of practical library work during library school are well documented. Students who work in Kent's Collection Management area gain valuable experience and learn skills specific to collection development and technical services work. They do not earn a high wage as student employees ($6.25 per hour), but they are provided with experiences that will serve them throughout their careers. Students can learn the practical skills that they would not learn in library school where the emphasis is on theory and where it is difficult to include sufficient hands-on practice. If they are successful in their work they may learn how to perform comfortably in OCLC and in the Innovative Interfaces Library system used at Kent State. They gain understanding of the structure of an integrated library system on a very practical level. They may have an opportunity to exercise the cataloging skills they learn in their library school curriculum. They begin to develop the professional judgment that is the hallmark of a well-trained technical services or collection management librarian. Even if they never work another day in a technical services or collection development unit, they will gain an understanding that will make them better librarians.

New student employees benefit from a structured employee orientation that is brief, but thorough. Librarians introduce the work rules and work culture to the students. Beyond that, training is tailored to match the job they will be performing. Much of this training is one-on-one with an experienced librarian walking him or her through the new process. Students are encouraged to read the professional documentation and bring back any questions they may have.

When the student leaves employment, the Library schedules an exit interview. This step accomplishes two purposes. First, it informs the department of the student's progress with his or her particular projects. Secondly, students are invited to assess the department's work with them and the experiences they have had. Their comments have contributed much to change employment processes.

This sounds like a lot of work and a first response to this might be to ask "Why bother?" However, it has been found that there are real benefits for the Library, benefits for the Library School, and benefits for the student. Since January of 2001, LMS has clocked at least 2,500 hours of graduate-level student employment. These students have originally cataloged library materials in a spectrum of formats including books, theses and dissertations, sound recordings, music recordings, and videorecordings. They have copy cataloged materials in all of these formats as well as materials accessed as remote electronic resources, and they have linked the catalog to those remote resources. They have filled gaps during temporary staffing shortages brought about by retirements and illnesses. They have taken on quality-control projects that have improved precision and recall in the catalog. And, they have performed countless repetitive tasks that have freed professional staff to take on more challenging work. Simultaneously, they have invented new ways of doing work and taught the full-time staff new tricks.

WORKING WITH PRACTICUM STUDENTS

Students in the Library School are required to complete a three-credit Culminating Experience which can take the form of a research paper, a research project, or a practicum. The practicum consists of 100 hours of on-site work experience plus 50 hours devoted to a paper or project. In the end, the student submits a packet of materials consisting of a statement of objectives, a summary reflecting on whether those objectives were realized, some samples of working documents, a journal accounting for the time spent on the job, and the final paper or project. The on-site supervisor also prepares a performance evaluation. All of this material is assessed by the academic advisor in the School.

If GSAs are temporary employees, then practicum students are very-temporary employees, sometimes working within technical services or collection development for as little as a month depending upon how they schedule their time. Others stretch their time out over a semester or more. Some of the same caveats regarding the management of the situation are true when working with practicum students. The more planning and organization that precedes the experience, the more successful it will be.

The best practicum experiences happen when a good match is made between the needs and expectations of the student and the needs of the library. Different practica emphasize different sets of skills. For example, a copy cataloging practicum will teach different things than will be learned from originally cataloging theses and dissertations. Consequently, different practicum projects have different requirements. For example, if the student wishes to learn how to do original cataloging, she or he must have already taken the cataloging class and be willing to work in the Cataloging Area for a minimum of 150 hours, 50 hours more than most other practica. The Library feels that it needs to get some benefit out of this process and that the additional hours will allow for that to happen.

A useful tactic is to provide the same experiences to a number of students, one after another, re-using the orientation and training material, equipment, and supplies. Therefore the department maintains a stable of practicum projects that it cycles students through until the projects are completed. Practica often involve tasks that the Library sees as important but for which it does not have adequate staffing to accomplish. A list of projects is maintained that includes a description of the project, which librarian the student would work with, as well as some information on the nature of the work. This list is reviewed each semester by Collection Management staff and is used to interview potential students and make the matches between them and the work available.

Collection Management librarians have learned to be very clear about what the work will entail for a specific project. Where the department has had unsuccessful practicum projects, and there have been a handful, it has either been because the student's expectations did not match the Library's or because the student was not suited to the work at hand. To make an effective match between the students seeking a practicum and an appropriate project, the Library interviews the students to ascertain their expectations, desires, experiences, and talents. Once the match is made and the practicum arranged with the Library School, it is important that the Library prepare for the arrival of the new practicum student by providing any resources needed to do the work.

In order to manage this process, LMS created the *Collection Management Practicum Student Checklist*, an eight-page document that lists the goals and objectives of the program and then provides a blueprint for the steps involved in each practicum including:

* Preplanning for program improvement
* Recruitment tasks
* Selection processes
* Equipment, software, and workspace needs
* Orientation materials
* Expectations and methods of assessment
* Training needs
* Supervision, and
* The student's professional experience assessment.

The department also suggests that its librarians limit their face-to-face training for each student to 25 hours. This requirement was born out of experience and ongoing assessment. Spending time training practicum students can become burdensome. By setting expectations at the beginning of the process, the library keeps the training focused and efficient and helps maximize benefits.

Since the program's inception in the fall of 1999 through spring 2004, a total of 25 practicum students in Collection Management have worked nearly 3,000 hours. Since only one-quarter of that time was spent with library employees, with the remaining work done on their own, the library gained an additional 2,250 hours of work through this program. To put this in perspective, when these numbers are added to the figures reported above for GSAs it represents approximately the equivalent of one full-time employee for two years.

Practicum students have originally cataloged musical sound recordings and streaming videos, have assisted with authority control work, have written collection development policies, have copy cataloged gift books, and have set up access to electronic journals by reviewing license agreements. One intrepid practicum student learned how to originally catalog on OCLC, taught herself how to transliterate Ukrainian (she was a native speaker) and either copy or originally cataloged 450 Russian or Ukrainian language titles (a gift collection). Another made significant contributions in the area of Afro-Pop music cataloging, supporting a unique course of study offered by Kent State.

Students generally have a good experience during their practica. A cataloging practicum student wrote that her practicum experience

> . . . presented me with a valuable opportunity to practice the skills I gained through my cataloging class in a real life setting. It gave me a unique possibility to explore KentLINK, OCLC and professional cataloging tools. It introduced me to professional catalogers whose kind help was always available to me during the course of my practicum. Interactions with these professionals contributed greatly to my learning experience.

A collection development practicum student commented that "I began to understand how collection development worked, why the policies are important and what goes into the approval plan for the different departments. It is important as a librarian to understand collection management."

Another commented that

> As many job postings state that candidates for library positions have at least familiarity with basic cataloging it was very important to me, as a soon-to-be-graduate of SLIS and job applicant, to be able to say with confidence that I knew MARC formats, was familiar with the OCLC database, and had experience using LCSH. I did not feel after my cataloging class that I could legitimately say I had experience in any of these areas, but am now confident that I have the necessary skills to be able to claim knowledge in all these areas—even perhaps some small measure of expertise.

"When I started I was a raw well-educated, well-meaning rookie," another student wrote. "Now I feel like a librarian."

The majority of the students work with one librarian. Recently the department has begun to experiment with split practica in which the students work with two different librarians on separate projects, or perhaps, work with librarians from other units. A recent collection development practicum involved working with faculty from the KSU Visual Communication Design Department and the Collection Development Librarian.

In addition to the skills they learn, many students also benefit from an opportunity to assemble a portfolio of original work which they can take with them to job interviews. The Library feels that it is contributing to the profession by providing training in collection development and technical services that leads to the development of new professionals in these fields. Librarians are also asked to act as references and become the foundation stones for the students' professional networks. Students also benefit serendipitously from any training that the Library happens to be providing its employees during their practicum.

At the end of their practica, students are evaluated by the librarian as required by the Library School. The students, in turn, are asked to assess their experience in Collection Management by filling out the *Practicum Student Evaluation*. In this evaluation the department asks the students to list experiences they valued and experiences they did not value, as well as ways the department could improve the training and the experience. These evaluations are taken very seriously and are discussed at managers' meetings, with worthwhile changes, as suggested by the students, implemented. For example, students suggested that the Library create personal web pages for students containing the resources they need for their specific projects. The department has done this and has found it to be a very successful tool for training.

WORKING WITH OTHER VOLUNTEERS

There is a great deal of professional literature on working with volunteers in libraries and a discussion of this in any depth is not the subject of this paper. At Kent State it has been found that in order to work successfully with volunteer library school students there has to be a commitment on the library's part to treat them as well as paid employees are treated. If the intake process for volunteers is not almost as carefully planned and executed as the process is for employees, then the library will make some expensive mistakes. While it is easier to tell a volunteer that his or her services are no longer needed than it is to fire an employee, the process of getting to the realization that the situation is failing is long, convoluted, and one that should be avoided if possible.

Students who wish to volunteer in Kent's Collection Management area are subject to many of the same intake processes that we perform for other sorts of students. They are interviewed and matched with a project or task, and they are provided with the training and resources that they need to do their work. Volunteers perform tasks that are similar to the work performed by GSAs and practicum students.

CURRICULUM COLLABORATIONS

Direct collaborations between SLIS students and librarians in the library's Collection Management division have been highly successful, but they have not been the only point of collaboration. Library faculty and staff have directly participated in the SLIS curriculum. For example, Wicks' "Selections and Acquisitions" classes have been touring the Collection Management area here at Kent since the year 2000.

When the Library was first approached about providing the tours, a chief management concern was finding a way to minimize workflow disruption caused by touring students. The managers did not want to impact productivity more than what was needed. One way this was accomplished was through splitting the class in half. While one group was touring the other was listening to presentations on collection development. This minimized the herd impact of the group. While on the tour, only one librarian remained with the students the entire time. The students toured Acquisitions, Bindery, Serials, Cataloging, Mailroom, Gifts, Authority and Quality Control, and Collection Development. At each point Collection Management staff would stop their work and talk briefly to the students, explaining their work, describing the materials they worked with, and answering questions.

The students learned about the nature of collection development and technical services work from seasoned professionals. The librarians saw it as an opportunity to attract future student employees and practicum students, and as a recruitment opportunity for technical services and collection development careers. A sense of pride in the work was also communicated. Responses from the tour by students have generally been positive. To include distance education students in the experience, the authors are planning to make a video, thus creating a virtual tour.

Maurer also organized a presentation on technical services work that was given to the "Organization of Information" class on at least three separate occasions from 2000 through 2003. The presentations featured technical services librarians from an academic library, a public library, and a special library describing their work and professional concerns. The librarians shared information about work in their diverse environments and their presentations afforded a recruitment opportunity to students considering technical services as a career choice. The students learned a great deal about the day-to-day aspects of technical services as well as what the individual presenters enjoyed about their work.

In 2003, Maurer was hired by the Library School to teach a course on "Technical Services." The course had not been offered for two years and had to be completely redesigned for the current circumstances with an emphasis on the management of technical services.

The Collection Development Librarian has also been a guest in Wicks' "Selection and Acquisitions" class. Plans are to move to a cooperative presentation which will include the librarian and a representative from Kent State's primary vendor, YBP, including a demonstration of its software and an explanation of how approval plans work.

ADDITIONAL COLLABORATION

SLIS and LMS personnel have also collaborated in scholarly and professional publications and presentations. The Wicks, Bartolo, and Swords article mentioned earlier is one example of this cooperation, as is this article. In addition, presentations at an ACRL conference and conferences of the Academic Library Association of Ohio (ALAO) have involved SLIS and LMS personnel.

It might be said that the Library, by virtue of its mission, contributes to the School through its collection, and that the School, by virtue of its mission, provides staff for the Library. The School also contributes to the Library Collection Development department through its faculty member who acts as the Departmental Representative. The Representative, with help as needed from the Collection Development Librarian, selects materials for the collection.

The two units also benefit from the positive and encouraging disposition of the School Director and the Library Dean. The two entities share the third floor of the Library building, and the Library has even yielded space and relocated part of its collection to allow the School to expand its facilities. This sharing of resources would not be possible without the collaborative attitude of the Director and Dean. Library staff have served the School not only as adjunct instructors but also as guests in the classroom and as members of the School's advisory board. Through their assessments of their practicum and student employment experiences, students have also assisted the Collection Management Division in its application of the University's Academic Quality Improvement Program (AQIP).

These mutual contributions are illustrated in Table 1, *Collaborations in Collection Management at KSU*. In the table, "Gives" signifies that either SLIS or LMS gives benefit to the other unit, and "Receives" means that one of those partners receives benefit from the other. In most areas the giving and receiving are mutual. In a few it is one unit which does most of the contributing.

For example, with respect to practicum projects, LMS gives an experience and receives productive work from SLIS students, while SLIS provides the students who do the work and gains educational opportunities for their students. Regarding recruitment to the profession, LMS provides an occasion for students to experience librarianship and receives the benefit of work done. SLIS produces potential librarians and receives a market for its graduates. Adjunct faculty and guests in classes give the benefit of their experience to the

TABLE 1. Collaborations in Collection Management at KSU

LMS		ACTIVITY	SLIS	
Gives	Receives		Gives	Receives
✓	✓	Practicum projects	✓	✓
✓	✓	Student volunteers	✓	
✓	✓	Graduate student assistants	✓	✓
✓	✓	Potential staff recruitment	✓	✓
✓	✓	Cooperative attitude at upper levels of management	✓	✓
✓	✓	Research, publications, and conference presentations	✓	✓
✓	✓	Students develop professional references and form the beginning of their professional network	✓	✓
✓	✓	Relationship between SLIS library representative and library liaison	✓	✓
✓	✓	Tours of technical services by SLIS classes		✓
✓	✓	Presentations by LMS Faculty in SLIS classes		✓
✓	✓	LMS Faculty as SLIS adjunct faculty		✓
	✓	Practical experience at assessment	✓	

students and receive an opportunity to better their skills as they prepare for the presentations. Finally, the Library makes use of SLIS students to fulfill its responsibility to the University to assess its programs.

CONCLUSIONS

It can be said that the two entities share in their desire to serve librarianship by helping students learn about working in libraries. Though the School can work towards this goal through its classroom instruction and lab work, plus its required readings and assignments, it needs the living laboratory of the neighboring academic library to round out the practical education of its students. The literature suggests that students are undertrained without the on-the-job training which the library provides. Much of that training will come only after employment, but some, certainly, can be gained before the student graduates.

The discussion in this article has focused on one department in one academic library. In the same Library, there is additional collaboration with other departments, such as reference and special collections. Such collaboration serves to deflect some of the criticism found in the literature of a perceived lessening of preparation in areas like cataloguing. As graduate programs, schools like SLIS, of necessity, include theory and research design in their curriculum. As professional programs, these same schools also include practice or application. Similarly, libraries such as Kent's LMS look for well-grounded *and* specifically-trained candidates for open positions. It is to both parties' benefit to cooperate. The example of these two bodies says that collaboration can be extensive and multi-faceted.

BIBLIOGRAPHY

Association for Library Collections and Technical Services. Web site. http://www. ala.org/ala/alcts/alcts.htm. Accessed May 24, 2004.

Aulik, Judith L. et al. "Online Mentoring: A Student Experience at Dominican University." In Janet Swan Hill, ed. *Education for Cataloging and the Organization of Information: Pitfalls and the Pendulum.* New York: The Haworth Press, Inc., 2002, 289-292.

Brine, Alan and John Feather. "Supporting the Development of Skills for Information Professionals." *Education for Information* 20 (December 2002), 253-262.

Coe, D. Whitney. "Recruitment, A Positive Process." In Sheila S. Intner and Janet Swan Hill, eds., *Recruiting, Educating and Training Cataloging Librarians: Solving the Problems.* New York: Greenwood Press, 1989, 53-72.

Coleman, J. Gordon, Jr. "The Role of the Practicum in Library Schools." *Journal for Education in Library and Information Science* 30, 1 (Summer 1989), 19-27.

Department of the Interior, Bureau of Education. *Public Libraries in the United States of America: Their History, Condition, and Management: Special Report, Part I.* Washington: Government Printing Office, 1876.

Futas, Elizabeth. "The Practicum in Collection Development: A Debate." In Peggy Johnson and Sheila S. Intner, eds., *Recruiting, Educating and Training Librarians for Collection Development.* Westport, CT: Greenwood Press, 1994, 145-156.

Genovese, Robert. "The Use of Library School Students for Technical Services Projects." *Technical Services Quarterly* VIII, 4 (Summer 1984), 63-69.

Gorman, Michael. "Technical Services, 1984-2001 (and before)." *Technical Services Quarterly* I, 1 (Fall 1983), 65-72.

Harcourt, Kate and Susan M. Neumeister. "Online Distance Learning with Cataloging Mentors: The Mentor's Viewpoint." In Janet Swan Hill, ed. *Education for Cataloging and the Organization of Information: Pitfalls and the Pendulum.* New York: The Haworth Press, Inc., 2002, 293-298.

Harralson, David M. "Recruitment in Academic Libraries: Library Literature in the '90s." *College & Undergraduate Libraries* 8, 1 (2001), 37-68.

Hill, Janet Swan. "What Else Do You Need to Know? Practical Skills for Catalogers and Managers." In Janet Swan Hill, ed. *Education for Cataloging and the Organization of Information: Pitfalls and the Pendulum.* New York: The Haworth Press, Inc., 2002, 245-262.

Hill, Janet Swan. "Education and Training of Catalogers: Obsolete? Disappeared? Transformed? (Part I)." *Technicalities* 24, 1 (Jan./Feb. 2004), 1, 10-11.

Hill, Janet Swan. "Education and Training of Catalogers: Obsolete? Disappeared? Transformed? (Part II)." *Technicalities* 24, 2 (Mar./Apr. 2004), 1, 9-13.

Intner, Sheila S. and Janet Swan Hill, eds. *Cataloging: The Professional Development Cycle.* New York: Greenwood Press, 1991.

Intner, Sheila S. "Persistent Issues in Cataloging Education: Considering the Past and Looking Toward the Future." In Janet Swan Hill, ed. *Education for Cataloging and the Organization of Information: Pitfalls and the Pendulum.* New York: The Haworth Press, Inc., 2002, 15-29.

Joudrey, Daniel N. "A New Look at US Graduate Courses in Bibliographic Control." In Janet Swan Hill, ed. *Education for Cataloging and the Organization of Information: Pitfalls and the Pendulum.* New York: The Haworth Press, Inc., 2002, 59-102.

Koh, Gertrude S. "Innovations in Standard Classroom Instruction." In Janet Swan Hill, ed. *Education for Cataloging and the Organization of Information: Pitfalls and the Pendulum.* New York: The Haworth Press, Inc., 2002, 263-288.

Moynahan, Sharon A. "Walk in My Shoes: The Case for a Practicum with a Publisher." *Library Acquisitions: Practice and Theory* 21, 2 (1997), 107-114.

Mugridge, Rebecca L. and Kevin A. Furniss. "Education for Authority Control: Whose Responsibility Is It?" In Janet Swan Hill, ed. *Education for Cataloging and the Organization of Information: Pitfalls and the Pendulum.* New York: The Haworth Press, Inc., 2002, 233-244.

Robinson, William C. "Time Present and Time Past." *Journal for Education in Library and Information Science* 26, 2 (Fall 1985), 79-95.

Rubin, Richard. *Foundations of Library and Information Science.* New York: Neal-Schuman Publishers, 2000.

Wicks, Don A., Laura Bartolo, and David Swords. "Four Birds with One Stone: Collaboration in Collection Development." *Library Collections, Acquisitions, & Technical Services* 25 (2001), 473-483.

Reeling 'Em In:
How to Draw Teaching Faculty
into Collaborative Relationships

Melissa Moore

SUMMARY. All academic librarians can be easily convinced from studies and personal experience that the best way to help students learn lifelong research skills is by collaborating with teaching faculty. The author explores the need for this collaboration to be relational rather than circumstantial, with a long-term focus. She explores practical ways to develop and maintain these relationships throughout the campus community. *[Article copies available for a fee from The Haworth Document Delivery Service: 1-800-HAWORTH. E-mail address: <docdelivery@haworthpress.com> Website: <http://www.HaworthPress.com> © 2004 by The Haworth Press, Inc. All rights reserved.]*

KEYWORDS. Academic libraries, collaboration, faculty-librarian collaboration, library instruction, college and university libraries/relations with faculty and curriculum, interprofessional cooperation

---

Melissa Moore, MSLS, BA, is Reference Librarian and Team Leader for Public Services, Summar Library, Union University, Jackson, TN, where she currently teaches graduate courses in the School Library Media Endorsement Program.

Address correspondence to: Melissa Moore, Box 3159, Summar Library, 1050 Union University Drive, Jackson, TN 38305 (E-mail: mmoore@uu.edu).

[Haworth co-indexing entry note]: "Reeling 'Em In: How to Draw Teaching Faculty into Collaborative Relationships." Moore, Melissa. Co-published simultaneously in *Resource Sharing & Information Networks* (The Haworth Information Press, an imprint of The Haworth Press, Inc.) Vol. 17, No. 1/2, 2004, pp. 77-83; and: *Libraries Within Their Institutions: Creative Collaborations* (ed: William Miller, and Rita M. Pellen) The Haworth Information Press, an imprint of The Haworth Press, Inc., 2004, pp. 77-83. Single or multiple copies of this article are available for a fee from The Haworth Document Delivery Service [1-800-HAWORTH, 9:00 a.m. - 5:00 p.m. (EST). E-mail address: docdelivery@haworthpress.com].

http://www.haworthpress.com/web/RSIN
© 2004 by The Haworth Press, Inc. All rights reserved.
Digital Object Identifier: 10.1300/J121v17n01_07

REFLECTIONS ON A FISHERMAN'S LIFE

As long as I can remember, my father has been a fisherman in his "down" time. He works a busy schedule as an internist, but each week during fishing season he takes short day trips to local fishing holes–either a friend's private lake, or Kentucky Lake, or Pickwick Dam. My mother says she learned early on not to quibble about these trips, that they are necessary for Dad's peace of mind and enjoyment of life. They provide him with a respite from the difficult issues surrounding medical practice in the 21st century.

Occasionally, he has taken longer trips. Two weeks ago, he spent a few days at Pickwick Dam with a fishing buddy, sleeping in a cabin and eating fresh fish. When I was growing up, our annual family trek to Florida was planned around football and cheerleading camps, but location and time were also determined in part by when the fish would be biting. Over the years, he has traveled to Mexico, Canada, Panama, Costa Rica, and Belize to fish for bonefish and permit, marlin and sailfish, bass and walleye.

Each of these various trips has common elements. My dad never just "goes fishing"–he plans for the experience, choosing where he will go the next day and what he wants to catch, selecting the right tackle and assembling his gear, even packing his cooler with cold drinks and sandwiches. According to him, the planning is work necessary for ensuring (inasmuch as the fish will cooperate) a successful trip.

LIBRARIANS AS FISHERMEN?

Those of us who are involved with college-level library instruction already know that *the most successful group instruction which takes place is in the context of a course, with the involvement and support of the teaching faculty member.* We know this intellectually, based on the studies which have been done (Rader,[1] Raspa & Ward,[2] Christe, Glover, & Westwood,[3] and Farber,[4] among others). We know this from personal experience–we've seen the difference instruction makes to students with specific projects to complete, because at the end of our instruction session, these students know what questions to ask, what resources to use, and how to evaluate what they find. And we can know this from collaborating faculty who share with us (anecdotally or formally) the difference in quality they find in those projects.

But how do we get the faculty to the point where they can see the evidence for themselves in the papers they are grading? How do we get them to surrender to us one of their coveted class periods for something as "rote and mundane" as a library instruction session? The answer is collaborative, long-term relationships. I am convinced that we can borrow some wisdom from fishermen like my father to reel teaching faculty into these relationships which benefit students, teaching faculty, and the library as a whole.

PREPARING FOR THE TRIP

For starters, you have to assemble all the gear you will need. Part of the gear is your library's collection. Whether print or online, you need to know what you have and how it complements the academic needs of various disciplines. You have an obligation to use your budget wisely to ensure a collection which matches the needs of diverse populations and programs. Programs tailored to non-traditional students should be supported by a network of online databases, electronic books, and web-based tutorials. Print collections should be up-to-date, well organized, and easily accessible to students. Consortial agreements which increase the number of resources available to your students can be invaluable.

An essential piece of your gear is the support of your library team leader or director. Don't underestimate the value of a supervisor who understands the need for developing relationships and provides you with outlets to pursue those connections. Professional relationships resist analytical measurement and take quality time and attention to develop. You and your supervisor must be in agreement on the priority this outreach is to have, so that your time and efforts in this arena aren't given away to visible, measurable tasks like additional reference desk hours or placing more ILL requests.

Finally, librarians need to be prepared educationally for their excursion. This includes not only an MLS/MIS degree but also training to be effective teachers in your library instruction sessions. This training can come in the form of education courses or workshops designed to increase teacher effectiveness. Typically, librarians are only given an hour to teach students the research skills they need for their specific project, report, or course. You need to know how to make the most of that precious slice of time, and the proper training is an essential step in that direction.

KNOW THE DESTINATION AND THE ROUTE

Whenever my father is planning a fishing trip, he has to decide where he's going, how he's going to get there, and how long it will take. The same holds true for librarians who want to make their instruction programs more successful.

You have to know your fishing hole–where you want to go. The ideal goal for instruction librarians is not having an information literacy program that is part of the academic core at their institution, nor is it doing such a terrific job that you have more requests for instruction than you can handle and more librarians have to be hired to teach the overflow. *The destination, or goal, is relationships with teaching faculty–significant, professional, long-term relationships as peers.* In the nearly eleven years at this fishing hole called Union University, I have developed in-depth relationships with faculty teaching in a variety of disciplines that have, in turn, opened doors of instructional opportunity I thought forever closed. Throughout that time, my goal has been building personal bridges from the library to distinct departments and individual faculty members, so that I can, in turn, help their students conduct quality research.

In addition to knowing your destination, you have to know how to get there. I have had many opportunities to develop relationships with faculty over the last decade. In addition to what I have written elsewhere,[5] let me suggest that you seek out opportunities to interact with faculty outside of the library's hallowed walls, whether through task teams or university-level committee work, working with faculty conducting research, or taking on for-credit teaching opportunities in academic departments. You may have to sell yourself to teaching faculty, particularly if you are young or new to the campus. But you have an obligation to your library, to your university, and to your profession to demonstrate that you understand pedagogy, that you can add significantly to their students' research processes, and that you are their peer. Embrace the challenge.

Finally, you have to know how long the trip's going to take. It can take time to "arrive" at your destination of quality, peer-level relationships with faculty. Some of the ideas you try will work great, right off the bat. The students will be animated and involved in what you are teaching them, the faculty member praising you for your work and lining you up for three other classes next semester. There's also going to be a day when something that worked so well for a colleague fails horribly at your initial attempt. The students are sneaking onto the Web to IM rather than listening enraptured to your spiel and laughing at the appropriate pauses. The faculty member wanders out of your instruction lab or sits in the corner grading papers. No one gets what you are teaching except the brainy female in the front row, and since you see her in the library every day you figure she already knew most of it anyway. For most of us, though, neither of these extremes happens very often–usually, it takes trial and error, lots of practice and a learned flexibility to match up your instructional methods with the students in a particular discipline. That's why we have to persevere, waiting at the toll booths when necessary, coasting down the hills with the top down at those moments of connective harmony, but mostly driving 30 in a 30 mph zone, making headway with ourselves and our students.

KNOW WHAT YOU WANT TO CATCH

Choosing a fishing hole and preparing a tackle box necessitates knowing what kind of fish you are going after. If marlin is the goal, you better have at least 50-pound test line and an excellent quality rod-and-reel with you if you want to be successful. Similarly, as librarians we have to know what we want to catch.

By nature, that implies knowing what you don't want to catch. Several times in the last decade, I have received phone calls from professors who are going to a conference next week and want their class to come to the library so they don't have to pay for a sub or cancel the class entirely. When the time frame has permitted me, I have indulged these individuals and tried to make the best of an unproductive situation, spending the hour talking with the students to determine their needs in the course and seeking to fill in the (large) gaps. But I am not looking for more babysitting jobs when I set out to establish quality relationships with faculty. Nor do I want to spend time trying to convince teaching faculty who don't value the library or what I have to offer that they are wrong. Thankfully, those faculty are few and far between, and I have a multitude of others who do value the ways I can help them and their students.

Your best bet is probably to "fish for" individual faculty members, rather than going after an entire pond (department). Think of the faculty you see in the library on a regular basis. Seek them out—what are they currently teaching? Find out their area of specialization and when they are next teaching a course in that area. Would they benefit from some tailored online or print resource lists which they could share with their students? Is there a new reference set in the library that would enhance their students' learning? Do they have some research project in the works? Is there anything you could do to help them?

In 1993, I signed up for the senior seminar class, taking it for graduate credit, and the faculty member constructed one of my "extra" assignments around my skills and job: I was to teach three one-hour classes, showing my classmates library resources and search strategies that were directly related to our shared assignments. The faculty member was so pleased with both the instruction and the results (on reports, a large portfolio, and a twenty-page research paper) that she invited me to do similar instructions for other classes and (as department chair) promoted my work and availability to the rest of the English department. For the last several years, every member of Union's English department has called on me and the other reference librarians for assignment-specific class instruction, course-specific bibliographies, and one-on-one research help.

KEEPING THE POND STOCKED

Sometimes, my father has a great day fishing but comes home empty-handed. Maybe he's too tired or busy to clean the fish when he gets home. Maybe the freezer's full or my mother's tired of eating fish. But it's important that, at times, he throw the fish back into the pond to keep it stocked for future trips and other fishermen.

Librarians need to look for ways to "keep the pond stocked" as well. We need fresh ideas to try, fresh opportunities to develop relationships with teaching faculty and bring them on board to the importance of library instruction. We need to get the word out that what we are doing is crucial in the lives of our students.

Sharing with other colleagues is crucial in this process. Certainly new ideas appear in the professional literature all the time–new ways of teaching, new ways of reaching out to teaching faculty, specific information literacy or collaboration goals with an academic course or faculty member. Conferences and workshops, both regional and national, abound on these topics. I have found that the sharing of "what works, what doesn't" happens best in the context of–you guessed it–relationships with other librarians whom you know well and are willing to be unguarded with. Discussing "flops" with a librarian in another environment can be extremely beneficial; they can frequently see what you can't because they don't know the professor's idiosyncrasies or the class expectations.

In order to develop relationships with teaching faculty, you have to interact with them and know what their issues are. Serve on those ad hoc committees, attend the greater faculty or faculty senate meetings, eat lunch with them in the cafeteria or sit with them at ball games. In the last few years, I have been fortunate to work with our Center for Faculty Development, teaching faculty workshops on plagiarism and information literacy issues and preparing packets of library materials to be given to new faculty during their orientation process. This, in turn, has given me greater visibility among the teaching faculty and administration, allowing for the development of new relationships.

In conclusion, let me encourage you to give satisfied faculty opportunities to "tell the tale," whether through the library newsletter, a bulletin board, or at a library open house. A few years ago, I was asked to lead a workshop for librarians on ways to reach out to teaching faculty. I had worked with a certain history professor in several venues–teaching information literacy segments for upper-division courses, developing bibliographies of print and online re-sources for specific courses, and aiding him on a personal research project. I asked him to attend the workshop and share his concerns and suggestions with the group. His primary piece of advice was this: *Market yourself and your library. Go after teaching faculty with zeal and purpose. Tell them all the things you can do for them and their students, and then do it well.*

I couldn't have said it better myself. Prepare your tackle, cast your line, and reel 'em in!

NOTES

1. Rader, H. B. Faculty-librarian collaboration in building the curriculum for the millennium–the US experience. 64th IFLA General Conference August 16-21,1998. Available at http://www.ifla.org/IV/ifla64/040-112e.htm (May 20, 2004).

2. Raspa, D. and D. Ward, eds. (2000). The Collaborative imperative: Librarians and faculty working together in the information universe. Chicago: ACRL.

3. Christe, Katherine B.; Glover, Andrea ; Westwood, Glenna (2000). Infiltration and entrenchment: Capturing and securing information literacy territory in academe. *Journal of Academic Librarianship*: pp. 202-208, May.

4. Farber, E. (1999) College libraries and the teaching/learning process: A 25-year reflection. *Journal of Academic Librarianship*: pp. 171-77.

5. Moore, M. (2003). If you build it, will they come? *College & Research Libraries News*: pp. 455-57, July/August.

Formal and Informal Structures for Collaboration on a Campus-Wide Information Literacy Program

Jordana M. Y. Shane

SUMMARY. Information literacy initiatives provide a vehicle for academic librarians to become agents of positive change. A campus-wide Information Literacy Initiative can improve teaching and learning, and further the mission of the institution. The Instruction Librarian may travel across literal and figurative boundaries. Librarians charged with designing and implementing Information Literacy initiatives must develop strong leadership and interpersonal communication abilities, to build effective collaborative relationships across campus. Furthermore, they must be able to work within the strictures of present campus bureaucracies and campus perceptions of roles and responsibilities. *[Article copies available for a fee from The Haworth Document Delivery Service: 1-800-HAWORTH. E-mail address: <docdelivery@haworthpress.com> Website: <http://www.HaworthPress.com> © 2004 by The Haworth Press, Inc. All rights reserved.]*

Jordana M. Y. Shane is Electronic Instruction/Reference Librarian, Paul J. Gutman Library, Philadelphia University, School House Lane and Henry Avenue, Philadelphia, PA 19144 (E-mail: ShaneJ@PhilaU.edu). She is also adjunct faculty, College of Information Science and Technology, Drexel University.

The author wishes to acknowledge Steven J. Bell for suggesting the topic of this paper.

[Haworth co-indexing entry note]: "Formal and Informal Structures for Collaboration on a Campus-Wide Information Literacy Program." Shane, Jordana M. Y. Co-published simultaneously in *Resource Sharing & Information Networks* (The Haworth Information Press, an imprint of The Haworth Press, Inc.) Vol. 17, No. 1/2, 2004, pp. 85-110; and: *Libraries Within Their Institutions: Creative Collaborations* (ed: William Miller, and Rita M. Pellen) The Haworth Information Press, an imprint of The Haworth Press, Inc., 2004, pp. 85-110. Single or multiple copies of this article are available for a fee from The Haworth Document Delivery Service [1-800-HAWORTH, 9:00 a.m. - 5:00 p.m. (EST). E-mail address: docdelivery@haworthpress.com].

KEYWORDS. Information literacy programming, instruction librarians, collaboration

INTRODUCTION

Achieving radical change within higher education is notoriously slow and commonly met with resistance. However, modern colleges and universities have been forced to change, sometimes rapidly and on many fronts, in order to remain relevant, solvent, and competitive. Over the past decade, the academic library landscape has experienced considerable changes of its own. All campus bodies are charged with justifying their existence, the library included. The academic library, too, must produce, and market its contributions to the overall university mission (K. Smith 2000). These contributions must be made consistently, with a high degree of quality, and often within the constraints of stagnant or shrinking budgets. Competition with the Internet, Barnes & Noble, and university departments that get bigger pieces of the budgetary pie has created new obstacles for the modern academic library. Trying to provide knowledgeable, well-trained staff, on top of the best services and resources possible, all within the budget allotted, is a major task in any age. However, today's academic library is challenged to do more with less, at a time when there is so much more to have and so much more to do.

As a result of pressures both internal and external, academic librarianship has also undergone transformation (Farber 1999). Reflecting the times, the 1996 ACRL theme was *Every Librarian a Leader.* In 1999, the ACRL National Conference theme was *Racing Toward Tomorrow.* The ensuing years have seen librarians developing their leadership skills, increasing their marketing skills, and honing their teaching and communication skills. Political savvy and involvement in the campus bureaucracy have also become necessities for academic librarians, whether or not they possess formal faculty status. This is a departure from previous views academic librarians might have had of themselves, their duties, and what they deemed to be the necessary skill set for professional success. The skill set for academic librarianship, as in all areas of librarianship, is expanding. Academic librarians are traveling in directions they might not have thought they would need to go–both figuratively and literally–when they originally signed on to the profession. Underscoring this fact is the upcoming 2005 ACRL conference, entitled *Currents and Convergence: Navigating the Rivers of Change.*

CHANGING ROLES AND RESPONSIBILITIES

Over the past decade, the phrase "paradigm shift" has occurred repeatedly in the literature, often in relation to library instruction (R. Smith 1997). The 1990s saw the formal, widespread movement in academic librarianship away from Bibliographic Instruction to the broader domain of Information Literacy (IL). IL expands on basic user training, simple information retrieval skills, and other technological tools training to encompass critical thinking and problem-solving skills, a broader understanding of the information universe, and the ethical and appropriate use of information, thus promoting users to view themselves now more as creators of new knowledge and accept the notion that they need to become lifelong learners (ACRL 2000).

This transition from Bibliographic Instruction to Information Literacy has also been a slow and gradual change, evolving naturally on some campuses, and less smoothly on others. Benchmarks like Earlham College have been, in many ways, doing it "right" all along, with their long-standing, course-integrated approach. Other institutions have had to devise and implement IL programs rapidly, sometimes with little or no history of BI from which to progress (which can serve to make the task easier in some respects).

New professional positions–"Information Literacy Librarian" or "Instruction Librarian"–have also been a result of the IL movement and philosophy. The "new skills" necessary for all "new millennium" academic librarians are, perhaps, even more crucial for the newly minted Instruction Librarians on campus, as well as for those not-so-new, who are charged with the educational mission of the library, even if these duties are not reflected in their official titles.

Figure 1 illustrates some of the factors that affect the academic Instruction Librarian's quest to initiate and sustain a campus-wide information literacy program. Depending on the institution, there are sure to be more than those listed. The various elements listed in Figure 1 are interconnected, and have the potential to cross-fertilize each other. Inroads made with one can draw upon another to achieve further progress. The Instruction Librarian, in particular, must be aware of ALL of the factors, and discern how exactly to exploit each area to achieve the ultimate goal, and use influence in one area to introduce greater progress into another. Politically, Instruction Librarians need to identify the key players, and enlist the support of those on campus who have influence in each of the various realms. Sometimes, one individual might be influential in more than one factor area. The Instruction Librarian must recognize that all combinations of External/Internal and Formal/Informal structures are necessary for success. All angles can be leveraged to move the IL initiative

FIGURE 1. Formal and Informal Internal/External Factors Affecting the Creation and Implementation of a Campus-Wide Information Literacy Program

	INTERNAL	EXTERNAL
FORMAL	*Campus Governance Structure* *Librarian Faculty Status/Lack Thereof* *Institutional Mission Statement* *Library's Mission Statement* *Library Director's Commitment Level* *Budgetary Constraints*	*ACRL Guidelines: "National Standards"* *IL Competency Standards* *IL Best Practices Guidelines* *Accrediting Bodies* *Statewide Mandates* *Need for Information-Literate Workforce* *Job Placements for Graduates*
INFORMAL	*Campus Culture and Politics* *Librarians' Leadership and Marketing Skills* *Existing Collaborative Relationships* *Collaborations in Development* *Library's Campus Image and Perceptions* *Librarians' Self-Image*	*Peers' Perceptions of Library/Librarians* *Graduates' Perceptions of Library/IL*

forward, and the more angles the librarian capitalizes upon and plays, the more deeply institutionalized the IL initiative can become.

FORMAL INTERNAL STRUCTURES

Two statements that can be made about all academic libraries are that they are all different, and are all undergoing constant change. Each academic library functions as its own entity, but within the context of an institution with an established hierarchy. This larger context influences the library and its status on campus, the way the library is perceived by its constituents. The internal reality and staff of the library also help shape these perceptions. For example, the formal element of whether or not librarians have faculty status can affect perceptions of the library for some members of the constituency, but not matter at all to other members. Such perceptions directly affect the depth and strength of collaboration possible between faculty or administration and librarians. Formally, within the campus governance structure, there may be administrative obstacles for the Instruction Librarian arising from a lack of faculty status. It is, however, possible to overcome such obstacles largely by focusing on productive alliances within the campus hierarchy.

Key individuals can function as champions for the Instruction Librarian's cause, and the information literacy initiative. Expending "top-down" efforts by approaching those with formal power is also an efficient method of marketing information literacy programming. Awareness of the formal structures on campus helps the librarian to identify course coordinators, those in charge of overseeing numerous sections of either the same course or clusters of related courses. Chairs of school or programmatic curriculum committees are other individuals holding real influence and authority. Sometimes a librarian is fortunate enough to have access or interaction with a Dean or Provost, either directly or via the Director or Dean of the Library.

McMillen, Miyagishama and Maughan's (2002) experiences at Oregon State University's Valley Libraries to initiate an instruction program exemplify the importance of such strategic alliances. Their efforts entailed collaboration with faculty to incorporate information literacy into freshman composition courses. At the time, library instruction was not formally a part of the course. Individual faculty teaching the course might require students in their particular section to conduct outside research, and thus, request a library instruction session, while other instructors did not. Therefore, student learning experiences differed, according to the instructors' requirements. The library's Instruction Workgroup approached the coordinator for freshman composition to discuss the possibility of formally incorporating IL components into *every* section of the course, as opposed to the current, uneven and faculty-dependent approach. The Workgroup discovered that their actions were timed perfectly: the coordinator related that the course was currently being retooled, and would require all students to write a research-based paper. The experience of Oregon State illustrates how important it is for Instruction Librarians to be proactive, in addition to how efficient and powerful targeting and making connections with the "right" individuals can be.

Offering to become part of existing activities is not a new idea, but broadening the scope of where possible opportunities lie is necessary. There may be several formal internal vehicles that can be infused with IL programming. Articulating a common ground on which to approach the key individuals requires Instruction Librarians to be informed about what is happening on campus, and also to ply their marketing skills.

For example, Boff and Johnson (2002) conducted a study of First Year Experience (FYE) programs and the involvement of the academic library. FYE programs exist on campuses of all sizes and types, and their strength as vehicles for IL programming lies in the fact that they are commonly required of *all* first-year students. Although there are wide institutional variations among the FYE programs examined, Boff and Johnson's findings were heartening. Of the 315 programs examined, 86% included the library in *some* form, although most of the libraries' involvement was limited to a range of only one to two hours of programming. However, the inclusion of the library component indicated that the library and librarians are viewed as having something worthwhile and important to offer in the larger context of institutional and FYE programmatic goals. Furthermore, collaboration was occurring between FYE program directors and librarians, concerning the content of the library's portion of the FYE programming (Boff and Johnson 2002, 285).

FORMAL EXTERNAL STRUCTURES: ACCREDITATION AND ACRL IL COMPETENCY STANDARDS

Academic librarians are aware that most regional accrediting agencies have recently shifted their focus from "bean-counting" to outcomes assessment. With the advent of online teaching and learning and the rise of digital libraries, the physical library building and its contents have given way to what the academic library *does*, as opposed to what it *houses*. Bonnie Gratch-Lindauer (2002) examines the accreditation standards of the various regional accrediting agencies for higher education in the United States. She notes the increased emphasis, with the newly revised versions of these standards, on outcomes assessment, information literacy, and collaboration between librarians, faculty, administration, and other departments on campus. Instruction Librarians are thus charged with familiarizing themselves with such larger-context issues, particularly student learning outcomes and outcomes assessment (Dugan and Hernon 2002).

The ACRL IL Competency Standards serve as general guidelines and are written broadly; Instruction Librarians usually need to put a spin on them to get local buy-in from their own faculty and administration. Standards and guidelines from programmatic accreditation bodies present a formal external structure that can help promote IL in a discipline-specific manner to which faculty and administration might more easily relate. At California State University at San Marcos, requirements from the Association to Advance Collegiate Schools of Business (AACSB) were used to rationalize the infusion of IL into the curriculum of the School of Business (Fiegen, Cherry, and Watson 2000).

According to the authors, the AACSB has a "requirement that mission-driven competencies be identified for business school graduates" (p. 307). At San Marcos, four core courses in the business curriculum were targeted, and information literacy outcomes were merged with course objectives. The ACRL Competency Standards were then invoked, to define specific IL outcomes appropriate to the targeted courses and stated course objectives. The entrée was gained through existing external guidelines from a formal entity (the AACSB), recognized by business school faculty. Via the guidelines of the AACSB, librarians were able to turn to the ACRL and incorporate "their" guidelines into the curricular design.

INFORMAL INTERNAL STRUCTURES

Alongside formal governance structures, and just as influential, is the prevailing campus culture. As stated above, the actual librarians and library staff help shape the perceptions of the library as an entity on campus. The individual librarian is ALWAYS representing their library, whether he or she is in the library itself, out and about campus, or acting in a professional capacity at a location off-campus, such as at a conference or workshop.

Changing a long-standing set of norms and creating new "institutional memories" is not easy in any organization. Politics are inescapable. Fortunately, many of the fundamental elements necessary for successful collaboration do not depend on the formal position of the instruction librarian within the campus governance hierarchy. These elements, such as motivation, initiative, marketing skills, and leadership abilities reside within the individual librarian. These elements are under the personal control of the librarian, and can be developed and improved if necessary.

THE INSTRUCTION LIBRARIAN'S ROLE: MAKING IT HAPPEN

In presenting the plan for a campus-wide information literacy program, the Instruction Librarian can pull various campus entities together through collaboration, hold the program together through leadership, and play a vital role to effect widespread change and improvement in student learning and faculty teaching. At Oregon State (McMillen, Miyagishima and Maughan 2002), some of the "lessons learned" from their brand-new initiative included "the functions and competencies vital to providing instructional leadership in an academic library" (p. 288). Instruction Librarians are commonly expected to have classroom teaching experience or degrees in education. However, the authors write that important considerations for successful development and implementation of an instruction program include "strategic planning, interpersonal skills including communication and an ability to articulate the importance of information literacy in the curriculum, organizational skills, assessment skills, and finally, teaching knowledge and experience" (p. 297). Furthermore, topping their list of the ideal instruction coordinator is the "ability to think strategically and work locally to identify program partners within the library and the institution at large" (p. 297).

Awareness of the numerous internal and external structures that can be leveraged is necessary, in addition to the willingness to engage in political maneuvering. As Bellman (2001, 49) states, "Politics involves knowing who to work with and how to work with them. If you want to change the system, you had better understand how it works." Bellman continues, saying, "There are no rulebooks about how to play the political games of your organization" (p. 49).

Christine Bruce expresses a similar sentiment, reminding Instruction Librarians that "It is critical that institutions promote an integration of information literacy with the underlying values and philosophies of the educational institution" (2002, 12). Adrianna Kezar's 2001 ASHE-ERIC report explains the characteristics distinctive to institutions of higher learning, and points out elements that can affect organizational change in higher education organizations. Kezar also details numerous models of organizational change and their applications to the environment of higher education (2001, 79-123).

To ensure the success of their programming and marketing efforts, Instruction Librarians must, therefore, be familiar with the "big picture," fitting their IL agendas into the larger context, and working in consort with the agendas of others on campus. Librarians must also work with sensitivity and awareness of the viewpoints of faculty and administration. Administrative values include "bureaucratic norms and structure, power and influence, rationality, and control and coordination of activities." According to Kezar (2001), faculty place greater emphasis on "collegiality, dialogue, shared power, autonomy and peer review" (p. 72). However, "Faculty also have divided loyalty between disciplinary societies, professional fields, and other external groups in which they participate" (p. 72). Mindfulness of these differing perspectives and values will help Instruction Librarians to devise approaches to explaining and marketing IL programming that resound with both faculty and administration, answering for each individual in either group the question "How does this affect *me*?"

Politically, becoming a conduit for the different entities on campus to communicate with each other is something that the Instruction Librarian is positioned to do. Similar concerns about student learning might be held by faculty from various divisions or schools, by librarians, and also by the administration. Faculty and administration might not understand that what they see as a myriad of separate problems are all part of "Information Literacy: The One Skill" (Goad 2002, 21-40). Information Literacy can be the overarching, unifying cause drawing together what might seem like distinct concerns, such as: students' technological fluency, issues of academic integrity, critical thinking, and skills involving the evaluation of information that has been retrieved from any number of different sources. A campus-wide Information Literacy Program provides the structure for a unified cause that actually has a name. For the Instruction Librarian, this may serve as a pathway into the hierarchy for those without official entrée into the existing formal structures.

COLLABORATION

Well-documented in the literature is the sentiment that for a campus-wide IL initiative to be successful and enduring, true collaboration, although elusive and difficult to achieve, is an inescapable necessity. Bottom-up approaches based on informal internal structures need to be used in conjunction with formally mandated top-down approaches. With or without internal or external support, Instruction Librarians will often be the people spearheading these activities, whether or not they are in a formally recognized position of leadership or political authority.

At Auburn University (Jenkins and Boosinger 2003), librarians took upon themselves the task of leading the campus in developing Information Literacy Outcomes. As a result, the librarians experienced how a combination of top-down and bottom-up methods helped them to gain deeper entrée into the formal campus governance structure. Auburn University librarians realized at the outset that their IL program was weak in the area of administrative buy-in and support. Therefore, marketing and consciousness-raising efforts concentrated more heavily on the campus administration (a top-down approach) than on the faculty (a bottom-up approach). Again, impending SACS accreditation was a prime vehicle to jumpstart discussions of information literacy programming between library and campus administration. The resulting chain of events included participation by the Instruction Coordinator and the Chair of Reference and Instruction in a meeting where SACS accreditation requirements for IL in the core curriculum were discussed. Subsequently, the two librarians were then invited to make a presentation to the Core Curriculum Oversight Committee. After this presentation, a plan for assessing learning outcomes in English Composition courses was devised. Thus, via formal structures, librarians were able to travel down to the course/instructor level for an enhanced, mandated, and officially supported collaborative relationship with Composition instructors, the Assistant Director of Composition, as well as the Director of the First Year Experience program (p. 27).

True collaboration is a multi-faceted enterprise, and–although this may present discomfort to some librarians–involves interactions that reach beyond the professional into the personal realm. The professional and personal are intertwined in the individuals with whom the librarian must build these relationships. Going a step beyond mere coordination of efforts requires one to find out what is important to the other person. Iannuzzi summarizes the situation succinctly, "In a truly collaborative environment, participants must agree to a great deal of negotiation, a submission of egos, and a merging of agendas" (p. 100). When asked by a workshop attendee about how exactly to get a collaborative relationship started with faculty, Carla List, of the State University of New York at Plattsburgh, replied, "I went to lunch a lot."

CHARACTERISTICS OF SUCCESSFUL COLLABORATIONS

Manuel, Molloy and Beck (2003) state, "What is lacking though, and perhaps impossible to attain, are criteria librarians might be able to use to identify potential partners for collaboration with some degree of predictive accuracy" (p. 6). Before partners are identified, however, librarians need some fundamental skills and awareness about collaboration in general. *The Collaborative Imperative* (2000), edited by Dane Ward and Dick Raspa, presents a collection of essays that provide valuable guidance. Indeed, there do seem to be some characteristics of successful collaborations that can be applied to a variety of campuses and their corresponding governance structures.

Raspa and Ward introduce the "5 P's of Collaboration": Passion, Persistence, Playfulness, Project, and Promotion (p. 8). "Passion" refers to the particular strengths the librarian can contribute to the collaboration. Perhaps it is research skills, content knowledge, or using technology to teach that can be offered up to the faculty member. "Persistence" is self-explanatory, and is, as previously mentioned, vital in the slow-to-change arena of higher education. An Attitude of "Playfulness" is desirable in that it allows one to be more open to possibility, less guarded and therefore more able to listen and actually hear the other person. "Playfulness" does not imply a lack of commitment to the cause, or Project. "Project" is that around which the group rallies, a clearly articulated problem that needs to be solved, or visionary challenge that needs to be met. Project gives the group focus and a reason to exist. "Promotion" is, again, that old friend "Marketing" in a more personal form. The Passion of an "IL Agenda" that guides every interaction can be powerful. Talking one-on-one with a faculty member is Promotion; slipping in any element of IL into the discussion is generally rather easy, provided the Project vision is clear.

INITIATING COLLABORATION

Raspa and Ward cite *listening* and *trust* as key elements necessary for collaboration. They also say, "By nature, collaboration is a fragile relationship possibly destined for great achievements. But powerful collaboration requires significant effort, lots of time, and a desire to make things happen" (p. 7). Patience, therefore, is not just a virtue, but a necessity. Building trust through active listening occurs over time, not overnight. Nor can collaboration be mandated or forced from above. Therefore, steady, continuous, and incremental progress is, indeed, progress. Capitalizing on every opportunity to work with faculty in *some* positive, mutually beneficial fashion is a step towards deepening the collaborative relationship.

Librarians cannot dictate to faculty, but they can regard themselves as "information consultants" who know their worth and what they have to offer. Most academic librarians are liaisons with one or more schools or academic departments on campus. If librarians are proactive in their liaison roles, faculty are often startled by how much and how quickly a librarian can help them and their students. The zeal of the newly converted often gathers additional supporters from across campus, through word of mouth. These zealots (or "satisfied customers") will understand IL in the manner that it most resounds *with them*. It is necessary to allow each convert to understand IL *in his or her own way*: there are some basic tenets, but IL is a very broad philosophy. For example, there will be "general IL" and "IL in the disciplines" (Grafstein 2002). There is no "cookie-cutter solution" to creating and implementing an IL program (Ratteray 2002, 6). When viewed in its totality, the program needs to be cohesive and make sense, in the context of the institution. Each program will be unique, and there is no hard and fast "right" way to "do IL," just some guiding target outcomes and best practices guidelines.

At California State University, San Marcos, mentioned previously, the authors related one of the benefits of the librarian-faculty collaboration as follows: "The librarian was given the opportunity to observe professors reflect on course objectives and how information competencies matched those objectives" (Fiegen, Cherry, and Watson 2000, p. 316). Furthermore, from their work with the business school faculty, "The activity of matching information competencies to course objectives and of designing an assessment instrument to measure learning outcomes in a test case provided insight into course design not usually available to librarians" (p. 316). Librarians at San Marcos learned the importance of discipline-specific IL, and how effective instructional design needs to be a collaborative and locally-tailored endeavor.

Ultimately, faculty-initiated collaborations are more powerful than librarian-initiated ones or attempts at officially mandated ones. If collaborating is the *faculty members'* idea, they are ready and receptive. *They* have ownership of the collaboration. The faculty member, in her or his own time and fashion, needs to come into alignment with the librarian's IL agenda. Eventually, "good candidates for collaboration" will reveal themselves as such, by stating to the *librarian* where their classroom/content learning goals are compatible with certain (probably oft-stated by the librarian) IL target outcomes. The faculty members need to be given adequate time and space in which to see this, while the librarian (gently) prods them along, sometimes for several semesters running.

One tactic for initiating collaboration is to use the existing formal structure to help get a foot in the door. In terms of marketing the library and the librarians and their expertise: approach the administration of the school with which you liaise, approach course coordinators, request five minutes of departmental meetings, and ask for the distribution list from the administrative assistants of your departments. Bold and daring moves? Uncomfortable actions? We live in dangerous times, my friend, where leadership and marketing are tied together.

Beyond discussion (or drafting) of goals for student learning, the librarian might try an informal foot in the back door, such as discussing with faculty members their area of research expertise. Faculty are deeply committed to their areas of expertise, and librarians can often provide research assistance and greater awareness of potentially helpful information sources.

Through discussions and invitations to collaborate on even routine activities, a rapport can be built with the faculty member that, over time, can lead to substantive IL-focused conversations. Via the competent delivery of everyday library services, trust and respect can be garnered. For instance, collection development, a common duty of the librarian liaison, can be viewed through the lens of IL: to teach online catalog searching skills, there need to be items for the students to find. Should the library include "controversial" items, and allow the students to select from within the circulating collection, ILL partners, and WorldCAT for themselves, instead of guiding them to a carefully constructed Reserve shelf? Every opportunity needs to be evaluated for its potential as a vehicle for introduction of both lower-order and higher-order IL skills and competencies. Every exchange with faculty and administration needs to be fully exploited for its ability to build stronger collaborative ties and potential to open the door to discussion of information literacy at both the curriculum level and at the level of individual classroom assignments.

LEADERSHIP

Terrence Mech, Director of the D. Leonard Corgan Library at King's College, conveyed the sentiment that leadership is necessary for ALL librarians, not just the library director (Mech 1996). He also acknowledges that most librarians tend to be Introverts on the Myers-Briggs scale of personality types. However, Mech notes, this "predisposition does not absolve us" from our responsibilities to ourselves–both personally and professionally–to develop our leadership skills (p. 352).

A hallmark of effective leaders is that they truly subscribe to the saying "know thyself." Glenna Westwood, of the University of Lethbridge, realized early on that she needed to engage in *self-reflection*, as opposed to trying to adopt wholesale the collaborative styles of colleagues (Chiste, Glover and Westwood 2000, p. 203). Awareness of one's own strengths, weaknesses, preferences, and interests is the foundation for developing a genuine and sincere approach to leadership and initiation of librarian-faculty collaborations.

VISION:
YA GOTTA BELIEVE

As the late, great Phillies pitcher Tug McGraw said, "Ya gotta believe." Austin (2002) defines vision as "a projection of a positive image of the ultimate consequences of proposed changes for the service organization and for the organizational stakeholders" (p. 435). Leadership is fueled by vision, and the ability of the leader to effectively articulate and market the vision. An Instruction Librarian does not have to possess the formal title of "Leader" in order to lead (Bellman 2001). From wherever the librarian stands on campus and within the library, it is possible to express a clear vision, and retain that vision in the face of confusion (and in the presence of confused faces). Every conversation with faculty or administration and every action taken as a result thereof should be a step toward the ultimate, long-term goal, provided it is clear *exactly what that goal is*. When the overall vision is clear, it is easier to see potential in what might seem like commonplace duties or routine classroom assignments. "Regardless of the type of institution, a leader's vision comes from one part foresight, one part insight, plenty of imagination and judgment, and often a healthy dose of chutzpah" (Riggs 1997, p. 8).

Consequently, Instruction Librarians must develop thorough awareness of the campus culture, institutional context, and all informal/formal structures that can be tapped. To achieve widespread acceptance, the IL vision that is articulated should be harmonious with other institutional issues already competing for attention and resolution. As Patricia Iannuzzi suggests, "Identify the key campus initiatives and answer the question: *How can the information literacy agenda help this initiative succeed*" (p. 99). This is in contrast to presenting an IL vision that calls for sweeping reform, yet does not resonate in any meaningful fashion with those faculty, administration, and staff called upon to participate in effecting the vision.

Florida International University (FIU) provides an example of how formal internal and external factors were identified and leveraged to expand the reach and positive effects of IL programming (Iannuzzi 1998). Existing campus issues of concern to the administration and to which IL could be attached included The Southern Association of Colleges and Schools (SACS) Accreditation, University Strategic Plan, Student Retention (in the context of the First Year Experience program) and Technology in the Classroom (p. 101). Information Literacy speaks to each of these issues, and was promoted as part of the solution to each. SACS accreditation guidelines and the university's strategic plan both contain language formally recognizing the importance of information literacy and the need to graduate information-literate students. First Year Experience course developers included librarians. Therefore, the incorporation of a strong IL component, and faculty development programming to help support that component, were both possible. Finally, faculty often love technology and learning how to improve their research and teaching skills through the use of technological tools. Faculty development programming using these tools is often popular and much-appreciated on many campuses, including FIU's.

Not uncommon is the attitude among faculty that Information Literacy is just another issue competing for their attention, an add-on to their overloaded courses that sounds as though it will necessitate even more work. However, the careful alignment of IL programming as a means to other ends which faculty hold more dear can efficiently enact the Instruction Librarian's vision.

MARKETING

In addition to playing politics, promoting collaboration, and practicing good leadership, proactive internal and external marketing efforts must run continuously, during and beyond the initial development of the IL program. Vision (leadership) and marketing are interconnected, the former feeding the latter. A strong sense of purpose and sincere commitment to the cause will be perceived as such by the audience. Chuck Broadbent has commented, "I find if you act like an equal, you will be treated as one" (Mech 1996, 347). Such a mind-set can be beneficial to librarians who are trying to enter areas of the governance structure where they may not have an officially recognized place, in order to market their vision. Librarian Glenna Westwood remarks, "If you attend enough meetings where faculty treat each other with disrespect, you understand that some faculty act this way towards everyone, not just towards librarians" (Chiste, Glover and Westwood 2000, p. 204). Again, understanding of the institutional milieu can help Instruction Librarians muster the necessary perseverance to market their IL vision.

The broader the institutionally-accepted definition of IL, the easier infusing IL into the curriculum can be. Christine Bruce (1997) provides a broad model that is inclusive of various conceptions of IL. Conversely, at some institutions, narrower definitions might be more understandable at first. There are many facets of IL on which emphasis can be laid, to find initial common ground with faculty and administration. However, as Grafstein (2002) states, "The manifest importance of these skills notwithstanding, their broad, general character makes it difficult to characterize in any specific way where classroom faculty can fit this enterprise" (p. 198).

For successful, widespread marketing to faculty, and a program that is truly "IL Across the Curriculum," sooner or later it will be necessary for Instruction Librarians to promote IL from the perspectives of the individual disciplines. Such marketing from within the disciplines allows for customized instructional designs that delve into IL skills and competencies using the language and approaches to knowledge creation of that particular discipline. Thus, an immediate connection of IL to faculty and students can be achieved. After an initial level of acceptance is achieved on campus, "generic IL" can indeed be difficult to market, as neither students nor faculty are interested in doing anything "for their own good" or because it will be useful in the future.

COMBINING THE ELEMENTS

Collaboration, leadership, and marketing efforts are simultaneously necessary, and serve to reinforce one another. For all of these elements to be attended to by one person is not an unusual expectation for the academic library. "Moreover, the decision to pursue a far-reaching, contested transformational organizational change objective without the political/power resources to ensure its implementation may only result in an extended period of conflict and struggle" (Austin 2002, 440). Ultimately, a collaborative team effort is necessary for changes to be deep-rooted and enduring. However, at first, only a handful of people will be the instigators of change. For many people, change is perceived as threatening. Therefore, the agents of change need to plan their movements carefully and politically, and anticipate potential roadblocks to success. The following is a case study of Philadelphia University's present experience with planned, transformational change, and the outcomes achieved thus far help illustrate this point.

EFFECTING CHANGE:
THE PHILADELPHIA UNIVERSITY STORY

Philadelphia University is a small, private campus, undergoing growth and change. Via fortuitous timing and strong leadership from the Library Director, the librarians were able to capitalize on a perceived need to build informal collaborative relationships with faculty and administration. These collaborative relationships have ultimately led to formal structures and curricular change. The collaborative model for the IL initiative at Philadelphia University takes advantage of formal, informal, internal, and external structures. All were tapped to ensure the IL program would be instituted as firmly and effectively as possible. An infrastructure was built that easily allowed collaboration to occur, and influence to be exerted in the various structural domains (see Figure 2).

A COURSE-INTEGRATED APPROACH

What appeared to be a difficult situation from Formal and Informal points of view actually held the potential for a best-case scenario. Due to local campus governance structure, the timeliness of the university's accreditation self-study and the university's location in the Middle States region, and the lack of degree-granting programs in the humanities and social sciences, Philadelphia University was forced to take a difficult, but ultimately better road to Information Literacy programming. As opposed to developing a stand-alone course, the Instruction Librarian needed to clearly articulate the vision of an entirely course-integrated, tiered approach to IL programming, and repeat the message until faculty and administration understood it, albeit in their own way, from their own vantage points. Faculty interpret the IL goals most closely from their perspective of teaching in the classroom, the administration from the overall campus-wide view, in light of accreditation, stated institutional learning outcomes, and the IL activities of peer institutions and competitors.

From the librarians' viewpoint, IL needed to be institutionalized in a manner that would be at once non-threatening to faculty, enduring, and immediately relevant for the students. "Effective" IL programming at Philadelphia University cannot be measured by programming delivered to students of political science, history, or literature. Course projects in the humanities and social sciences are typically formal research papers, and the process of producing a written paper is easily recognized as aligning closely with many aspects of IL. Instead, designing successful course-integrated, assignment-driven programming aimed at students majoring in such areas as textile design, architecture, and fashion apparel management would be the task. Students needed to be provided opportunities to "do IL" in a context meaningful to *them.*

As opposed to numerous, disjointed course-related, or even course-integrated, one-shot instruction sessions, an overall plan for curricular change (change that can use the one-shot as a delivery mechanism) would be more en-

FIGURE 2. Formal and Informal Internal/External Factors Affecting the Creation and Implementation of a Campus-Wide Information Literacy Program at Philadelphia University

	INTERNAL	EXTERNAL
FORMAL	Campus Governance Structure Lack of Faculty Status for Librarians Library Administration Mandate/ Mission	Accrediting Bodies Workplace IL/Job Placements for Graduates
INFORMAL	Leadership Skills of Librarians Marketing Skills of Librarians Existing Collaborative Relationships Collaborations in Development Campus Image and Perceptions	Peer Perceptions of Library, Librarians, and Library Director

during and effective. Inculcating IL into the curriculum prevents it from being a bureaucratic problem. If the IL is seamlessly delivered via existing courses, there is no budget line to cut, there is no course to push through the approval process, no new faculty to hire. Librarians at Philadelphia University do not have faculty status, and therefore could not teach a stand-alone course on campus. Since the degree-granting programs are professionally oriented, a course-integrated approach directly delivered via classes in students' major courses of study is necessary. The practical nature of the student body in relation to their education and goals for employment upon graduation also shaped the IL goals delineated in a campus-wide *Information Literacy Framework* to guide the initiative through four years of undergraduate study.

A FORMAL INTRODUCTION

Beginning with a faculty development program in the Fall of 2000, the impending changes to the Middle States accreditation guidelines were used as a point of discussion to introduce IL to the campus community at large, and to begin to pave the way for curricular change. The Middle States region, to which Philadelphia University belongs, directly states that Information Literacy and IL programming are necessary for accreditation and re-accreditation today. Middle States does not like, as Ratteray writes, to "lay down the law," but rather, to let colleges and universities "drive their own engines for change" (Ratteray 2002, 369). Student learning and learning outcomes are paramount to the Middle States approach to self-study and accreditation. The question of whether or not the students are learning what the institution has stated that they are supposed to be learning is now at the forefront: student learning now comes *first*: the "inputs and outputs" of yore are now being scrutinized and evaluated in relation to their effectiveness at supporting student learning. The academic library is included as an important part of the endeavor. Information Literacy and the library's IL plan are part of the General Education require-ments portion of the Middle States Region's guiding document for accredita-tion, revised in 2002 and entitled *Characteristics of Excellence*.

Since the Middle States Commission's Oswald Ratteray served on the ACRL Task Force charged with developing the *Information Literacy Compe-tency Standards for Higher Education*, it is not surprising that Middle States is keenly interested in and aware of information literacy and its role in higher ed-ucation and the institutional enterprise. *Characteristics of Excellence* reiter-ates the need for collaboration between faculty, librarians, and administration to successfully deliver a sound IL program and achieve desired outcomes and levels of student learning. IL is not, therefore, a "library thing," but an institu-tion-wide concern. Faculty, administrators, and librarians must all work to-gether in a coordinated and mutually supportive fashion. To have this "ideal world" mandated from an external source is indeed a plus for librarians in the Middle States region, while at the same time it is a challenge to librarians' po-litical skills, interpersonal skills, and professional self-image.

TLTR:
THE FIRST VEHICLE FOR CHANGE

The semi-formal structure of the campus Teaching Learning & Technology Roundtable (chaired by the Library Director) was exploited to make initial in-roads. The TLTR is not, strictly speaking, part of the formal governance struc-ture, but it is officially recognized, and reports to the Faculty Senate at the Senate's monthly meetings. The TLTR serves in an advisory capacity to the Dean of Academic Affairs, on matters of technology and its role in the educa-tional enterprise. The membership is representative of all of the schools on campus, in addition to members representing the Administration and Office of Information Technology. The TLTR is a good example of how groups can benefit from cross-campus collaboration. It is important to recognize the fac-ulty membership in these groups by making their contributions count in a fash-ion that is *formally* noted and by giving credit to those who serve. As in the IL Task Force, the TLTR membership is diverse, including librarians and the li-brary's Instructional Technologist. The viewpoints offered create discussions and lead to actions that are more informed, better planned, and more success-fully executed.

Since technological and "tool literacy" aspects of IL were recurring themes in TLTR meetings, an "in" was found to introduce the more comprehensive idea of IL to a cross section of campus faculty and administrators already interested in technology, teaching, and student learning.

Through the TLTR, a proposal to establish a campus-wide Information Literacy Program was introduced. A faculty member serving on the TLTR provided a formally recognized "voice" to the initiative by presenting the proposal at a meeting of the Undergraduate Curriculum Committee in the Fall of 2000. The proposal was adopted.

In the Fall of 2000, Information Literacy was formally introduced to the campus community through a faculty development luncheon, an annual fall event with different topics each year. The revisions Middle States was planning, including Information Literacy as a vital component of accreditation, were used as a formal means of connecting with faculty on the issue. This presentation led to informal discussions and connections between all of the librarians and faculty from the schools with which they liaise. The door was opened for librarians to approach faculty and discuss with them issues of assignment design and the use of library resources and the improvement of student research skills. The faculty got started with their understanding of Information Literacy and why it is important. Faculty were allowed to approach information literacy according to their own opinions and from a point of view that resounded most deeply with them. Librarians did not dictate to faculty, but, rather, presented basic, broad definitions and allowed for flexibility in the development of a campus-specific, working definition of IL.

INFORMAL RELATIONSHIPS AND MORE FORMALITY

In the Fall of 2001, the Teaching and Learning Subcommittee of the Undergraduate Curriculum Committee was resurrected. The Teaching and Learning Subcommittee was an official part of the bureaucratic structure but was dormant at the time, waiting for a project to lead. Among those enlisted to serve on the T&L Subcommittee were the Director of the Library, Dean of the School of General Studies, Assistant Vice President of Academic Affairs, and the Instruction Librarian. Faculty members with whom the librarians already had good working relationships were tapped to serve as representatives of their schools, and communicate the aims and activities of the Sub-Committee to their respective faculties.

The common misconception that "technological fluency" is synonymous with Information Literacy was the first hurdle to overcome. Separating Information Literacy from the TLTR, and providing the Information Literacy initiative with its own committee helped to convey the proper message and vision. A conscious effort was made *not* to have a faculty member from the

School of General Studies chair the committee: on the surface, IL competencies align most closely with General Studies (Humanities and Social Sciences) courses. Philadelphia University has a campus-wide initiative, delivered entirely via course-integrated instruction. This conscious and political decision was made to help aid buy-in from faculty within the four professional schools (see appendix), and prevent the initiative from being dismissed as a "General Studies thing." Therefore, a faculty member from the School of Architecture and Design served as the original chair for the first year. Although it is a formal part of the campus governance structure, the Sub-Committee was sustained, again, through the informal, intangible structures such as faculty perceptions of librarians, their roles, and contributions to the university at large.

EMBEDDING IL IN THE CAMPUS CULTURE

In 2002, a reform in the governance structure eliminated the Teaching and Learning Subcommittee, and the Undergraduate Curriculum Committee was renamed the Undergraduate Education Committee. However, the Teaching and Learning Subcommittee continued, under the name of the Information Literacy Task Force. A new chairperson–the faculty member representing the School of Textiles and Materials Science–steered the Task Force through the next two years. (The original chair moved on to become the Chair of the Graduate Education Committee.) Since the IL Task Force is recognized as a formal entity on campus, members of the Task Force with faculty status are allotted credit towards their requirements for university service. This fact is vital for the success of the initiative: active *faculty* participation is how the initiative is implemented in the classroom.

Marketing the IL plan is an ongoing task. All aspects of the marketing campaign seek to formalize the initiative in the minds of the campus constituents. In its initial year, the (Teaching and Learning Sub-Committee) Chair named the plan the *Information Literacy Project@PhilaU*. The Instruction Librarian designed a brochure to raise awareness of what Information Literacy is, and about the campus-wide initiative. The brochure was distributed at the orientation sessions provided to new and adjunct faculty, and also given to faculty from the School of General Studies.

Also created by the Instruction Librarian was the *Information Literacy Project@PhilaU* website. The website is intended to serve as a marketing and communication tool for the Task Force, including content aimed at faculty, students, and administrators. A page dedicated to "Faculty Development & Support" is an important recent addition. Originally, the *Information Literacy Project@PhilaU* website was a sub-web of the Instruction Librarian's own personal site. Eventually, the site was given its own space, and is not a link off of the Library site or the Instruction Librarian's site. This is important in terms of image: the *IL Project* is viewed with more respect, as its own entity, not as a "library only" concern, or worse, as the concern only of the Instruction Librarian. A sign of formal acceptance of the Information Literacy Project and its importance came in the Spring of 2003, when the Instruction Librarian was asked to supply text concerning Information Literacy for the 2003-2005 Philadelphia University Undergraduate Catalog.

Finally, a formal victory with great potential is the newly amended and faculty-approved Course Proposal Form, resulting from the efforts of the Director of Writing Across the Curriculum. Originally, the Course Proposal Form did include a space for the Director of the Library to sign off, indicating that the library had access to sufficient materials to support the proposed course, and no inordinate strains would be placed on the library budget, were the course approved. New language has been introduced where, in addition to the above, the Director of the Library or designee (read "Instruction Librarian") will also examine proposed syllabi and assignments to determine if any aspects of Information Literacy can be incorporated into the course. This "consultation stage" allows an opportunity for discussion of IL to occur. The success of the discussions is, again, up to the collaboration skills of the librarians and faculty members involved, but the formal "foot in the door" is, at least, a start.

NEW IMAGES AND ROLES FOR CAMPUS LIBRARIANS

Currently, the university librarians enjoy greater respect from faculty and administration than had been afforded them in the past. The professionalism and integrity of the library administration and the librarians have garnered them esteem on campus and promoted a positive image of the library. Rules and norms are changing: in addition, the Director, the Instruction Librarian, and the library's Instructional Technologist have been invited to the first and second annual all-university Faculty Retreat, to take an active part in the planning process and discussions concerning the overarching mission and future directions of the University. Through informal collaborative relationships built by each librarian with those outside the library, a positive cycle has been created, and is being sustained and exhibited in formal, public venues. Finally, there is movement on the part of the Dean of Academic Affairs to allow the Instruction Librarian to chair, or–in conjunction with a faculty member, to co-chair–the IL Task Force. Since campus librarians do not have faculty status, they are not eligible to chair groups within the formal governance structure. In this situation, there are institutional rules and norms to consider, and thought needs to be applied as to whether or not such a precedent can and should be set. Such is the way of the world of higher education, where change is incremental and fraught with politics, and such events and deliberations as these should not be taken personally, regardless of the outcome.

CONCLUDING REMARKS

Since Philadelphia University is a small, private university, relatively rapid progress and change are possible. Each institution experiences different obstacles and potentialities borne of campus culture and formal governance structure. However, the necessity for the Instruction Librarian and/or those responsible for instruction to be leaders in the academy remains. Although the *initiation* of an IL program might result from formal internal or external structures, formal structures cannot, of themselves, *sustain* an IL program over the long term.

The elements sustaining the program and helping it to grow are the informal structures, including the dedication of the librarians themselves. Progress continues, via librarian initiative, to build collaborative relationships with faculty, based on creating classroom assignments that necessitate library-based research. More challenging are the collaborative efforts to design assignments aiding development of higher-order thinking and information literacy skills and competencies. As faculty create their unique definitions of IL and shape their assignments accordingly, the whole initiative moves forward.

Extensive literatures are dedicated to librarians and leadership, marketing, and collaboration. There is much in the library literature concerning all facets of IL and the components necessary to design and deliver IL programming, as well as many discussions of the nature of Information Literacy itself, and how to explain it to campus constituencies. There are numerous examples of different approaches taken, successes, failures, and suggestions for implementing IL at different types of institutions.

Instruction Librarians might not have envisioned themselves as leaders, especially if they are not in formally recognized positions of leadership or power within their formal campus structures. However, it is quite likely that Instruction Librarians will end up being leaders. They need, at this point, to turn also to the business literature and examine more closely how leadership, project management, organizational dynamics, "learning organizations" (Senge 1990), organizational change, and marketing are written about outside of the library context. It is not necessary to reinvent the wheel, and it is helpful for the Instruction Librarian to develop perspective on these topics, to better understand the library as an entity in itself and as part of the academy. Furthermore, instruction librarians need to read the general literature of higher education on a regular basis: recent events and trends are not the exclusive concern of top-level library and campus administrators. Being proactive requires being informed, and being positioned to capitalize on emerging developments. Instruction Librarians must, as the Nike slogan says, *"Just Do It."*

REFERENCES

Association of College and Research Libraries. 2002. *Information Literacy Competency Standards for Higher Education.* Available at http://www.ala.org/ala/acrl/acrlstandards/informationliteracycompetency.htm.

Austin, David M. 2002. *Human services management: Organizational leadership in social work practice.* New York: Columbia University Press.

Bellman, Geoffrey M. 2001. *Getting things done when you are not in charge.* San Francisco: Berrett-Koehler Publishers.

Boff, Colleen, and Kristin Johnson. 2002. The library and first-year experience courses: A nationwide study. *Reference Services Review* 30: 277-287.

Bruce, Christine. 2002. *Information Literacy as a Catalyst for Educational Change: A Background Paper.* White Paper prepared for UNESCO, the U.S. National Commission on Libraries and Information Science, and the National Forum on Information Literacy, July 2002. Available at http://www.nclis.gov/libinter/infolitconf&meet/papers/bruce-fullpaper.pdf.

Bruce, Christine. 1997. *The seven faces of information literacy.* Adelaide: Auslib Press.

Chiste, Katherine B., Andrea Glover, and Glenna Westwood. 2000. "Infiltration and entrenchment: Capturing and securing information literacy territory in academe." *The Journal of Academic Librarianship* 26: 202-208.

Dugan, Robert E., and Peter Hernon. 2002. Outcomes assessment: Not synonymous with inputs and outputs. *The Journal of Academic Librarianship* 28: 376-380.

Farber, Evan Ira. 1999. College libraries and the teaching/learning process: A 25-year reflection. *The Journal of Academic Librarianship* 25: 171-177.

Fiegen, Ann M., Bennett Cherry, and Kathleen Watson. 2002. Reflections on collaboration: Learning outcomes and information literacy assessment in the business curriculum. *Reference Services Review* 30: 307-318.

Goad, Tom W. 2002. *Information literacy and workplace performance.* Westport: Quorum Books.

Grafstein, Ann. 2002. A discipline-based approach to information literacy. *The Journal of Academic Librarianship* 28: 197-204.

Gratch-Lindauer, Bonnie. 2002. Comparing the regional accreditation standards: Outcomes assessment and other trends. *The Journal of Academic Librarianship* 28: 14-25.

Iannuzzi, Patricia. 1998. "Faculty development and information literacy: Establishing campus partnerships." *Reference Services Review* 26: 97-102.

Jenkins, Jim, and Marcia Boosinger. 2003. "Collaborating with campus administrators and faculty to integrate information literacy assessment into the core curriculum." *The Southeastern Librarian* 50: 26-31.

Kezar, Adrianna J. 2001. *Understanding and facilitating organizational change in the 21st century: Recent research and conceptualizations*. San Francisco, Jossey-Bass.

Kotter, John P. and Dan S. Cohen. 2002. *The heart of change*. Boston: Harvard Business School Press.

Manuel, Kate, Molly Molloy, and Susan Beck. 2003. *What faculty want: A study of attitudes influencing faculty collaboration in library instruction*. ACRL National Conference, Charlotte, North Carolina, April 10-13.

McMillen, Paula S., Bryan Miyagishima, and Laurel S. Maughan. 2002. Lessons learned about developing and coordinating an instruction program with freshman composition. *Reference Services Review* 30: 288-299.

Mech, Terrence. 1996. Leadership and the evolution of academic librarianship. *The Journal of Academic Librarianship* 22: 345-353.

Middle Sates Commission on Higher Education. 2002. *Characteristics of excellence in higher education: Eligibility requirements and standards for accreditation*. Philadelphia: Middle States Commission on Higher Education.

Raspa, Dick, and Dane Ward, eds. 2000. *The collaborative imperative: Librarians and faculty working together in the information universe*. Chicago: Association of College and Research Libraries.

Ratteray, Oswald M. T. 2002. Information literacy in self-study and accreditation. *The Journal of Academic Librarianship* 28: 368-375.

Riggs, Donald E. 2001. The crisis and opportunities in library leadership. *Journal of Library Administration* 32: 5-17.

Riggs, Donald E. 1997. What's in store for academic libraries? Leadership and management. *The Journal of Academic Librarianship* 23: 3-8.

Schreiber, Becky, and John Shannon. 2001. Developing library leaders for the 21st century. *Journal of Library Administration* 32: 35-57.

Senge, Peter. 1990. *The fifth discipline: The art and practice of the learning organization*. New York: Doubleday.

Smith, Kenneth R. 2000. "New Roles and Responsibilities for the University Library: Advancing Student Learning Through Outcomes Assessment." Association of Research Libraries, New Measures Initiatives: Higher Education Outcomes Research Review. Available at http://www.arl.org/stats/newmeas/outcomes/HEOSmith.html.

Smith, Rise L. 1997. "Philosophical Shift: Teach the Faculty to Teach Information Literacy." ACRL 8th National Conference Contributed and Featured Papers, April 11-14. Available at http://www.ala.org/ala/acrlbucket/nashville1997pap/smith.htm.

WORKS CONSULTED

Black, Christine, Sarah Crest, and Mary Volland. 2001. Building a successful information literacy infrastructure on the foundation of librarian-faculty collaboration. *Research Strategies* 18: 215-225.

Booth, Austin, and Carol Ann Fabien. 2002. Collaborating to advance curriculum-based information literacy initiatives. *Journal of Library Administration* 36: 123-142.

Boyce, Mary E. 2003. Organizational learning is essential to achieving and sustaining change in higher education. *Innovative Higher Education* 28: 119-136.

Bruce, Christine. 1998. The phenomenon of information literacy. *Higher Education Research & Development* 17: 25-43.

Hardesty, Larry. "Faculty Culture and Bibliographic Instruction: An Exploratory Analysis." *Library Trends* 44 (1995): 339-468.

Howe, Eleanor B. 2001. Ten tips for leadership. *Knowledge Quest* 29: 16-19.

National Research Council (U.S.) Committee on Information Technology Literacy. 1999. *Being fluent with information technology.* Washington D.C.: National Academy Press.

Paglia, Alison, and Annie Donahue. 2003. Collaboration works: Integrating information competencies into the psychology curricula. *Reference Services Review* 31: 320-328.

Quinn, Brian. "Librarians' and Psychologists' View of Leadership: Converging and Diverging." *Library Administration and Management* 13 (1999): 147-157.

Senge, Peter et al. 1999. *The dance of change: The challenge of sustaining momentum in learning organizations.* New York: Random House.

Shane, Jordana. 2004. "Information Literacy Project@PhilaU." Available at http://www.philau.edu/infolit.

Whyte, Susan Barnes. 2002. Conversations betwixt and between: Guiding principles. *Reference Services Review* 30: 269-276.

Young, Rosemary M., and Stephena Harmony. 1999. *Working with faculty to design undergraduate information literacy programs.* New York: Neal-Schuman.

APPENDIX. Philadelphia University Information Literacy Initiative Organizational Chart

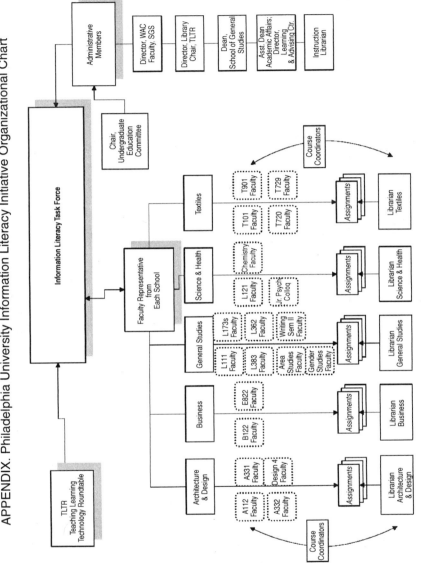

A Campus-Wide Role
for an Information Literacy Committee

Trudi E. Jacobson
Carol Anne Germain

SUMMARY. The current Middle States Commission on Higher Education accreditation guidelines suggest an enhanced role for faculty members in information literacy instruction. A campus-wide information literacy committee can play a key role in accomplishing this. Such a committee at the University at Albany, SUNY, has been critical in addressing this recommendation, and in advancing a general education information literacy requirement. The committee serves as a source of information and as an organizer of workshops for faculty members who would like to tailor their courses to fit the general education information literacy requirement. It also serves as a syllabus review body and advocates for collaboration with librarians in this distributed model of information literacy instruction. *[Article copies available for a fee from The Haworth Document Delivery Service: 1-800-HAWORTH. E-mail address: <docdelivery@haworthpress.com> Website: <http://www.HaworthPress.com> © 2004 by The Haworth Press, Inc. All rights reserved.]*

Trudi E. Jacobson, MLS, MA, BA, is Coordinator of User Education Programs (E-mail: tjacobson@uamail.albany.edu), and Carol Anne Germain, MLS, BA, is Networked Resources Education Librarian (E-mail: cg219@albany.edu), both at University Libraries, University at Albany, SUNY, 1400 Washington Avenue, Albany, NY 12222.

[Haworth co-indexing entry note]: "A Campus-Wide Role for an Information Literacy Committee." Jacobson, Trudi E., and Carol Anne Germain. Co-published simultaneously in *Resource Sharing & Information Networks* (The Haworth Information Press, an imprint of The Haworth Press, Inc.) Vol. 17, No. 1/2, 2004, pp. 111-121; and: *Libraries Within Their Institutions: Creative Collaborations* (ed: William Miller, and Rita M. Pellen) The Haworth Information Press, an imprint of The Haworth Press, Inc., 2004, pp. 111-121. Single or multiple copies of this article are available for a fee from The Haworth Document Delivery Service [1-800-HAWORTH, 9:00 a.m. - 5:00 p.m. (EST). E-mail address: docdelivery@haworthpress.com].

http://www.haworthpress.com/web/RSIN
© 2004 by The Haworth Press, Inc. All rights reserved.
Digital Object Identifier: 10.1300/J121v17n01_09

KEYWORDS. Information literacy programs, librarian-faculty collaboration, general education, colleges and universities, partnerships

Librarians have taken on the role of promoting and implementing information literacy (IL) for years. This is not surprising since the American Association of School Librarians, the American Library Association, and the Association of College and Research Libraries sowed the early seeds of IL decades ago (Hope, 25). Certainly, library instruction, also known as bibliographic instruction, was not a new concept during that time. However, IL introduced the concept of information in a more holistic perspective. It embraced the idea of teaching library constituents about information resources, including non-library materials and electronic resources. IL teaches the user to address an information need, to access and locate that information, to evaluate it and to effectively use and communicate this information. This was, and still is, an important undertaking since library patrons are citizens of the information age and need to be information literate. While it is essential that librarians remain key players in IL instruction, a better approach is to develop campus partnerships and collaborative ventures with faculty members and administrators. At the University at Albany, this model has been accomplished under the auspices of a university-wide committee that focuses on IL issues, including course criteria and the number of IL courses offered.

INFORMATION LITERACY/COLLABORATION LITERATURE REVIEW

The Middle States Commission on Higher Education's accreditation guidelines emphasize the need for broad-based IL instruction. In a section entitled "Fundamental Elements of Educational Offerings," the Commission emphasizes "collaboration between professional library staff and faculty in teaching and fostering information literacy skills relevant to the curriculum" (Middle States Commission on Higher Education, 2002, 33-34). The guidelines also indicate that "evidence of information literacy incorporated in the curriculum with syllabi, or other material appropriate to the mode of teaching and learning, describing expectations for students' demonstration of information literacy skills" is a method for gauging an "institution's own analysis relative to this accreditation standard" (Middle States Commission on Higher Education, 2002, 35-36). Middle States provides further information about how to successfully incorporate IL into the curriculum in *Developing Research & Communication Skills: Guidelines for Information Literacy in the Curriculum*

(2003). This source outlines the responsibilities that both faculty members and librarians have to ensure that students learn six key IL skills: know; access; evaluate sources; evaluate content; use; ethically/legally (Middle States Commission on Higher Education, 2003, 23).

The Association of College and Research Libraries' core document on IL, "Information Literacy Competency Standards for Higher Education," also encourages collaboration. It notes that the best efforts are met by "incorporating information literacy across curricula, in all programs and services, and throughout the administrative life of the university, [which] requires the collaborative efforts of faculty, librarians, and administrators" (ACRL Task Force on Information Literacy Standards, 209). A review of the literature emphasizes the importance of cooperation between these main campus stakeholders. Edward Owusu-Ansah highlights the history of academic librarian/faculty/administrator partnerships and the continued need for these alliances for the development of IL programs (Owusu-Ansah, 7). Charity B. Hope and Christina A. Peterson stress that "collaboration–especially collaboration on campus–is clearly a central and growing area of concern for advocates of information literacy" (Hope, 22). In a recent article, Gary Thompson notes "Information literacy represents the highest level of collaboration, where faculty and librarians recognize and act upon their joint responsibility for ensuring that students acquire information competencies" (Thompson, 236). Through these types of partnerships IL can be realized.

The literature also points to the extensive efforts college and university librarians have made in initiating IL programs (Rader, 243). They have been strong advocates with campus administrators, faculty, and members of curriculum committees for the integration of IL into the general education curriculum. Prototypes included stand-alone courses as well as the integration of IL into preexisting discipline-based courses. Until recently, many of these strategies have originated with librarians and not campus administrators or faculty members. This was not the case at the University at Albany, where the IL initiative has been instituted from the top down.

IL REQUIREMENT AT ALBANY

The impetus for this initiative came in 1998 with a resolution passed by the Board of Trustees of the State University of New York (SUNY). Resolution #98-241 mandated that all SUNY colleges and university centers establish a core general education program that included the requirement that students "complete a minimum of thirty credits in ten knowledge and skill areas." These included mathematics, Western and other world civilizations, foreign language, basic communication, natural sciences, social science, American history, humanities, and the arts, as well as the infusion of critical thinking and information management into the curriculum. Since the information management competency, originally conceived as a mandated course, reflected the national standards for IL, the University at Albany chose that terminology for consistency with assessment (University at Albany, 2000). Because the University moved so quickly to implement this particular new general education requirement, the course requirement remained intact.

Information Literacy Subcommittee

Through the direction of the Office of the Dean of Undergraduate Studies, the University's General Education Committee created a subcommittee to address the IL requirement. Initially, the subcommittee included faculty from the Center for Excellence in Teaching and Learning, the School of Information Science and Policy, and the University Libraries. The team worked to design a program that was not "one-size-fits-all," and encouraged IL to be taught through a variety of courses. The subcommittee used the IL competency standards developed by the Association of College and Research Libraries that identify the six key characteristics of IL proficiencies (ACRL Task Force on Information Literacy Standards, 207) to draft a course description and criteria for approved courses. The University at Albany IL course definition states that:

> Approved courses introduce students to various ways in which information is organized and structured and to the process of finding, using, producing, and distributing information in a variety of media formats, including traditional print as well as computer databases. Students acquire experience with resources available on the Internet and learn to evaluate the quality of information, to use information ethically and professionally, and to adjust to rapidly changing technology tools. Student[s] must complete this requirement within the freshman or sophomore year. (University at Albany, Information Literacy Subcommittee, 1999)

The subcommittee developed a proposal for a University-wide IL program that was overwhelmingly passed by the General Education Committee. Faculty who opt to teach IL skills develop or revise courses to include three characteristics:

1. Classroom activities on finding, evaluating, citing, and using information in print and electronic sources from the University Libraries, World

Wide Web, and other sources. Courses should address questions concerning the ethical use of information, copyrights, and other related issues that promote critical reflection.
2. Assignments, course work, or tutorials that make extensive use of the University Libraries, World Wide Web, and other information sources. Assignments should include finding, evaluating, and citing information sources.
3. At least one research project that requires students to find, evaluate, cite, and use information presented in diverse formats from multiple sources and to integrate this information within a single textual, visual, or digital document (University at Albany, Information Literacy Subcommittee, 1999, revised 2001).

Advantages of the Campus-Wide Subcommittee Approach

Our Information Literacy Subcommittee has worked well owing to the composition of the committee and the commitment of its members. Currently, there are four faculty members, two librarians, and the associate dean responsible for the General Education program. The chair of the subcommittee also heads the University's first-year experience program, Project Renaissance. Two of the other faculty members are also strong proponents of IL. The Assistant Director of User Services and the Coordinator of User Education Programs are the librarians who serve on the subcommittee. Many of the subcommittee members teach or have taught a course meeting the University at Albany IL requirement.

The diverse backgrounds of the members have ensured that the campus does not perceive the IL initiative as being the sole concern of librarians. We have found this broader support to be critical in increasing our IL course offerings on campus. In addition, the subcommittee's faculty members have raised significant issues that have advanced our discussions and strengthened the IL requirement. For example, one major discussion involved the research project required of IL courses. The original criterion specified that the required research product be an annotated bibliography, with set categories of material and information types to be included. This product initially worked well, but as the number and range of IL courses increased, it began to prove limiting. The faculty members' perspectives on what would be valuable for a number of courses, while heeding the librarians' emphasis that a range of research materials be consulted, led to the current research project criterion. The new requirement of a "single textual, visual, or digital document" provides a great deal more flexibility to professors, who may select what works best for their fields.

The subcommittee's faculty members were also instrumental in shaping the other two criteria. This was a result of the faculty members puzzling over how they would actually implement the various components based on the two librarians' explanations of successful IL integration. They felt that it would help their colleagues if we clearly specified that it is necessary to have classroom activities, assignments and other outside class activities, as well as a research project, and enumerated what should be included within these areas. While the two librarians were fully cognizant of these needs, the other subcommittee members provided suggestions about how to lay out the issues in the clearest possible manner for those who have less expertise.

The subcommittee also enhanced this general education initiative by providing structure and assistance to faculty members who are exploring the IL requirement. Faculty members on campus understand there is a clearly defined procedure for submitting an IL course proposal, and can use the subcommittee's criteria to shape their new or revised courses. Subcommittee members provide direction on developing IL courses, and sometimes even solicit course proposals. The IL Subcommittee chair has the responsibility for determining that there are a sufficient number of IL General Education "seats" available through various courses to meet the needs of our students. This has served as a spur to approaching other departments about developing such courses.

Information Literacy Course Approval Process

A number of course proposals have come through the subcommittee in the last four years. They fall into several categories: first-year experience courses, first-year developmental skills courses, generic IL courses, and discipline-specific courses. Courses have been accepted from a range of fields, including East Asian Studies, Information Science and Policy, Linguistics, Communication, and Geography and Planning. Students are often enthusiastic about meeting their IL requirement within their major, because they see the immediate relevance of the material. Unfortunately, the initial influx of disciplinary proposals has stalled, and the subcommittee will need to do more outreach to faculty members in key departments.

The subcommittee takes the criteria seriously and does not rubber stamp courses for approval. It has returned proposals for further work, with information about how they might be revised to meet the criteria. One recommendation may be that the course professor work with the appropriate librarian: the bibliographer for subject resources or the University Libraries' Coordinator of User Education for assignment design and other pedagogical assistance. Subcommittee members feel that it is critical that courses meet the established

standards, but willingly work with faculty members so that most proposals ultimately succeed.

One professor took the unusual route of instituting all of the IL criteria in his
course a full year before he applied to have the course officially approved. Because this is typically a large class of over one-hundred students each semester,
it had a significant potential impact on the number of IL "seats" available, and
on the library as students fulfilled the course requirements. For two semesters,
students and librarians alike struggled as the students worked on their assignments. Finally, when the course was submitted for approval, the subcommittee
recommended that the faculty member work with a librarian on the subcommittee to smooth out the assignment problems. The professor and his teaching
assistant (TA) met willingly with the librarian, and came to the meeting with a
number of ideas for making the assignments flow more smoothly. In addition,
the librarian suggested several strategies, including proposing that the TA
hold some of her office hours in the library, a model pioneered by the largest
IL course on campus. The professor and TA also met with the subject bibliographer, during which time they further refined the course assignments.

General Education Assessment

One piece of the SUNY Board of Trustees' general education mandate is an
assessment of courses in all general education categories. The University at
Albany developed learning objectives for each general education category.
Faculty members teaching courses in the same general education category
were brought together to develop these learning objectives, a very time-intensive but rewarding process. In the case of the IL category, the subcommittee
served as the group which developed the learning objectives:

- The ability to locate, evaluate, synthesize and use information from a variety of sources
- An understanding of basic research techniques appropriate to the course
  discipline and an ability to use those techniques
- An understanding of the various ways in which information is organized
  and structured
- An understanding of the ethical issues involved in accessing and using
  information (University at Albany, Learning Objectives/Outcomes)

Developing these learning objectives, which required us to distill those elements that we believed to be critical, provided an excellent opportunity for
subcommittee members to revisit our goals for the requirement, and to provide
additional background for newer committee members.

SUPPORT OFFERED BY LIBRARIANS

Since the IL course criteria emphasize that students utilize a variety of library resources, librarians have worked vigorously to help support these needs. When faculty members begin to investigate the process of meeting the IL course requirements, subcommittee members are able to describe what resources and services are available through the University Libraries. Examples include several new interactive tutorials: Evaluating Internet Resources 101, a University Library Virtual Tour, and Plagiarism 101 (http://library.albany. edu/usered/tut.html) developed by members of the User Education Unit. Faculty may assign these tutorials, in addition to the prototype Researching 101, as homework or as in-class exercises. Students follow the fundamental lessons of these guides at their own pace; upon completion they fill in a form to identify themselves and their instructor. Librarians designed a database that collects this data and produces reports that are sent to faculty to verify that their students have completed the assigned tutorial(s). These tutorials have been very effective, especially in meeting the needs of larger classes. An example of this situation involves use of the University Library Virtual Tour, which is completed by over 750 students each semester: it would be impossible for instruction librarians to conduct live tours for so many students. Students may return to the tutorials at any time to refresh their knowledge and/or review for tests.

The "research project" component of the criteria is still being fulfilled in many courses by an annotated bibliography assignment. Most instructors call for a particular number (usually 10) of specific resources, which may include a mix of primary and secondary sources, popular and scholarly articles, Websites, and books. This assignment generates increased traffic at the University Library reference desk. Reference librarians take very seriously their role in advancing students' IL skills, yet students frequently ask the same questions, such as "What is the difference between a scholarly article and a popular article?" and "How do I find a print article?" This causes reference interviews to become very repetitive, as one of the key IL courses has approximately 400 students enrolled each semester. By working with faculty members, User Education librarians developed a number of course-specific pathfinders to help make these types of reference interviews more efficient.

In addition, librarians quickly noted that students in the new IL courses, like other courses, are not immune to procrastinating. The reference desk was therefore inundated with last minute users during the due date crunch. While many of these students needed reference help, it was found that some needed additional course-related assistance (e.g., access to electronic homework assignments). To help facilitate meeting this need, the professor teaching the largest IL course was contacted and offered space in the Library's Reference area so that his TAs could conduct office hours at this point of service. TAs are situated at a computer workstation, with a sign to identify their availability and location. Depending on the wishes of the course professor, TAs might hold office hours in the library throughout the semester, or only during the weeks when students are working on an IL assignment. This has worked so successfully that the librarians on the subcommittee now encourage faculty to consider having their TAs do the same. This arrangement benefits many constituents: students, librarians, TAs, and faculty. Students are able to maximize their research efforts by being able to get help in one convenient location. Librarians can refer students to their TAs for on-the-spot assistance related either to their course or to a specific assignment. TAs get to work with many more students, who are much more likely to seek them out in the library. Faculty members note better student performance on their assignments.

Other collaborative efforts have been undertaken to educate faculty about implementing IL courses. *Resources for Information Literacy Courses* (http://library.albany.edu/usered/faculty/infolit.html), a Web page created and maintained by one of the authors, provides pertinent information to help instructors get started. The page collects together all online tutorials offered by the University Libraries and provides a link to a form through which faculty members can register their courses, so that they automatically receive reports of which students have completed the tutorials. The page also links to a fact sheet about the services offered by User Education librarians, a collection of guides and handouts developed for student use, and key information relating to IL on campus and in the state university system. A link is also provided to the ACRL Information Literacy Competency Standards for Higher Education.

Members of the Libraries' User Education Department have conducted several different IL workshops in collaboration with the University's Center for Excellence in Teaching and Learning. One workshop, which has been offered several times, encourages faculty members to consider adapting existing courses to meet the IL requirement. The workshop leaders, who are all members of the Information Literacy Subcommittee, introduce the three criteria discussed earlier in this article. Faculty subcommittee members who teach IL courses talk about the mechanics of incorporating these criteria into their courses. The librarian outlines what resources the libraries provide to support IL courses, and the chair of the subcommittee explains the course review process. Another workshop highlights "best information literacy practices" on campus, by bringing together faculty members who have very successfully adapted their courses. These programs focus on innovative and engaging strategies which help to introduce information and library resources into the classroom.

Through the methods described above and through direct instruction of students, the University Libraries and librarians play a significant role in IL courses, while not dictating exactly how librarians must be involved. This gives both faculty members and librarians pedagogical flexibility, while encouraging collaborative ventures. Without the subcommittee, librarians would play the narrower, traditional role of being the only group on campus advocating for IL instruction. The support materials developed by librarians are critical for most faculty members teaching IL courses, including University librarians who teach credit courses. Bibliographers and User Education librarians are available for faculty members who request assistance, though the criteria and the review process ensure that courses that do not call upon librarians in person still contain the required IL elements.

CONCLUSION

The Information Literacy Subcommittee at the University at Albany has been instrumental in helping the campus meet the goal of requiring an IL course of all students in their first two years. Librarians have played a significant role in IL initiatives, but they have done so in conjunction with both the campus administration and with faculty members. It has enabled a full-scale IL effort that has not overwhelmed librarians, and that encourages buy-in from a range of participants. This cooperative venture has led to an environment that is very much in the spirit of the Middle States Commission on Higher Education's recommendations, which emphasize the broad scope of IL with a central role for faculty ownership of IL instruction. The University at Albany has been able to foster that ownership, while acknowledging the key role of librarians in the process.

REFERENCES

ACRL Task Force on Information Literacy Competency Standards. "Information Literacy: Competency Standards for Higher Education." *College & Research Libraries News* 61.3 (2000): 207-215.

Hope, Charity B. and Christina A. Peterson. "The Sum Is Greater Than the Parts: Cross-Institutional Collaboration for Information Literacy in Academic Libraries." *Journal of Library Administration* 36.1/2 (2002): 25-38.

Middle States Commission on Higher Education. *Characteristics of Excellence in Higher Education*. Philadelphia: The author, 2002.

Middle States Commission on Higher Education. *Developing Research and Communication Skills: Guidelines for Information Literacy in the Curriculum*. Philadelphia: The author, 2003.

Owusu-Ansah, Edward K. "Information Literacy and Higher Education: Placing the Academic Library in the Center of a Comprehensive Solution." *Journal of Academic Librarianship* 30.1 (2004): 3-16.

Rader, Hannelore B. "Information Literacy 1973-2002: A Selected Literature Review." *Library Trends* 51.2 (2002): 242-259.

Thompson, Gary B. "Information Literacy Accreditation Mandates: What They Mean for Faculty and Librarians." *Library Trends* 51.2 (2002): 218-241.

University at Albany. (2000). *University at Albany Self-Study Report: A Decade of Progress, 1990-2000.* Albany, NY: University at Albany.

University at Albany, Information Literacy Subcommittee. (1999). University at Albany: The New General Education Program: Communication and Reasoning Competencies. [cited April 10, 2004]. Available from World Wide Web <http://library.albany.edu/usered/faculty/newgencomp.doc>.

University at Albany. Learning Objectives/Outcomes: The *New* General Education Program. [cited May 10, 2004]. Available from World Wide Web: <http://www.albany.edu/gened/learnoutcome.html>.

Talking Toward Techno-Pedagogy: IT and Librarian Collaboration– Rethinking Our Roles

Juliet Habjan Boisselle
Susan Fliss
Lori S. Mestre
Fred Zinn

SUMMARY. A Mellon workshop created teams including faculty, librarians, instructional technologists, and students from nine educational institutions to incorporate technology into curricula. Instructional technologists and librarians from Mount Holyoke and the University of Massachusetts Amherst recount initial and subsequent collaborative efforts in infusing technology and information literacy into curricula. Their experiences illustrate differences and challenges of collaboration in small colleges and large universities. Regardless of size of institution,

Juliet Habjan Boisselle, LITS, Mount Holyoke College, 50 College Street, South Hadley, MA 01075 (E-mail: jboissel@mtholyoke.edu).

Susan Fliss, 6025 Baker-Berry Library, Dartmouth College, Hanover, NH 03755 (E-mail: Susan.Fliss@Dartmouth.edu).

Lori S. Mestre is Head, Research and Instructional Services, W. E. B. Du Bois Library, 154 Hicks Way, University of Massachusetts, Amherst, MA 01003 (E-mail: lori. mestre@library.umass.edu).

Fred Zinn, University of Massachusetts Amherst, 740 North Pleasant Street, Amherst, MA 01003-9306 (E-mail: zinn@oit.umass.edu).

[Haworth co-indexing entry note]: "Talking Toward Techno-Pedagogy: IT and Librarian Collaboration–Rethinking Our Roles." Boisselle, Juliet Habjan et al. Co-published simultaneously in *Resource Sharing & Information Networks* (The Haworth Information Press, an imprint of The Haworth Press, Inc.) Vol. 17, No. 1/2, 2004, pp. 123-136; and: *Libraries Within Their Institutions: Creative Collaborations* (ed: William Miller, and Rita M. Pellen) The Haworth Information Press, an imprint of The Haworth Press, Inc., 2004, pp. 123-136. Single or multiple copies of this article are available for a fee from The Haworth Document Delivery Service [1-800-HAWORTH, 9:00 a.m. - 5:00 p.m. (EST). E-mail address: docdelivery@haworthpress.com].

http://www.haworthpress.com/web/RSIN
Digital Object Identifier: 10.1300/J121v17n01_10

both experiences resulted in changes in the way these constituents across campus participate in teaching and learning. Former support staff roles of instructional technologist and librarian evolved into dynamic roles based on partnership. *[Article copies available for a fee from The Haworth Document Delivery Service: 1-800-HAWORTH. E-mail address: <docdelivery@haworthpress.com> Website: <http://www.HaworthPress.com>* © 2004 by The Haworth Press, Inc. All rights reserved.]

KEYWORDS. Information literacy, information fluency, faculty collaboration, faculty outreach, collaborative partnerships, instructional technology, integration of technology, instructional design, course management systems instruction

On a train bound for Pennsylvania in mid-June, 2000, a librarian, an instructional technologist, a faculty member, and a student from Mount Holyoke College chatted amicably together about what the next week at Bryn Mawr and participation in Talking Toward Techno-Pedagogy (TTTP) would hold, while separately, the members of the University of Massachusetts team looked around at unfamiliar faces, each trying unsuccessfully to recognize the other members of their team. Both teams completed the TTTP program and returned to their perspective campuses and found success from this collaborative effort . . . but success happened in different ways for the two teams.

TALKING TOWARD TECHNO-PEDAGOGY

Through a grant from the Andrew W. Mellon Foundation, nine college and university teams gathered on the Bryn Mawr campus to participate in Talking Toward Techno-Pedagogy: A Collaboration Across Colleges and Constituencies[1] (http://serendip.brynmawr.edu/talking/). Centered around revising a course taught by the faculty member on the team, the goals of the TTTP program, as stated on the Web site are to

- foster communication across constituencies who are often separated by institutional structures
- encourage each team member to reconsider what he or she as well as what other participants in the workshop have to contribute to the teaching and learning goals of a particular course
- identify/share vocabulary and ways of talking to one another

- ensure that teams leave the workshop with a specific curricular project to be implemented in the coming year
- help build foundations for future, long-term collaborative relationships.

Information technology is changing teaching and learning on campuses; the roles of those involved in teaching and learning are changing, also. This workshop encouraged each team member to investigate his or her role and the role of the other constituent groups. Alison Sather-Cook, and the other cofounders of the workshop, posed such questions as "Who has what roles in teaching and learning at the college? What is the nature of interactions among people in old and new roles in that educational context? How can we revise our understanding of role, moving from a notion of something prescribed and fixed to something more complex and responsive?"[2]

After an exhausting and enlightening week of reflection and collaboration, the Mount Holyoke and University of Massachusetts teams returned to western Massachusetts to continue the collaborative work begun in Pennsylvania. The instructional technologist and librarian from each team will present an overview of their collaborations and lessons learned. The Mount Holyoke experience demonstrates the collaborative process involved in redesigning a course. The University of Massachusetts team efforts turned from a course-specific focus towards new collaborative efforts on campus.

MOUNT HOLYOKE EXPERIENCE

Mount Holyoke College is a liberal arts college for women with approximately 2,000 students. The first Mount Holyoke College collaborative team to attend the Talking Towards Techno-Pedagogy workshop series dedicated itself to the support of an Experimental Methods in Psychology course. The overall spirit gained from the week at Bryn Mawr was a reminder of the vast resources available from different constituencies on campus–constituents can continue to learn from one another and navigate this sea of constant change together. Specifically, librarians, instructional technologists, faculty, and students should not plod onward in isolation.

The workshop series at TTTP provided a safe space for breaking down barriers and getting to know one another away from daily routines and stresses. The week's discussions, which were really just a beginning, provided an opportunity for the faculty member to articulate goals and needs for the class, and for the student, librarian, and instructional technologist to participate in discussions surrounding the implementation of these goals and needs. The student was familiar with the course and her feedback was very helpful to the rest of the team. The librarian and instructional technologist had not yet worked with the faculty member although they knew each other.

From these collaborative discussions, two clear goals regarding the Psychology course emerged for the team: (1) increase communication between students in the class, particularly group work communications and (2) help the students posit themselves in the ongoing research process and develop an understanding of how research fits into the world of scholarly publishing and communication. Put simply, improving the student group work logistics and inserting what in retrospect can be identified as an "information fluency" component to the course.

The collaborative team of faculty, student, instructional technologist, and librarian collectively developed a plan for the next offering of the course. The College had just purchased the course management system WebCT, and everyone on the team agreed that it had great potential to address the group work logistics that had been so frustrating to busy students–it also offered a promising forum for integrating research information and gateways to library resources.

Mount Holyoke installed WebCT over the summer of 2000 and held training sessions for faculty including the team members and the course lab director. The instructional technologist was eager to find interested faculty to pilot the use of WebCT, but since it was new to the College, the entire team would be learning the system intricacies at the same time. True to the planning that took place at Bryn Mawr, the faculty member invited the librarian and instructional technologist to the first labs and classes and introduced them to the students as a "team" that was supporting the course. The instructional technologist who provided training for the students during their first lab gave an in-class introductory assignment on the use of the discussion tool. The librarian met with the class in the Psychology and Education Department building to teach information literacy principles, including evaluating types of sources within the context of the publishing and scholarly world, considering them in the context of a literature review, and also analyzing one's topic in order to most effectively engage in the search and retrieval process. As a separate session, the class then met as smaller lab groups at the library itself to gain hands-on experience with the appropriate resources, completing a fairly structured lab assignment that walked them through the tools.

ASSESSMENT OF COLLABORATIVE INITIATIVE

The team of faculty, student, instructional technologist, and librarian met at the close of the first semester and assessed the new model for supporting the course. The faculty member shared mid-semester evaluations that she posted within WebCT. Reflections included: the students adapted easily to WebCT and did not need as much assistance navigating the system as was initially expected; the new research instruction seemed to offer a stronger base from which the students could work (previously the librarian's role involved a short 15-20 minute "demo" of one just one tool, PsycInfo); and the hands-on lab was received well by students and teaching assistants alike–but they didn't care for the rigid structure of the "library" assignment. This information in hand, the team adjusted and re-tooled some of the components and offered a slightly different approach the second semester. This model, one of coming together as a collaborative team in between semesters to assess and re-evaluate the technology and research components of the course, is a model that has been maintained for the past several years, with just a few exceptions. While the backbone and the goals have remained steady in the past four years under this model, it is fair to say that the nature of the librarian and instructional technologist's interactions with the class has evolved from semester to semester–and this is exciting. The collaborative model effectively draws from different perspectives and inherently includes regular assessment and resulting growth.

CHANGING ROLES

The role of the instructional technologist in the team has changed; because of the usability of WebCT and increased faculty and student comfort with the tool, the instructional technologist no longer needs to spend time with the class teaching them how to use it. In this instance, the lab director for the course eagerly embraced this role and the instructional technologist is now more of an advisor and available as needed. After two years, a different person took on the instructional technologist responsibilities for the course. In contrast, the librarian's level of involvement has remained steady. The same librarian is working on the team and a librarian's continued close participation is necessary due to the increasing number of research tools; however, the nature of the content taught has changed somewhat.

While the student perspective has been very present from semester to semester via both formal evaluations and informal dialogues that the faculty member has collected, the collaborative team notes the absence of a steady student voice within the "team" to provide candid and informed feedback in a safe setting with the other educational partners. One possibility of reintroducing the student perspective centrally into the collaborations has recently emerged–the new Mount Holyoke Technology Mentor Program–a course-oriented, peer-based program modeled on a highly successful writing mentor program on campus. Paired with a faculty member and assigned to a particular course, a student technology mentor might offer support in a variety of ways, including: holding office hours for project consultation with students enrolled in the course, offering training workshops on specific software or equipment associated with assignments, and even providing faculty feedback on the effectiveness of a particular technology-based assignment. The team looks forward to exploring the possibilities of this new role within the context of the Experimental Methods in Psychology course in fall 2004.

Increased collaboration at Mount Holyoke was also one of the goals of the 2004 merger of the instructional technologist's and the librarian's separate departments into one. Through numerous stages, collaborations have formalized into strategic coordinated planning. What had been two distinct departments, Curriculum Support and Instructional Technology (CSIT) and Reference Services, are now Research and Instructional Support (RIS). Instructional technologists and reference librarians not only collaborate closely on particular projects, but they also share office spaces, weekly meetings, and water coolers. Traffic patterns have changed and shared visions, identity, and culture are emerging. On a typical day, a faculty member may visit with an instructional technologist to develop a course in WebCT and find herself an hour later deep in conversation with the librarian who was seated within earshot, talking about information fluency. Collaboration is almost seamless (www.mtholyoke.edu/lits/ris/).

The composition of the "collaborative team" flexes and the roles within the team may ebb and flow; however, the goal remains the same: to support the changing curriculum and faculty and student needs. This can be done through regular conversation, mutual respect, and frequent assessment. The team of educational partners needs to be aware of the faculty member's educational objectives, make regular efforts to reflect on these objectives, and determine how best to support them.

LESSONS LEARNED

This collaboration to redesign a Psychology course did not happen seamlessly or smoothly. There were times of anxiety, of not knowing how to broach a topic, of technical glitches with WebCT, of slow communication among the team members, etc. However, perhaps because of the shared TTTP week, or perhaps because of the members themselves, the team members had confidence in each other and supported this project through a bumpy first term.

Late in fall 2000, the faculty member invited the instructional technologist and the librarian to the end-of-semester poster sessions where the students explained their experiments and findings. Curious to see the finished student projects, the two guests were interested in identifying projects or research areas where their participation might have had an influence. Other questions they hoped the poster sessions would clarify included: How do the students describe their experiences throughout the semester? Are there areas where they might have offered more/different support? In viewing the student work, they felt proud of the students' achievements and found gratification for their supportive efforts. In the end, they left the poster session with a better understanding of the teaching and learning that happens in the course. This invitation was a valuable "thank you" gesture by the faculty member. By jointly attending a few of the students' end-of-semester poster-sessions the librarian and instructional technologist were prompted to think about what additional unarticulated technology needs existed that might be addressed. Attending the poster sessions sparked the idea for the possibility that this course might be a good fit for a student technology mentor.

Other Mount Holyoke librarians and instructional technologists who attended the TTTP week in the two following years also shared their lessons learned for this article.[3] Attendees of the TTTP week agree that the time spent together strengthened the bonds among the team members. The question is how to re-create that opportunity on a busy campus? How does one create times away from the office or library where conversations can happen–go for a coffee, go for a walk on campus?

In talking with faculty, when they ask a question, think about their teaching process when framing your answer. What is the faculty member trying to achieve? Think of the process from the perspective of the teacher and the learner before proposing solutions. Be direct with faculty about the time it will take to use or do something new in their teaching. Forget the cheerleading; garner enthusiasm by promoting how the changes can work in the course–i.e., students communicating, exchanging ideas and papers, getting access to help and to materials more easily. To get started, or to find new faculty to partner with, one has to make time for outreach and put continued effort into forming relationships.

UNIVERSITY OF MASSACHUSETTS AMHERST EXPERIENCE

In contrast to Mount Holyoke College, the University of Massachusetts Amherst is a large research university with 18,000 undergraduates and 6,000 graduate students. The 893 acres of land encompass 16 miles of roadways and

348 buildings. Needless to say, collaborating with individuals outside one's own domain requires time and effort. The distance between the UMass Amherst Office of Information Technology (OIT) and the Library is a seven-minute walk, and this is short compared to the walk to some faculty offices. This may explain why, prior to the TTTP experience, the representatives from OIT and the Library didn't know each other.

The TTTP experience was eye-opening to the information specialist and librarian. Both individuals were embarrassed to admit that it took a conference to get them to know each other, despite their common interests and job functions. At the opening reception, they were each discreetly looking at nametags to locate the other representatives from UMass Amherst. In contrast, all of the representatives from the small colleges at the event were not only already familiar with each other, but were clustered together, chatting personably about past events common to them. This is a stark demonstration of the difference between the staff and faculty relationships at the smaller colleges and the relationships (or lack thereof) at the larger university. Considering that staff and faculty often encounter this kind of isolation at a large institution, how does one even begin to change this culture and collaborate?

Coming back from the cozy collaborative environment of the TTTP event, the librarian and the information specialist were immediately reminded of the size of their institution. What had been easy conversations in the halls of the conference center at Bryn Mawr now required comparing calendars, setting up meetings, and crossing the campus. Such efforts change the nature of conversations; they become meetings with agendas and action items. For example, the members of the collaborative group set up at TTTP to work on a specific course quickly fell back into their traditional roles of faculty member, student, librarian and information specialist. What had been a casual face-to-face exchange of ideas at Bryn Mawr gave way to the pressures of distance and conflicting schedules and became a series of e-mails arranging very specific tasks to support the class. Eventually, each participant in the group was back to addressing their own specific specialty from their separate locations. The course moved forward, but it was largely unchanged by the collaborative efforts introduced at the TTTP workshop.

For the librarian and the information specialist, the collaborative themes presented at TTTP led them to look beyond their specific project into other areas where a similar style of collaboration could help transform the campus culture. Specifically, they looked at the common goals that existed in their respective offices. Most of all, they had a common goal of wanting to see the faculty and students achieve the best possible outcome, whether it was using something on the computer, writing an excellent paper, or completing a project. The goal they both had was an improved course for all. Once they defined this common goal, it was easy to list all of the skills that the librarian and information specialist had in common, or that could be used to support each other. It was obvious that by acting as a team, the two could provide a much richer outcome for the faculty and students.

With this awareness, the librarian and the information specialist set out to bring more of the collaborative spirit of TTTP into their everyday efforts to support faculty and students. Overall, this meant actively overcoming the distance between their offices to set up more possibilities for casual exchanges of ideas and collaboration. As new collaborative relationships developed, several overlapping areas emerged where IT staff and librarians were able to work together to address changes in their roles on campus. The main area was adapting to the new role in which both information specialists and librarians are called upon to be teachers.

LAYING THE GROUNDWORK
FOR COLLABORATION BETWEEN LIBRARIANS
AND INSTRUCTIONAL TECHNOLOGISTS

In order to develop collaborative relationships between their two groups, the librarian and the information specialist decided to follow a simple mantra: "Get out of the office." The distance between offices made it too easy to forget about other people and resources on campus. In addition to this architectural distance, there were also the limitations of the org-chart-based "Office." Staff from different branches of the chart rarely crossed over to collaborate, perhaps because they assumed that all important communications were taking place at the upper levels of the organization. Based on their shared experience at TTTP, the librarian and the information specialist knew that by getting up and visiting each other's offices, the librarians and IT staff would discover that casual interactions would foster significant connections between the groups.

RETREATS AND WORKSHOPS

The first big event arranged for these groups was a "retreat" in which both groups got together to compare notes. The information specialist and the librarian who had been to TTTP introduced the concept of using collaborative teams of IT staff, librarians, and students when supporting faculty. Following the presentation, the attendees broke into small mixed groups of information technologists and librarians to discuss the ways they could work together. One of the primary themes that arose from this first meeting was the need for each group to learn more of the basic skills that the other group used. In this way, each had a better sense of what the other could offer to their faculty clients, and would know when to call in an expert from the other area. From this meeting each group arranged a series of workshops for the other. Librarians offered to the IT staff workshops on library services, searching strategies, and how material is organized into databases. The IT staff offered workshops geared to librarians on Web page design, planning and authoring, WebCT, and many other workshops geared to specific software products.

Once both areas had the experience of learning the other's "tools of the trade," they were much more comfortable with working with and promoting these tools to faculty. The librarians regularly use the Web and WebCT to provide training and resources to faculty and students. The IT group now includes a regular question in all faculty workshops: "Do you know your subject specialist?" This is often followed by an introduction to the services the library provides that can be of help to faculty using a specific technology in their classes.

INFORMAL DISCUSSIONS

The librarian and information specialist encouraged a continuation of the casual conversations of the retreat by establishing monthly "cookie chats" (because they were often held over a plate of goodies). These meetings were casual and involved no set agenda. Most of the discussions involved swapping stories and describing current projects. Yet, these casual stories always ended up with the groups swapping solutions to problems, or discovering new ways that each area could be of service to the other. A space where the two groups collaborated regularly outside of the cookie chats was the "Multimedia Room" in the Library. This room provided hardware, software, and support for faculty working on multimedia projects. The librarians often consulted with the IT staff on purchases and technology issues. Each group referred faculty clients to the other if more appropriate services were available in the other area.

Because the two groups were collaborating so closely in this area, this collaboration facilitated working together to preserve the Multimedia Room function when it was threatened by budget cuts. The comfortable relationship and trust that had been built up through the "cookie chats" made it easy for the two groups to work together and arrange a transfer of the service from the Library to the IT group due to a drastic decrease in the library budget. IT proved to be a good location for this service because of a compatible mission of faculty support and a budgetary commitment to upgrading hardware and software on a regular schedule. Once the Multimedia Room in the library closed, the new room in IT was ready to handle referrals of the Library's clients.

ADJUSTING TO A NEW ROLE:
TEACHING EACH OTHER, TEACHING FACULTY,
TEACHING STUDENTS

Staff from the library and IT previously saw themselves as "support person-nel" whose jobs were primarily reactive–responding to specific requests for help from faculty and students. As conversations continued between the groups it became apparent that both felt that their roles had changed. In both cases, staff were providing more direct training of faculty and students. Their roles had grown to include "teaching." This teaching had gone beyond the simple demonstration of how to use a tool, and now included how to plan the process and use the tools effectively in the context of a course or topic. Their approach now had to include a careful awareness of individual learning styles and goals.

In the library, subject specialists were working with faculty to develop Web pages of resources specific to courses. They would also present demonstra-tions of database searches in classes that provided techniques that were spe-cific to the topic of the class. In IT, generic software workshops for faculty had been replaced with workshops that focused on specific ways that the software could be used in a pedagogical context. Demonstrations of software to classes now included content specifically addressing the project or the topic. When asked by faculty to present to a workshop or to a class, both areas now took the time to work with the faculty to customize the material to the needs of the stu-dents.

A primary reason for this change was the expansion of technology into all areas of campus. At one time, faculty using technology were in the same "tin-kerer" category of computer user as the librarians and IT staff; they enjoyed the challenge of figuring things out. Now the software for creating course ma-terials and performing searches is so ubiquitous and "user-friendly" (relative to the old days) that librarians and IT staff are faced with a new majority: users who want to use the technology themselves, but who don't want to deal with roadblocks or to figure things out. They want it to work the first time. For these people, anything that gets in the way of their goal is a source of painful frustra-tion. In many ways this is the source of the transformation of support roles into collaborative teaching roles; short quick answers are not enough. IT staff and librarians have to help their clients get to a level of comfort where they can use the technology with a minimum level of fuss.

Using specific examples from a discipline helps put the technology in a context the learners can more easily understand (such as using epidemiologi-cal data in a graphing demonstration for Public Health Faculty). During faculty workshops, for example, the librarians and IT staff display citations of published works of the faculty attending the sessions. They then proceed to show the faculty how they can create a persistent URL using those citations to the full-text article, if available, and then adding this link to a Word document, Web page, or within WebCT for use in their courses. These personal examples help make the connection to faculty about the usefulness of the technology. Reframing acronym-laden technological shorthand into plain English requires empathy and an ability to see the technology from an outsider's perspective. And most of all, the instructor needs to become a coach and mentor with an eye to the goal of self-sufficiency. This requires a very different approach from their original supporting role of handing out tips and results. Librarians and IT staff have to become teachers and coaches.

Because their areas are becoming increasingly intertwined, to be effective coaches, these Librarians and IT staff need to work closely. Each needs a basic awareness of the other's topics to provide as much of a one-stop shop as possible for each individual seeking help. In cases where an expert in the other area is needed, a close collaboration will make the referrals more personal and effective. Leaving clients hanging ("I don't know where you could get help with this") or with non-specific referrals ("Someone in the Library/IT should be able to help you") is a thing of the past.

With the planning of a new Learning Commons in the library, both groups are discussing cross-training in which all staff would have a similar set of basic skills when assisting students and faculty in the Commons. The ideal goal is that anyone acting as support staff in the Commons could help a client with any of the most common questions involving research, basic software use, or study and writing skills. Most important is that every helper in the Commons be a one-stop source of assistance; bouncing clients around to other helpers is to be avoided unless a client has a need that requires a very narrow specialized knowledge.

OTHER EXAMPLES OF COLLABORATIVE TEACHING

The librarians and IT staff now regularly present material about services and technologies to each other. Each group now feels more comfortable requesting individual or small group training with specific tools. Most recently the IT staff has learned about citation software from the librarians and the librarians have learned about CGI form processing from the IT staff. Both groups regularly collaborate on faculty training. A workshop on incorporating links to library resources in course Web pages is now in its third semester and is very popular. Collaborative student support mostly takes the form of be-hind-the-scenes efforts such as including sets of library-oriented links in the IT-administered WebCT course management system on campus. As both groups go forward they are looking for ways to work together when asked to present topics to faculty groups or classes.

LESSONS LEARNED

The UMass participants' most valuable lesson was that it is critical to get out of the office and meet other individuals in person. The face-to-face interaction is instrumental to developing good relationships. Sharing of information was also a vital necessity for developing successful and lasting relationships. Regular cookie chats and brown bag lunches have helped keep both departments informed of changes, plans, concerns, and possible joint projects. The success of these collaborative efforts has made an impact at the university level. Campus administrators now suggest representatives from these two departments to be involved in task forces and university committees. In this way, the upper-level planning process for several new initiatives on campus will regularly include collaborative teams from across campus. Task forces planning and coordinating Information Technology, Instructional Technology, and a new Learning Commons all include faculty, librarians, IT staff, Center for Teaching staff, and students. So while the original collaborative project did not go much further after the TTTP conference, the theme of collaborating across traditional boundaries has infused itself across this large campus.

A side effect of this success is that, as the collaborative efforts of these two groups have become more high-profile and formalized, the informal cookie chats have disappeared and been replaced with more formal meetings with agendas and action items. The original participants in this project have discussed bringing back the cookie chats for the "schmooze" value they offered. The informal chats and the informal relationships they helped build between the two groups were so valuable that they must be continued in order to lay the groundwork for future collaborations.

CONCLUSION

Members from these two teams arrived for the TTTP workshop with pre-conceived ideas of their current roles on campus. At the workshop they were given the opportunity to re-examine these roles and determine new possibilities. Returning to campus, each team, working within the culture of its institution, tested new roles, accepted some, changed some, and rejected others. As new collaborative teaching opportunities emerge, the roles may differ again. This process of "unrolling" roles[4] resulted in a change in the way constituents across campus participate in the process of teaching and learning. For instructional technologists and librarians, the former support staff roles are changing into roles based on partnership.

NOTES

1. The original participating institutions are Amherst, Bryn Mawr, Hampshire, Haverford, Mount Holyoke, University of Massachusetts Amherst, Smith, Swarthmore, and Vassar. A tenth institution, Hamilton, joined in 2001.

2. Alison Cook-Sather, "Unrolling Roles in Techno-Pedagogy: Toward New Forms of Collaboration in Traditional College Settings" 26, (2) *Innovative Higher Education*, 2001, p. 122. Other cofounders of Talking Toward Techno-Pedagogy are Susan Perry, Sandra M. Lawrence, and Elliott Shore.

3. Thank you to Aime DeGrenier, Mary Glackin, and Sandy Ward of Mount Holyoke for sharing their TTTP experiences for this article.

4. See Sather-Cook article.

REFERENCE

Alison Cook-Sather. "Unrolling Roles in Techno-Pedagogy: Toward New Forms of Collaboration in Traditional College Settings" 26, (2) *Innovative Higher Education*, 2001: 121-140.

Collaborating to Create the Right Space for the Right Time

Jill McKinstry

SUMMARY. From classroom, to study space, to collaborative work or laboratories, students seek spatial, social, and intellectual connections, and most importantly, they seek the right space at the right time. The challenge for libraries is to provide different types of integrated spaces that balance the need to reflect and to absorb with the need to communicate and to create. The Odegaard Undergraduate Library at the University of Washington is enhancing the 32-year-old vision for collaborative spaces of learning to set the right balance between contemplative and group space and 24-hour access to the latest tools and technology. *[Article copies available for a fee from The Haworth Document Delivery Service: 1-800-HAWORTH. E-mail address: <docdelivery@haworthpress.com> Website: <http://www.HaworthPress.com> © 2004 by The Haworth Press, Inc. All rights reserved.]*

KEYWORDS. Collaboration, undergraduate, library, technology, innovation, space, commons, research, transformation, exhibits

---

Jill McKinstry is Head, Odegaard Undergraduate Library, and Chair, Library Research Award for Undergraduates, University of Washington Libraries, Box 353080, Seattle, WA 98195-3080 (E-mail: jillmck@u.washington.edu).

[Haworth co-indexing entry note]: "Collaborating to Create the Right Space for the Right Time." McKinstry, Jill. Co-published simultaneously in *Resource Sharing & Information Networks* (The Haworth Information Press, an imprint of The Haworth Press, Inc.) Vol. 17, No. 1/2, 2004, pp. 137-146; and: *Libraries Within Their Institutions: Creative Collaborations* (ed: William Miller, and Rita M. Pellen) The Haworth Information Press, an imprint of The Haworth Press, Inc., 2004, pp. 137-146. Single or multiple copies of this article are available for a fee from The Haworth Document Delivery Service [1-800-HAWORTH, 9:00 a.m. - 5:00 p.m. (EST). E-mail address: docdelivery@haworthpress.com].

http://www.haworthpress.com/web/RSIN
Digital Object Identifier: 10.1300/J121v17n01_11

From classroom, to study space, to collaborative work or labs, students seek spatial, social, and intellectual connections. Most importantly, they seek the right space at the right time. Students seek spaces that balance the need to find, to reflect and absorb with the need to create and produce. As Joan Frye Williams reminds us, *"The library is part of an* open *infosystem, through which the people we serve move as hunters and gatherers, choosing what they want from a wide variety of sources. We are not the sole arbiters of the value of what we provide. We have serious competition."*[1] The student may find that on occasion the wireless coffee shop is an inviting, effective office away from home. But at some point, the coffee shop closes and there is more than a subtle suggestion that seat time is not free. The student moves on, looking elsewhere to find the right space.

While the student may not need to consult the vast print resources of a research library that day, he or she may be looking for a plotter to print the latest research symposium poster or need digital video and audio editing equipment to enhance the class multimedia project. In a race to capture and retain the ever-fickle student population of today, libraries across the country are transforming buildings and services to meet these new demands. As ubiquitous and unlimited access to information grows, students' expectations have risen. It is no longer sufficient to provide quiet space for study and research, even with access to print and electronic information. As students seek greater integration of their social and academic lives, both online and off, they search for the seamless continuum of space and service options. The challenge for academic libraries is to be one of those places—to stay relevant, to be valued, and to make real contributions toward enhancing the full educational experience of students.

The Odegaard Undergraduate Library (OUGL) at the University of Washington, one of the largest undergraduate libraries in the country, was built in 1972 to serve the curricular, research, and social needs of the undergraduate students. In an ideal central location, with multiple group study rooms, a media center, comfortable furniture, and a widely-circulating collection, OUGL was innovative by design from the beginning by creating inviting spaces that provided solitude without isolation, supported work in parallel, and set the right balance between contemplative and group study space for students.

But, after twenty-two years, Odegaard was ready for a change. In 1994, through a distinctive partnership with the Office of Undergraduate Education (OUE) and Computing & Communications (C&C), the University Libraries joined in a collaborative effort (formerly called *UWired*) to develop and support effective uses of technology in teaching and learning. The original location of this collaboration was the Odegaard Undergraduate Library with the construction of the first computing "collaboratory" or computer classroom in a library and the establishment of a partnership to focus on teaching and training fluency in information technology and literacy skills.

Now, ten years later, this collaboration has created the only 24-hour library on campus, a 356-seat general access computing lab, two computer classrooms or "collaboratories," a drop-in center for faculty to support teaching with technology and create a suite of online tools, a copy center, a digital audio workstation, a wireless network, electronic white boards, and 14 renovated group study rooms. Building on the concept of "one-stop shopping," the library combined computing help, printing, and reference (with 6,000 reference volumes) into a single point of service, in the middle of the computer lab, located on the second floor of the building.[2] The computing, study, and research needs of the students are also enhanced with a widely-circulating print and media collection of over 180,000 titles.

WHO ARE OUR PARTNERS?

The Office of Undergraduate Education (OUE) at the University of Washington (http://www.washington.edu/oue/) focuses on developing transformative educational experiences for all undergraduate students within and beyond the classroom. Enrichment of student learning is at the core of OUE which includes advising, counseling, service learning, honors and first year programs, classroom support, scholarships, and the Undergraduate Research Program (URP) which facilitates research experiences for undergraduates with UW faculty members across disciplines.

In an effort to provide the very best in technology and training in the service of teaching and learning, a new organization, Educational Partnership and Learning Technologies (EPLT), also known as *UWired*, was formed from the Office of Undergraduate Education. With a broader goal of serving the community and the university campus, EPLT is committed to the development of learning technologies and educational partnerships:

> Networked information technology is changing the way teachers teach and learners learn, and we are committed to assisting in this transformation in ways that support the goals and values of the University of Washington. We serve both students and faculty by providing access to tools and resources; promoting fluency with information and information technology; and fostering innovation in technology-enabled teaching and learning.

Educational Partnerships further connect the education and research expertise of the University of Washington to a range of communities, locally, statewide, nationally, and internationally and help create new forms of education and engagement. By forging genuinely reciprocal relationships between the UW and diverse communities, we aspire to provide educationally rich experiences for students, faculty, and community members and to advance knowledge and human potential.[3]

The partnership with EPLT and the Libraries was a natural one. The mission of the University Libraries to enrich the quality of life and advance intellectual discovery by connecting people with knowledge through a world-class portal of resources and technology complements the mission of EPLT to support innovative uses of the university's infrastructure to support faculty and student research, education, and clinical applications of information technologies.

The Odegaard Undergraduate Library had space to share and a commitment to take advantage of the new opportunities afforded through technological advances. In ten years, the willingness to experiment and innovate has created numerous partnerships on campus and enhanced services. The Program for Educational Transformation Through Technology (PETTT), another outgrowth of EPLT partnerships and housed in Odegaard, is a multidisciplinary funded initiative at the University of Washington that explores the interplay of technology and pedagogy in real settings, making strong connections between research, design, and practice in order to bring the sciences of learning to teaching with technology. Online tools have been developed, by EPLT and PETTT, such as "Catalyst Portfolio Tool" to help students create their own academic portfolio, "Video Traces" to annotate visual media, "Arthritis Source," a web-based tool for anyone with questions about arthritis, or "Catalyst VirtualCase," integrated Web applications that facilitate online problem-based learning, to name a few.[4]

The University of Washington Libraries has been using networked computing technology to expand the resources available for education and research for almost two decades. The infrastructure needed to provide access to this array of global resources is jointly supported by the Library Information Technology Services and Computing & Communications (C&C). Computing & Communications provides the expertise and infrastructure necessary to enable advanced network computing applications and rich information content access at the University of Washington and beyond. Behind the wall, in the ceiling, and often behind the scenes, C&C has helped realize our shared vision of broad and reliable bandwidth by insuring secure and dependable computer and network-based services, resources, and information technology infrastructure. During the early '90s, C&C and the Libraries jointly developed an online catalog and database interface, Willow, and locally loaded databases for uniform searching and commands. With the advent of web-based databases and access, the need to load databases locally diminished, but the working partnership has continued.

In addition to collaborating on issues of authentication, customizable portals, and wireless and upgraded networks, C&C and the Libraries joined other partners in producing a monthly online newsletter, *OnTechNews*, to inform UW faculty, staff, and students about new and interesting technology to use in teaching, learning, and work (http://www.washington.edu/computing/ontech/). The Libraries is on the editorial board and has a monthly submission of a highlighted electronic resource.

C&C is currently talking with the undergraduate library to serve as a location for an Access Grid Node. Access Grid (AG) is used for large-scale distributed meetings and collaborative work sessions in "designed spaces" that contain high-end audio and visual technology for high-quality exchange. It is important to note that C&C has contacted the library about this project not only because we might be willing to share space, but because of our ongoing collaboration and our track record of being good stewards, dedicated to service and maintenance, and our commitment to provide access to the entire university community.

None of the library innovations would have been possible without collaboration with our partners. We each bring to the table our particular focus and commitment, and after ten years, we are continually redefining our relationship, seeking common ground and goals, and renewing our vows to work together. Sometimes it's been harder to communicate than others, but at the end of the day, we celebrate our partnership, and realize that we would never have been able to offer the current level of services and spaces without our partners.

As a general rule, collaboration works best when members come together on a project or initiative that is new and has a certain level of complexity. This newness and complexity create a sense of challenge in solving a new problem. Group members tend to be more open to diverse solutions when they realize that the problem at hand is more complex or is unfamiliar to them and can't be easily solved using current or past designs.[5]

THE IMPORTANCE OF PLACE:
SPATIAL NEED

In the 2004 Triennial University of Washington Libraries Survey (http://www.lib.washington.edu/assessment/), 95.2% of undergraduates surveyed indicated that they had used the UW Libraries services or collections during the academic year. While the in-person visits by faculty and graduate students declined in 2004, the numbers slightly increased for undergraduates. On a weekly basis, 60.8% of undergraduates indicated that they visit the library in person (in 2001, the number was 60.4%). When asked what services they need in the library during evenings and weekends, 75.7% selected "place to work" and 65.5% indicated "computer access."

In addition to the Triennial University Libraries Survey, the Educational Partnerships and Learning Technologies (EPLT) conduct campus-wide surveys of students and faculty to find out what they want and how technology support can add to the resources available to students to get their work done. Not only is this information useful in planning, but it is a requirement when writing proposals for funding from the Student Technology Fee (STF) Group, another partner in the landscape. Each quarter, students must pay a "student technology fee" ($38.00) to have access to the campus computing facilities and network. Each year, this brings in over $4,000,000 to the campus. The student-run STF committee reviews proposals from departments to fund computing labs, laptops, servers, digital equipment, etc., and distributes funds based on the established criteria of improving general access computing for the greatest number of students. The proposals must include input from students that demonstrates the need and priority for funding. Funding from the Student Technology Fee Group has purchased three generations of computers, laptops, scanners, and editing equipment for the OUGL Computing Commons, totaling an investment of over $2,000,000 in the past six years. More recently, STF funded a unique digital audio workstation for OUGL, the only non-departmental audio editing studio for students on campus.

In a bold step, the Libraries partnered with EPLT to install and support a distributed lab model with computer clusters (locally named, "Access +") in five different libraries. These authenticated workstations provide fuller functionality than just access (hence the "+") by including productivity and communication software such as Microsoft Word, Excel, PowerPoint, and Access. The machines also come with CD-RW drives to read and write saved data and USB ports. While issues of branding (*Why is your logo at the top when the computers are in our library?*) and communication (*We didn't know you were going to upgrade the software over the weekend.*) do surface occasionally, the STF-funded cooperative venture has gone well, building on years of partnership and good communication between the parent organizations.

THE IMPORTANCE OF PLACE:
SOCIAL AND INTELLECTUAL NEED

Research Exposed! Approaches to Inquiry

The library is a place of convergence–a place to bring together divergent ideas, communities, and knowledge. It is a place to convey–to make connections to ideas and to people. It is also a crossroads.[6] To bring different disciplines together in a neutral space, the Odegaard Undergraduate Library and the Undergraduate Research Program in the Office of Undergraduate Education co-sponsor a weekly lecture series, "Research Exposed," to introduce students to some of the best minds and research on campus and the community. From the latest research on geophysics, oceanography, aeronautics, and cardiac research, to cutting-edge discoveries in intuitive visual design, digital music and art, students are challenged to follow their curiosity and get involved in research as an undergraduate (http://www.washington.edu/research/urp/exposed/index.html). Having a place such as the undergraduate library to showcase and promote the most exciting research creates a magnet for undergraduate teaching, research, and technology-enhanced study. The libraries are seen as an integral part of the research process and undergraduate education.

Exhibits and Displays

As Joan Williams is fond of saying, "Let students trip over ideas rather than stare at a blank wall."[7] At the Odegaard Undergraduate Library, the exhibition program has grown significantly. Over the last five years, thirty-four large exhibitions have been presented. One outstanding aspect of the program has been the presentation of artists and exhibitions reflecting diverse cultural interests and backgrounds. Peruvian artist Javier Vela Cancinco exhibited paintings in 2000, supported by the Latin American Studies Department, and in 2003, "The Face of Pakistan" photography exhibition by Phil Borges drew significant critical interest. Another popular exhibit (2004) "A Living Wall–Denmark, October 1943: The Rescue of the Jews" involved fifteen different community sponsors including the Swedish Cultural Center, Seattle, WA; the Museum of History and Industry, Seattle, WA; and the Mittleman Jewish Community Center, Portland, OR.

Last year in conjunction with the Seattle Art Museum, the library presented a special exhibit, "India: A Confluence of Cultures" involving visual displays, a film series and dance performances. For the summer of 2004, fifty engravings depicting traditional Jewish costumes worn during the Ottoman Empire in the 16th to 19th centuries are on display in Odegaard. The exhibit is sponsored by the UW Jackson School of International Studies; Consulate General of Turkey; Sephardic Bikur Holim Congregation; Turkish American Cultural Association; American Sephardi Federation; Assembly of Turkish American Associations; Ministry of Foreign Affairs of the Republic of Turkey; and the Jewish Community of Turkey.

Featured artists have been of national interest. *The New York Times* published an article on Sabah Al-Dhaher, a refugee from Iraq, who exhibited his sculpture in Odegaard Library throughout 2003. Exhibitions receive reviews in *The Seattle Times* and are regularly advertised in campus publications and small community newspapers including *The University Herald*.

New Book Displays

In an effort to optimize the serendipitous accidental discoveries, we have had book display tables custom made to highlight new books. It has been very successful and not infrequently, students stop and browse and chat around the new books.

University Libraries Undergraduate Research Award

To heighten the visibility and the importance of developing and using information literacy and research skills, and to partner with departmental faculty and the Undergraduate Research Program, the University Libraries offered monetary awards to the best examples of undergraduate research in any discipline. The awards were given to undergraduates for research completed during the academic year for a credit course. In the first year, there were 51 projects from varying disciplines. Six $1,000 awards were presented to undergraduate students for exceptional research and scholarship projects. The Library Research Award for Undergraduates Program (http://www.lib.washington.edu/researchaward) stimulated a wonderful recognition of the importance of a strong working partnership in academic learning between the faculty, students, and librarians. It is rare that librarians actually see the finished projects or papers of students. This program at the University of Washington followed the inspiring lead of University of California Berkeley's "Library Prize for Undergraduate Research," first initiated in 2002-2003 (http://www.lib.berkeley.edu/researchprize).

COLLABORATIVE SPONSORSHIP:
WHY THE LIBRARY?

Libraries make good partners. On campuses where there is fierce competition for funding and space, the library is often seen as a neutral party, an excellent steward and custodian of resources and services for all of the campus. While the library's real estate or extensive footprint on campus may be the target of intensive review for scarce space, the library is respected for its honesty, strong sense of responsibility, responsiveness to the entire campus, and expertise in running big operations. As Margaret Wheatley observes in her book, *Leadership and the New Science* (2001):

> Libraries are very much alive and integral to the communities they serve. They are living systems. In order to maintain their adaptability and take advantage of key changes in the environment, complex organizations encourage people to create and maintain many informal relationships. . . . The reinforcing leadership actions that make complex systems work are *connection*, *contribution*, and *collaboration*.[8]

In 2002, the director of University Libraries, Betsy Wilson, along with all other deans, was asked by the incoming interim provost to provide a list of departments and frequency with which she had communicated in the past year, and to indicate which of those interactions she had initiated. Not surprisingly, Betsy came in first. She far surpassed other academic deans on campus in the number of collaborative contacts and connections. Libraries have space, they have time, they have expertise in organization and management, and they have connections.

The Odegaard Undergraduate Library has been open to innovative uses of spaces and staff to support student learning in the most effective way. Often called the "Digital Sandwich," with books on the first and third floors and a digital filler in the middle, Odegaard has worked to keep core library resources and services in the building while offering state-of-the-art technology and access. One of the most significant developments from this partnering has been the dramatic increase in entry gate statistics. From an average of 5,000 to 6,000 entries per day, the gate counts are averaging 9,000 to 10,000 per day and some peak days reaching over 13,000 entries. The statistics for logins in the computer lab are about half that number, supporting the observation that students are using the library for non-computing purposes as well. Our gate count has become the highest in the distributed library system, accounting for over 1,776,560 visits per year. To integrate services and options for students in one place, to provide the spatial, social, and intellectual comfort in one location has been our goal. It is a place of strong community and collaboration. Many of our university partners come together in this building to create a rich learning environment for students and faculty.

According to Margaret Wheatley, organizations are often at their best when they operate more like chaotic or complex systems, taking advantage of change to allow growth and to reach target goals. "The goal of a complex organization is not to control change that is often out of our immediate or direct control, but to be opportunistic and respond to change."[9]

NOTES

1. Williams, Joan Frye. "Innovation and Risk-Taking." Strategic Planning Seminar. University of Washington Libraries, 8 June 2004, Student Union Building Auditorium, Seattle, Washington.

2. Jill Morrison McKinstry and Peter McCracken, "Combining Computing and Reference Desks in an Undergraduate Library: A Brilliant Innovation or a Serious Mistake?" *portal: Libraries and the Academy* 2.3 (July 2002): 391-400. http://muse.jhu.edu/journals/portal_libraries_and_the_academy/v002/2.3mckinstry.html.

3. University of Washington Educational Partnerships and Learning Technologies, "About Educational Partnerships and Learning Technologies," http://www.washington.edu/eplt/about/ (accessed June 20, 2004).

4. University of Washington, Program for Educational Transformation Through Technology (PETTT), "PETTT Projects," http://depts.washington.edu/pettt/projects/ (Accessed June 20, 2004).

5. Christi A. Olson with Paula M. Singer, *Winning with Library Leadership* (Chicago: American Library Association, 2004), 73.

6. Betsy Baker, "Values for the Learning library," *Research Strategies* 17 (2000): 85-91.

7. Williams, Joan Frye.

8. Olson, 6-7.

9. Olson, 4-5.

New Library Facilities:
Opportunities for Collaboration

Joan K. Lippincott

SUMMARY. As academic libraries renovate or build new spaces that provide services to users, they should consider opportunities to collaborate with other units on campus to develop collaborative services in the new space. These collaborative spaces, such as information commons, teaching and learning centers, and multi-media studios, offer advantages such as providing seamless services to users, leveraging the technology and information expertise of several professional specialties, and pooling resources from more than one campus unit. Careful attention to the planning process is needed in order to ensure mutual understanding of the project goals, responsibilities, resource contributions, and services. *[Article copies available for a fee from The Haworth Document Delivery Service: 1-800-HAWORTH. E-mail address: <docdelivery@haworthpress.com> Website: <http://www.HaworthPress.com> © 2004 by The Haworth Press, Inc. All rights reserved.]*

KEYWORDS. Collaboration, partnerships, collaborative facilities, library renovation, information commons, academic library facilities, library planning

Joan K. Lippincott is Associate Executive Director, Coalition for Networked Information, 21 Dupont Circle, Suite 800, Washington, DC 20036 (E-mail: joan@cni.org).

[Haworth co-indexing entry note]: "New Library Facilities: Opportunities for Collaboration." Lippincott, Joan K. Co-published simultaneously in *Resource Sharing & Information Networks* (The Haworth Information Press, an imprint of The Haworth Press, Inc.) Vol. 17, No. 1/2, 2004, pp. 147-157; and: *Libraries Within Their Institutions: Creative Collaborations* (ed: William Miller, and Rita M. Pellen) The Haworth Information Press, an imprint of The Haworth Press, Inc., 2004, pp. 147-157. Single or multiple copies of this article are available for a fee from The Haworth Document Delivery Service [1-800-HAWORTH, 9:00 a.m. - 5:00 p.m. (EST). E-mail address: docdelivery@haworthpress.com].

http://www.haworthpress.com/web/RSIN
© 2004 by The Haworth Press, Inc. All rights reserved.
Digital Object Identifier: 10.1300/J121v17n01_12

INTRODUCTION

Renovation or construction of technology-rich facilities such as information commons, teaching and learning centers, and multi-media studios is a high-profile topic on many campuses today. Facilities built or renovated from the 1960s through 1980s are ripe for renovation, and major developments in technology assist administrators in making the case for an investment in new facilities that will accommodate the technological needs of users. This article explores a subset of technology-rich facilities that provide services on campus, namely collaborative facilities in libraries. In these facilities, more than one campus unit or professional group shares space and cooperates or collaborates to develop a plan for seamless information and technology services to the user community.

The focus of this article is on collaborative facilities in which the library or librarians are likely to be involved, such as information commons, teaching and learning centers, and multi-media studios. These facilities have an emphasis on employing new technologies to deliver services and also have strong connections to content, generally in digital form, that supports teaching, learning, and research. A model for many collaborative facilities based in libraries is the Leavey Library at the University of Southern California, which is now approaching its tenth year of operation. Leavey's mission statement reflects its dual heritage as a library and information technology facility in its commitment to be a "guide to the world of information resources" and "a campus partner for integrating information technology into the curriculum," among other goals (Leavey). Most library-affiliated collaborative facilities are renovations and additions, such as the Integrated Learning Center (ILC) at University of Arizona <http://www.ilc.arizona.edu/>, but some are entirely new buildings, such as the Student Learning Center at University of Georgia, a partnership of the library and information technology <http://slc.uga.edu/facility.html>.

Many libraries have long housed other units, such as writing centers and centers for teaching excellence, as tenants. In such cases, the library may have a laissez-faire relationship with the occupant but, in other cases, there may be tension over the other unit's occupation of the library's space. These kinds of relationships are not collaborations. In a genuine collaboration, there are a number of factors present in addition to the mere sharing of a physical facility. They include development of shared goals by the parties, joint planning, an awareness of and a valuing of the expertise of each partner, and pooling of resources (Kanter, 1994; Katzenbach and Smith, 1993).

A recent survey found that there is a high proportion of new construction or renovations of library facilities that include such features as general computer labs (69.9%), multi-media production centers (45.1%), and educational technology centers (26%). Interestingly, the survey report characterizes these facilities as "nonlibrary facilities." In some cases, the facilities may be tenants of the library, wholly separate in administration and service delivery from the library. However, it is not a given that all of these should be characterized as "nonlibrary" as some could be collaborative endeavors or some could be library-run. The authors of the article note the positive impact of these features, stating that

> the trend toward inclusion of nonlibrary facilities within the building has changed the character of recently improved libraries in significant ways. Rather than having a few nonlibrary units occasionally occupying space in the building, the physical library is increasingly becoming the home base for a wide variety of operations. As such, it is becoming a more complex facility that attracts students for multiple purposes and must accommodate the needs of nonlibrary units. (Shill and Tonner, 2004)

"Accommodating the needs" of the other units ignores the opportunity that exists to develop genuinely collaborative facilities and services within library space.

On many campuses, technology-rich facilities, including information commons, teaching and learning centers, and multi-media studios are *not* collaborative facilities. Instead, they are planned and administered by a single campus unit such as the library, computer center, center for teaching excellence, multi-media unit, or other such campus department. This article will describe the rationale for collaboration in technology-rich facilities as well as describe the challenges in initiating such collaborations and making them work.

RATIONALE

Frequently, library administrators are asked by funders whether there is still a need for existing, renovated, or new physical space for the library. While the emergence of ubiquitous technology on many campuses may initially lead some to think that specialized facilities are no longer required, in actuality, technology drives the need for the renovation or development of new physical spaces that will facilitate the types of activities and services in which our user population currently engages. A recent article by library leaders describes a vision for a "transformed library" and lists ten characteristics of such an institution. Four of those characteristics are relevant to collaborative spaces in libraries:

provides both physical and virtual spaces to access information any time, any place; partners with other campus agencies to achieve the collective university goals; develops new and innovative learning environments and activities through collaboration with other academic and campus units; and provides community spaces for inquiry-based learning and out-of-classroom activities, including the creation and design of products by students. (Brewer, 2004)

This modern view of the library's space, role, and relationships emphasizes the continuing value of the library as "place" and the increased need for outreach and partnerships with other campus units.

Planning collaborative facilities requires vision and a leap of faith. At the University of Washington's library, where they have developed a "collaboratory" for teaching and learning, a collaborative Center for Teaching, Learning, and Technology, and the UWired Information Commons, library director Betsy Wilson comments, "Collaboration is a choice. It can't be mandated. It's hard work. It's fragile" (Wilson, 2002). The decision to collaborate should be carefully considered by all parties and discussed to ensure that all parties understand the goals and terms of the collaboration.

Some key rationales for developing collaborative facilities are: to provide seamless services to users, to leverage the various talents that different professional groups can bring to a service, and to pool institutional resources.

Most campus professionals operate within their departmental silos; generally, librarians work for libraries, information technologists work for computing centers, faculty work for departments. These professionals' focus, loyalties, and frames of reference are developed within these silos. Their funding stream is generally commensurate with their campus unit. It is entirely logical, from an administrative perspective, for each unit to develop its own priorities, policies, and services.

However, the user communities in higher education institutions do not necessarily understand how the administrative structures we've developed translate into service availability. For example, if a faculty member wants to arrange for someone to teach his/her class to access U.S. census data and analyze it using a statistical package, does he/she request that service from the library, the computing center, the campus data center, or some other entity? If a student wants to develop a multi-media presentation on the events of September 11, 2001, does he/she get assistance in finding digital content, understanding intellectual property rights issues, and using a multi-media presentation software package from the library, multi-media service, or computer center?

The answer would not only vary from campus to campus, but on any given campus, the student or faculty member might have to go to a number of physically separate facilities to get all of the assistance he or she needed. As Chris Ferguson notes in an important conceptualization of a new era of information services, "The particular challenge is to build unified service delivery models for both on-site and remote service that rely on common service providers and training programs, collaborative approaches to service, tools for collaborative service delivery, and a shared set of service values" (Ferguson, 2000). Collaborative facilities, jointly staffed by more than one campus unit, can be a means of achieving these types of service goals.

Developing facilities in a collaborative mode can help address the balkanization of services that is evident on many campuses. For example, at Northwestern University, a workshop series for faculty is framed this way: "The 2East Technology Series is intended for faculty who want to take advantage of the teaching and research capabilities of digital media, course management systems, online archives, advanced visualization technologies, electronic journals and other emerging technologies" (Northwestern University 2East). Staff from various units have combined in this facility, which is part of the library, to offer a workshop series that draws on expertise from many professional specialties. In addition, faculty do not have to check a multitude of department websites to find out who offers a workshop on a specific topic; it is all in one place, an example of seamless service to the users, in this case faculty.

Even in one professional specialty such as librarianship, it is difficult for librarians to keep up with all of the current technology and digital content developments in or related to their field. Yet many of the sophisticated applications of technology that today's users want require a multitude of skills. Two articles describing new or renovated library facilities discuss the problems faced by library staff who felt unprepared to deal with the new technology and the types of services required by users in their new facilities. Both articles mention increased attention to training, possibly by computer experts from outside of the library, as a possible solution to their problem, but recognize its limitation in a constantly changing environment. One proposes partnering with another campus unit, a teaching and learning center, to broaden the types of expertise available to provide services to users in the new facility (VanderPol and Fitch, 2002; Cowgill, Beam, and Wess, 2001). As libraries plan technology-rich spaces, they need to think in advance about the skills required by staff and consider collaborating with other units to offer services in the new facility.

Collaboration among groups of professionals with different skills can help solve the problem of keeping up with a never-ending stream of new developments. In a collaborative environment, professionals can divide and share expertise in order to offer a broader array of services in a mode that is seamless to users. At Indiana University, the CIO described the development of a new information commons in the library with these words:

> Today's great universities provide access to information that will expand teaching and research. IUTS staff, with their expertise in technology, and Librarians and Library staff, with their expertise in information access, worked together to design the IC with the goal of providing students with the services, tools, and the support they need to succeed academically and to prepare them for careers after graduation. (Campus Celebrates, 2003)

By combining the expertise of library and IT staff, Indiana University believed it could provide a wider range of tools and services for its students in their newly configured information commons than it could separately.

Resources are always limited in any academic institution, and the pooling of resources in a collaborative relationship is one way to meet user needs in an efficient manner. In a genuine collaboration, each unit contributes value to the relationship, but each does not need to contribute in identical ways. Therefore, the library might contribute space to a collaborative endeavor, the computing center might contribute equipment, and the center for teaching and learning might contribute funds for software licenses. Each unit could contribute staff expertise to be used for planning, administration, and service delivery.

These three rationales, providing seamless services to users, leveraging expertise, and pooling resources, offer strong incentives for collaboration among various service units or departments on campus. However, the road to collaboration is not easy and it requires support by top administrators and a spirit of cooperation and openness by those at the service level to achieve the desired results of collaboration.

BARRIERS TO COLLABORATION

Some of the same elements that provide the rationale for collaboration, viewed from a different perspective, can form barriers to collaboration. While various campus units share the overall mission of the institution, most staff identify instead with the mission of their particular department. When they develop goals for a facility or a service, they do so within the confines of their traditional units. It takes imagination to develop new facilities and services that are not necessarily "library" services or "computing" services but rather information and technology facilities or services for users.

The types of professional groups that may be involved in collaborative facilities based in libraries often have different organizational and work styles. Some professional groups work through a committee structure, others work through a hierarchical structure. Some have a project-based work style while others have an ongoing service perspective. They may have different norms concerning appropriate response time to user requests, the type of staff that can answer certain queries, and the scope of services that are offered to various user groups. They may have different values and expectations on policy issues such as charging users for services, privacy issues, and security issues. These types of style and norms issues should be explicitly discussed as part of the planning process for the collaborative facility.

Some professional groups have developed stereotypes about potential partner groups on campus. These kinds of attitudes can poison collaborations. In regard to partnerships between librarians and information technologists, while there is recognition that they need to work together, "There is also a deep, visceral division that must be overcome as these professionals begin to see each other in very different ways, recognizing what each brings to the partnership" (Hawkins and Battin, 1998). Achieving this understanding of the value of the skills that each group brings to a partnership is a hallmark of successful collaboration.

The administrative structure of the institution may, in itself, create barriers to collaboration. Heads of the units of potential partners may report to different parts of the administration, have competing budget needs, and have developed different relationships on campus. Sharing control of a facility is challenging and time consuming, and some administrators may dismiss this notion out of hand.

All of these factors are genuine concerns and should not be considered lightly. Developing collaborations requires a concerted effort on the part of the units and key administrators involved, openness to sharing professional perspectives, interest in developing new ways of conducting business, and a willingness to develop trust between or among the parties involved.

MAKING PARTNERSHIPS WORK

An important aspect to making collaborations and partnerships work is to start with the planning process. Collaboration should be an explicit goal of a renovation or new facility, and a public recognition of the value of the partnership is highly desirable. At Dartmouth College, planning for a renovation and expansion of the main library became a campus, not a "library," project. A task force was assembled to frame design goals for the facility and it included individuals representing many campus sectors. The task force report recommended that the campus develop a "library plan that could be claimed by everyone in the community, developed by a representative group that could give the plans a broad, institution-wide endorsement." The resulting design goals included a stipulation that the design "must allow for and enable the expansion of cooperation between the Library staff and the Computing Services staff" ("From the Start," 1998). The perspectives that technology was leading to convergence between many library and information technology services and that together the two campus units could offer the institution a new level of user support drove the joint planning effort, which resulted in all of academic computing services moving into the renovated and expanded library.

The University of Tennessee's Hodges Library has two collaborative facilities within its building, the Digital Media Service, which digitizes and stores instructional materials for faculty, and the Studio, which is a digital media production laboratory for use by faculty and students. From the first steps of the planning process, consideration was given to the campus partners for development and implementation of the plan and for operation of the facilities. The facilities are partnerships between the libraries and the Office of Research and Information Technology (ORIT). A memo of understanding was developed to formally describe the partnership arrangement, including governance, reporting relationships, service philosophy, timeline, and assessment of the service (Dewey, 2002 and Dewey, Planning Checklist and Memos, 2003). Such formal arrangements pave the way for collaborations based on mutual understanding and expectations.

Southern Illinois University at Carbondale (SIUC) clearly states its rationale for partnership between the library and IT in a "Statement of Partnership." The statement was developed in anticipation of the Information Technology Customer Service Center's move to the library. The statement stipulates that the

mission of the partnership–to provide faculty with effective support for teaching and learning initiatives in the classroom and in distance learning technology–can be divided into three goals: (1) to develop a seamless and equal partnership between IT and Library Affairs, so that customers are unaware of organizational complexities; (2) to set the trend for instructional technology for SIUC; and (3) to provide high-quality instructional technology development and support for campus faculty. A climate of collaboration and seamless support is essential to the success of this partnership. (Southern Illinois University, Statement)

The Statement further outlines the opportunities presented by the partnership, goals and objectives, benefits to be derived, key strategies, anticipated resources, potential risks to the partners, and the terms of the partnership agreement. It lays a very clear groundwork for collaborative initiatives within a common facility, emphasizing instructional technology.

Involving campus committees in the overall planning of collaborative facilities can put an imprimatur on the mission of the facility to leverage partnerships to provide new types of services to the campus community. Aligning the mission of the collaborative facility to the overall institutional mission, academic strategic plan, and institutional technology plan can provide a framework within which the specific plan for the facility can mature. While much attention generally is paid to developing the physical plan for the facility, sometimes little attention is given to the relationships between and among the partners who will be working together in the new facility. A parallel effort should be underway to plan for collaborative services, which will be offered in the facility or provided virtually from the facility.

Developing shared meaning among the partners in the facility can be an important aspect to building collaborative services. What does it mean to provide user support? How can complementary units provide seamless services both onsite and virtually? What kinds of workshops and instruction sessions should be offered to students, faculty, and staff? Which staff is best equipped to offer certain types of instruction and when are partnerships in the classroom needed? Professionals such as librarians, information technologists, multi-media specialists, and instructional technologists have different norms, cultures, and traditions of service. These need to be explored, respected, and valued while building new shared norms, cultures, and traditions.

The planning for collaborative facilities should include an assessment component that proposes mechanisms for measuring the degree to which the goals of the project are met after it has been operational for a given time period and at regular intervals thereafter. Assessment results can help refine both physical elements of the facility and the services offered in the facility; it cannot be assumed that the planners will get everything right on the first try. Collaborative facilities, as indeed all technology-rich facilities, need to have the capacity for relatively easy reconfiguration as needs will change over time.

CONCLUSION

Planning collaborative facilities requires an institution-wide vision and a willingness to think beyond the confines of administrative structures. Collaborative facilities offer the units involved an opportunity to provide a richer and broader set of services to users, leverage the technology and information skills of various professional groups on campus, and pool resources from various administrative units. By developing plans that encompass both the physical aspects of the structure and the services to be offered, the campus can achieve a genuine partnership that creates new value for its institution, serving users in new ways that take into account the current technology and information environment.

Collaborative facilities based in libraries are a relatively new phenomenon. However, there are some exemplars out there, and those considering collaborative facilities for their campus can learn from the experience of others. The Coalition for Networked Information (CNI), a joint project of the Association of Research Libraries and EDUCAUSE, has developed a Collaborative Facilities website with its partner, Dartmouth College, which hosts the site. Links to collaborative facilities, policies, and planning information are included on the site and provide some of the background for this article (Coalition for Networked Information; Lippincott, 2002). The CNI website at <www.cni.org> also includes presentations on collaborative facilities that have been given at many of the CNI Task Force meetings.

REFERENCES

Brewer, Joseph M. et al. "Libraries Dealing with the Future Now." *ARL: A Bimonthly Report on Research Library Issues and Actions from ARL, CNI, and SPARC*, number 234, June, 2004, pp. 1-9.

"Campus Celebrates Opening of Information Commons: New Technology and Information Center in Main Library." News Release, Indiana University UITS, September 13, 2003. < http://www.indiana.edu/-uits.cpo/lc091703/>.

Coalition for Networked Information and Dartmouth College. Collaborative Facilities web site. <http://www.dartmouth.edu/~collab/>.

Cowgill, Allison, Joan Beam, and Lindsey Wess. "Implementing an Information Commons in a University Library." *Journal of Academic Librarianship*, vol. 27(6), 2001, pp. 432-439.

Dewey, Barbara. "Planning Checklist" and "Memos of Understanding." Planning Collaborative Spaces in Libraries: An ACRL/CNI Preconference, Toronto, Canada, June 20, 2003. <www.cni.org/regconfs/acrlcni2003/handouts.html>.

Dewey, Barbara. "University of Tennessee's Collaborative Digital Media Spaces." *ARL: A Bimonthly Report on Research Library Issues and Actions from ARL, CNI, and SPARC*, number 222, June, 2002, pp. 4-5.

Ferguson, Chris. "Shaking the Conceptual Foundations, Too: Integrating Research and Technology Support for the Next Generation of Information Service." *College & Research Libraries*, vol 61(4), 2000, pp. 300-310.

"From the Start, Berry Planning Guided by Task Force Report." *Interface: Computing News of Dartmouth College*, vol. 29 (2), 1998.

Hawkins, Brian L. and Patricia Battin. "The Information Resources Professional." In *The Mirage of Continuity: Reconfiguring Academic Information Resources for the 21st Century*. Washington, DC: Council on Library and Information Resources and Association of American Universities, 1998, pp. 260-270.

Kanter, Rosabeth M. "Collaborative Advantage: The Art of Alliances." *Harvard Business Review*, vol. 72, July-August, 1994, pp. 96-108.

Katzenbach, J. R. and D. K. Smith. *The Wisdom of Teams*. New York: HarperBusiness, 1993.

Kratz, Charles. "Transforming the Delivery of Services: The Joint-Use Library and Information Commons." *C&RL News*, vol. 64, February, 2003, pp. 100-101.

"Leavey Library's Mission Statement." <http://www.usc.edu/isd/locations/undergrad/leavey/mvv.html>.

Lippincott, Joan. "CNI and Dartmouth Launch Collaborative Facilities Web Site." *ARL: A Bimonthly Report on Research Library Issues and Actions from ARL, CNI, and SPARC*, number 222, June, 2002, p. 6.

Northwestern University. 2East: Bibliographic Resources and Scholarly Technologies. <http://2east.northwestern.edu/>.

Shill, Harold B. and Shawn Tonner. "Does the Building Still Matter? Usage Patterns in New, Expanded, and Renovated Libraries, 1995-2002." *College & Research Libraries*, vol. 65(2), 2004, pp. 123-150.

Southern Illinois University. "Statement of Partnership." <http://www.dartmouth.edu/~collab/institutions/so_il/so_il.html>.

VanderPol, Diane and Megan Fitch. "Gearing Up: Technologies for Adventures in Library Learning." *Library Hi Tech*, vol. 20 (1), 2002, pp. 111-120.

Wilson, Lizabeth A. "Collaborate or Die: Designing Library Space." *ARL: A Bimonthly Report on Research Library Issues and Actions from ARL, CNI, and SPARC*, number 222, June, 2002, pp. 1-3.

Digital Preservation
of Theses and Dissertations
Through Collaboration

Gail McMillan

SUMMARY. While university libraries have a long tradition of preserving scholarship, they are less experienced in the technology-dependent and computer networked environment. By taking advantage of current activities and expertise that exist in various parts of the institution, policies and practices can be linked that will engender long-term accessibility. Under ideal circumstances preservation is not an isolated process; rather, it is built into the information life cycle beginning with a work's creation and continuing through to storage and access. Electronic theses and dissertations (ETDs) provide a good starting point to determine the processes and policies that will lead to confidence in digital preservation. *[Article copies available for a fee from The Haworth Document Delivery Service: 1-800-HAWORTH. E-mail address: <docdelivery@haworthpress.com> Website: <http://www.HaworthPress.com> © 2004 by The Haworth Press, Inc. All rights reserved.]*

KEYWORDS. Preservation, archiving, computer services, digital, ETD, electronic theses and dissertations, graduate school, library, university

Gail McMillan, MLS, MA, is Director, Digital Library and Archives, and Professor, University Libraries, Virginia Polytechnic Institute and State University, P.O. Box 90001, Blacksburg, VA 24062-9001 (E-mail: gailmac@vt.edu).

[Haworth co-indexing entry note]: "Digital Preservation of Theses and Dissertations Through Collaboration." McMillan, Gail. Co-published simultaneously in *Resource Sharing & Information Networks* (The Haworth Information Press, an imprint of The Haworth Press, Inc.) Vol. 17, No. 1/2, 2004, pp. 159-174; and: *Libraries Within Their Institutions: Creative Collaborations* (ed: William Miller, and Rita M. Pellen) The Haworth Information Press, an imprint of The Haworth Press, Inc., 2004, pp. 159-174. Single or multiple copies of this article are available for a fee from The Haworth Document Delivery Service [1-800-HAWORTH, 9:00 a.m. - 5:00 p.m. (EST). E-mail address: docdelivery@haworthpress.com].

http://www.haworthpress.com/web/RSIN
© 2004 by The Haworth Press, Inc. All rights reserved.
Digital Object Identifier: 10.1300/J121v17n01_13

PRESERVATION

Keep alive, intact, and safe from injury and harm; save from decomposition. These are standard definitions of preservation[1] but not necessarily formal practices in these early days of digital libraries and institutional repositories. Preservation, whether of born-digital works or scanned documents, should not be an isolated process or a single event. It is not a specific activity but the coalescing of procedures and policies that enable long-term access. Ideally preservation is built into the information life cycle beginning with a work's creation and continues through submission and acceptance for archiving and access. Electronic theses and dissertations (ETDs) can be used to prototype the activities and policies the academy needs to address to ensure long-term preservation and access to its unique scholarship.

INTRODUCTION

ETD initiatives have grown out of collaborations in a variety of environments–within a university, in regional consortia of universities such as Committee on Institutional Cooperation (CIC), in statewide consortia such as OhioLink, and in national programs such as the Australian Digital Theses. In each of these environments ETD initiatives developed through collaborations between dispersed units (known by various names) including the Library, Graduate School, Computer Services,[2] and Learning Technology.[3] This article focuses on ETDs within a single institution, a university setting, but a digital preservation initiative can be extrapolated across multiple collaborating universities.

Goals of ETD initiatives include improving graduate education, increasing the availability of student research by developing accessible digital libraries of theses and dissertations, and preserving them electronically. ETDs are a testament to the university so that institutions that are not legally bound to retain theses and dissertations find themselves ethically obligated to also preserve ETDs.

Among the members of the Networked Digital Library of Theses and Dissertations (NDLTD, www.ndltd.org), it is usually the university Library that hosts the ETD initiative. As the database develops, the Library stores and provides access in a variety of ways, including searching, browsing, and linking. Minimally, it stores multiple copies in several locations and routinely backs up the ETD database because this has proven to be sound practice in the evolving digital library. Procedures to better ensure long-term access have not necessarily been formalized, in part because the knowledge and expertise reside in disparate units of the university.

University libraries have a long tradition of preserving original scholarship produced by graduate students. Land grant universities like Virginia Tech also have a larger mission–a democratic mandate for openness, accessibility, and public service. In the computer-networked environment, libraries inadvertently provide access to ETDs for the benefit of society at large, not just to local users but also to users nationally and globally. There is evidence that when ETDs are available globally, readers outside the originating institution access them more frequently than do readers from the home institution or even the home nation.[4]

In practice, living repositories of ETDs have served researchers well for nearly a decade. In addition, Virginia Tech serves as an example that, without limiting the software that graduate students can use to submit their theses and dissertations, nearly 6,000 born-digital ETDs are available to typical Internet readers. However, libraries are looking for collaborators to share formal preservation responsibilities because such records of success are telling but limited. Universities can draw on units such as Computer Services and Learning Technology, along with the Library, to establish the network of preservation partners that can collaborate to ensure long-term access to digital works.

Preserving unique university works should be an institutional responsibility, not the responsibility of one unit. University libraries are designed, constructed, maintained, and function because of the interplay of various units of the university including the subject departments, the Graduate School, and Computer Services. Long-term preservation naturally follows from library activities such as collecting, identifying, and providing access to purchased and donated information resources. A unit such as Computer Services has the existing infrastructure (machines, staffing, routines) to facilitate more securely archiving these resources than currently exist elsewhere in the university or the library. Collaboration can lead to virtually centralized activities and reduce unnecessary duplication of efforts. Establishing preservation routines for static works such as ETDs can serve as a prototype for establishing them for other collections that have similar components including metadata, discovery, and access controls.

It is the early days in the life of digital works, and preservation is yet to be tested and to evolve into formal procedures. Sharing preservation policy development for the university at large with a pervasive unit such as Computer Services is a good place to start. A dark archive[5] as a repository of back-up ETDs can be one initial aspect that Computer Services can incorporate into its current security measures without any adverse effect on systems or staff.

Combined with the Library's people focus, preservation goals can be both pragmatic and evolutionary.

PRESERVATION IS NOT MAINLY A TECHNICAL QUESTION

Technology "is just a bunch of engineers solving problems."[6]

Several sources tell us that preservation is not just a technical question. In 2001, JSTOR's Kevin Guthrie wrote in *Educause Review* that archiving is not, and never has been, an issue fundamentally about technology; rather, it is about organizations and resources.[7] In the same year Henry Gladney, retired IBM scientist, expressed similar sentiments. "The greatest challenges to implementation [of digital document durability] are not technical, but rather economic and political."[8] Three years later Lavoie and Dempsy at OCLC wrote in *D-Lib Magazine* that preservation has less to do with technical issues and more to do with how preservation fits into the broader theme of digital stewardship.[9] Therefore, this article focuses on existing activities at research universities that can be extended to include digital preservation of their graduate students' ETDs.

The technology can address the range of functions of a preservation repository. Some works will be acceptable as recoverable intact bit streams that maintain access to the intellectual content but not to the artifact. Other works will require migration to new formats or the creation of emulators that will reproduce the look, feel, and functionality of the original work. The marriage of data and documents that can live together for a long time in durable formats such as PDF will satisfy some.

Beginning an ETD initiative should not be postponed while various communities come to terms with future technologies that promise long-term access. For example, fears about not being able to get data off previous media can be allayed by our colleagues in Computer Science who reassure us that, though the average person may not know how to get the data off five-inch floppy diskettes, the knowledge exists and can be deployed when necessary. Leadership in the Graduate School promotes the tens, hundreds, and thousands of accesses in the near-term that overcome the dearth of requests for paperbound theses and dissertations.[10] The threat of obsolete technology has not been realized in the first decade of ETDs, while the promise of vastly improved access has been accomplished. Rather than getting bogged down in future-limited technology, the Library mission of digital stewardship will be better served by tackling the challenges of collaboration.

ETD PRESERVATION THROUGH COLLABORATION

Within a university there are disparate units whose ongoing activities and processes are associated and, therefore, make them obvious collaborators for a long-term ETD preservation initiative. These units can be called the Library, Computer Services, Learning Technology, and the Graduate School. However, the Graduate School, which approves ETDs, does not have in its mission long-term access to theses and dissertations. Departments, colleges, and schools within a university may have varying formatting requirements, but the formal software training, already offered through a unit such as Learning Technology, can incorporate these various templates and/or formatting issues in training sessions. Computer Services is already performing back-up routines but it is not oriented towards handling continuous access and reference questions. The Library is designed for some of these activities but not others. Taking advantage of areas of expertise, distributing the workload, and sharing responsibilities required for long-term preservation will benefit every unit individually and the university as a whole. Collaboration among university units can enhance the productive capacity of limited funds and shared resources, eliminate unnecessary redundancies, exploit economies of scale, and foster long-term preservation and access. A digital preservation system with separate but interoperable and collaborative services has various layers (from top to bottom)[11] of shared and disparate activities that operate across appropriate university units.

- Access services (browsing, searching), validating access permissions, retrieval/delivery
- Preservation measures: monitoring changes in the repository that would affect access and use; initiating migration or emulation to mitigate changes
- More specialized services to manage the archived content, including metadata management, and validating the works' integrity
- Hardware, software, network infrastructure supporting ETD storage and distribution

ETD PRESERVATION AND THE LIBRARY

The Library's developing digital experience expands on its decades of keeping materials in exceptionally cool and dry environments that permit only appropriate access and protected handling. The Library's single decade of experience with born-digital and scanned materials has demonstrated its capability to provide near-term preservation. It has also demonstrated better than any other academic unit that it understands the preservation of digital files against reasonable contingencies through periodic back-ups and multiple, distributed copies.

The best archive may prove to be the active one like Virginia Tech and other NDLTD members maintain in a live environment that has continuous ingest and access to the original works. Resorting to reformatting will have its costs and delay access. Preservation processes should operate seamlessly along with access and retrieval processes, without impeding access or thwarting the sharing of ETDs. Even without guaranteeing long-term access, universities are fulfilling their goals to improve access to original scholarship as demonstrated by quantitative measures of near-term accesses recorded on the Library server's logs.

In part because the Library plays a role in the full information cycle, from creation to access, it is difficult to reduce the wide range of library activities into separate and distinct aspects. However, a summary of the university library's preservation-related activities includes the following.

Areas of Expertise

Access Control. Libraries regulate access through controlled stacks such as Periodical Reading Rooms and through closed collections such as Rare Book Rooms. With the advent of online subscription databases within the last decade, license agreements have required libraries to similarly control online access by identifying appropriate users, usually through IP address and university-level PIDs[12] and passwords. When ETD authors choose to temporarily limit or withhold access, computer programs maintained in the accessible library database must be mirrored in the dark archive or preservation database.

Authentication is multi-faceted. Authors and their committees and/or advisors (i.e., students and faculty) are validated against existing university-wide computer-networked human resource systems maintained by Computer Services. Likewise, the Graduate School reviewer must be authenticated to allow approving new ETDs and moving files from temporarily restricted access to permanent worldwide access. The Library systems administrator must be authenticated to copy a work from the dark archive into the publicly accessible and active ETD database. Similarly, centralized records of the university's IP addresses must be available along with PIDs to distinguish members of the university community from nonmembers. Collaborating to use these centralized and networked resources is more efficient and cost effective than creating and maintaining duplicate systems that can easily get out of sync, for example, with each address change.

Because the Library and Computer Services will maintain duplicates, they must be able to share files, and information about them through interoperable systems. ETDs must have unique and persistent identifiers, such as handles[13] and PURLs.[14] An identifier is a permanent name for the object that is unique and unchanging and that distinguishes it from other ETDs. This unique identifier will also be used to link it with its metadata record as well as other related files.

Back-ups and security. Copying databases (i.e., back-ups) is a standard operating procedure and part of current computer routines for the accessible ETD database. Every two weeks, for example, the database is copied and the previous copy is replaced. Unfortunately, this removes the trail of changes while ensuring new additions are backed up. Preservation routines are for security and must add new files to the dark archive without overwriting previous files. Computer Services back-ups are in addition to other routines that periodically verify the veracity of the archive.

Discovery. Libraries provide access through services such as searching, browsing, and reference, as well as opportunities for serendipity. Searching can lead to information about the work (metadata and front matter) or take the user directly to the work (full text or entire object). Google-type search engines have also provided discovery resources, as have traditional publications like *Dissertation Abstracts* and newer online services such as Dissertation.com. But, the Library provides the first line of discovery that enables all of the others and it is the Library database that leads to replacements from the preservation archive.

Format Registry. Through the submission scripts, the Library server initially receives the ETD files that will be approved by the Graduate School. The source of information about the file formats that authors used to create their works and/or to submit them for final approval is important to all of the collaborators in ETD and preservation initiatives. In addition, the Library looks out for the interests of the reader so that it can provide the software that will enable access to its electronic information resources.

Levels of format support can be established to facilitate long-term preservation and access. Delineating formats that are more likely to persevere through time should not preclude authors having control of their digital works. A three-tiered preservation concept of software formats is a wise approach and is becoming common in other digital initiatives such as DSpace.

1. *Supported Formats* will be guaranteed for future access through long-term preservation by whatever means is necessary or available, including refreshing, migration, emulation, and recreation. These formats are standards based and many are documented by ISO, the International Organization for Standardization. However, it is generally accepted that

TIFF and PDF, while not ISO documented, will be supported and there may be, or may develop, additional formats.

2. *Known Formats* may not be guaranteed though they are accepted. The Library can recommend these based on currently supported formats and the Graduate School can refine or expand this list through its experience in reviewing each ETD. What may be guaranteed is that the content will survive even if the originating software does not.

3. *Unsupported Formats* may be accepted but they are not guaranteed. The Graduate School accepted ETDs with these formats because at that time they could review them. Therefore, the Library assumes that users will have access at least in the short-term. The content may survive but not the look and feel of the original work and the approved ETD.

Defining standards/formats that are most likely to persist well into the future is not meant to stifle creativity and limit how authors present their ideas. However, the better defined the standards, the more likely it will be for universities to support those formats for a longer period of time. Recommended file formats should come after considering creativity, access, preservation, and affordability.

A student might want to include a file type that might not migrate because the increased value for the document *now* is worth the risk. A program also might want to restrict these variations to appendices, asking that the student craft the document so that it can stand alone, should the appendix not migrate.[15]

Legal issues. Libraries, particularly at universities without law schools, are often the source of legal information about copyright law, mainly *U.S. Code Title 17* (especially sections 107-108). In addition to providing guidance to students and faculty about using copyrighted works appropriately and about their rights as authors, Library activities conform to copyright law in terms of preservation copies.

The *Digital Millennium Copyright Act* revised U.S. copyright law, expanding the legal circumstances under which libraries may make preservation copies to include when a format becomes obsolete. When libraries make preservation copies of unpublished works, such as theses and dissertations, preservation copying is permitted if:

1. The copy is solely for preservation or security.
2. The work is currently in the collection of the library making the copy.
3. The digital copy is not distributed or not made available outside the premises of the library.

Copies made by libraries as allowed under Section 108 are generally limited to single, isolated instances, but Congress recognized that the practical reality of preservation copying usually necessitates making back-ups. [16]

Metadata have multiple roles. Some are drawn from the submission forms authors complete. Librarians and skilled para-professionals enrich this metadata to enhance descriptive information for improved access through the library's online catalog. Metadata mapped to MARC provide online catalogs with the information users need about what is available and what is not.

In addition to description, metadata play a role in administration, reuse, and preservation. Administrative metadata such as transaction date and time are automatically supplied. Assumptions must be made about what output information will be necessary to manage preservation in the future. Fortunately, appropriate bodies such as the OCLC Office of Research with the Research Libraries Group, and the National Australian Library, are specifically tackling preservation metadata. [17] The NDLTD (which has members on its Board from OCLC and Australia) is also beginning to consider the issues and will become an important source specific to these digital works.

Redundancy. This article avoids, as much as possible, naming specific technologies, but without any computing redundancy, losing, misplacing, or deleting files is all too easy. A minimal level of redundancy should include using a RAID[18] controller card to overcome even a single drive failure. A higher level of security would come with a second and duplicate standby server. If this secondary server also has the RAID architecture, both servers would have to fail simultaneously to eliminate archive access. It is best to physically separate redundant servers, having one on site (e.g., in the Library) and one off site (e.g., in Computer Services). Of course, redundant mechanical parts like fans and power supplies are also necessary components for stable and long-term performance.

Server. At the same time that having these duplicate servers is a good thing, having ETDs distributed across multiple unnecessary servers may cause problems. The Graduate School does not need an ETD server when the Library houses the primary server because, once the Graduate School approves an ETD, it does not need to store it.

Submissions. The Library receives theses and dissertations directly from graduate student authors though they are submitting them to the Graduate School. A decade ago when computer networks were slower and less reliable, we eliminated the need to move files from the Graduate School to the Library. Anticipating that one day ETDs may require considerable bandwidth, we also precluded file transfers by providing the Graduate School with secure access to the active ETD database on the Library server.

Training. Faculty and graduate student development initiatives provide opportunities for collaboration between Learning Technology and the Library. Instruction in using software and desktop technology is within the purview of Learning Technology, while instruction in accessing and using information resources is appropriate for the Library. Whether or not the library has a role in broad training initiatives, there are teachable moments while providing reference services. The virtual reference desk and other online reference services such as e-mail also provide venues for help with many aspects of ETDs.

ETD PRESERVATION AND COMPUTER SERVICES

For decades or longer, libraries have made theses and dissertations available to their immediate constituents as well as to a larger research community. Responsibility and care for these works have evolved within the university library (enhanced by interactions with other units or institutions preserving historical materials). Libraries, like Virginia Tech's, have also accumulated more than a decade of experience with born-digital electronic information resources and have developed expertise with the numerous issues surrounding ETDs.

Computer Services is mostly about employing technology to support the various missions of the university. Long-term preservation can be coupled with, or separate from, long-term access. Computer Services units are by and large more comfortable with providing dark archives, that is, a preservation database infrequently accessed. Collaborations between Computer Services and the Library should take advantage of their existing areas of expertise and university resources and not duplicate them for a single set of e-information resources such as ETDs.

Write once read many (WORM) is an available technology that does not preclude the need for preserving and limiting access to an ETD. Back-ups are part of current routines and should be applied to the dark archive without replacing the Library's back-up routines for its live ETD database. Computer Services back-ups should be in addition to the other routines that periodically test the veracity of the archive and should not over-write the original of each ETD that is available for long-term preservation. If the originating software becomes unavailable, then Computer Services ensures that the content of the work survives at least as readable bits.

Authenticating users is necessary to identify members of the university community and to distinguish between members and nonmembers. It ensures that only the home institution's students submit ETDs, that only legitimate members can sign off on a thesis or dissertation, and that only the community has access when authors choose to temporarily restrict availability. Authentication programs such as LDAP and Kerberos are run at the university level by Computer Services to draw on information from the Registrar's Office that knows who is a student and the Human Resource Department that knows who is a staff or faculty member. Similarly, Computer Services maintains centralized records of the university's IP addresses. Centralized and networked resources are more efficient and cost effective than creating and maintaining duplicate systems that will frequently be out of sync.

Dark archives: Storage. Without added equipment or staff, Computer Services can initially provide storage of original works for future access when exact copies are needed, and for migration or conversion as necessary. Redundancy is a part of current routines and should be applied to the dark archive to the extent deemed appropriate by the experts in Computer Services. Redundancy routines should not replace the library's copying (i.e., back-up) routines until appropriate tests determine that multiple redundancy systems are not necessary. Several strategies are being tested including approaches such as LOCKSS (Lots of Copies Keep Stuff Safe) that would extend sharing caches beyond serials to historical artifacts.

Equipment and infrastructure: Support systems. Computer Services provide university-wide support systems that include equipment and the infrastructure of routines and staff. This support is a long-term commitment and considered by many to be for the good of the institution, somewhat like library services. Computer Services may lack a formal mandate to specifically provide long-term digital preservation assurances beyond that required or established at the highest administrative levels of the university. But, because Computer Services has in place the infrastructure, it would be efficient and cost-effective not to duplicate this in dispersed units that lack the expertise. Shared administration and technology services increase effectiveness, lower costs, and allow affiliated units to focus on their missions, to hone their areas of expertise, and to effectively manage their resources.

Security is an important issue for the Computer Services dark archive because this is meant to be the reliable source if anything happens to the library's active ETD database. The Computer Services archive is not meant to deal with authors submitting their works and vast numbers of frequent accesses. The Library, however, must have ready access when necessary to replace files in its active ETD database.

ETD PRESERVATION AND LEARNING TECHNOLOGY

While libraries provide informal instruction when users seek assistance at the Reference Desk, formal instructional technology resides with the Learning

Technology unit. Technology training should lead, among other things, to authors preparing sustainable works for long-term access, not just documents that will survive the Graduate School's approval process. Learning Technology provides computer labs with knowledgeable staff. Students and faculty will find instructors expert in how to use software and desktop equipment. Departmental formatting requirements for their students' ETDs can be part of instruction about the appropriate software to author new works. In addition, Learning Technology also teaches about digitizing text, images, video, and audio. Providing graduate students with a level of comfort in submitting their ETDs is also a function of Learning Technology's classroom instruction.

If Learning Technology training would include making graduate students aware of preservation issues along with the importance of using standards-based software, long-term access could be incorporated into the earliest stages of the information cycle to the benefit of the author as well as current and future library users. By collaborating with the Graduate School and the Library, and by being aware of the software popular in the various subject departments, Learning Technology is in an important position to influence ETD authors.

Faculty must also receive training in appropriate software for preservable works. They heavily influence their graduate students, so informing faculty about appropriate software is the most significant way to influence students' selection of software to prepare their ETDs for long-term accessibility.

The vast majority of ETDs to date have been submitted as PDF files, whether it is the required, recommended, or easily available format. Even before PDF was a save feature in word processing, it was readily accepted by libraries, in part because Acrobat has made the source code for its Reader available. Several PDF readers already exist so libraries are not tied to the originating proprietary software.

It is not hard to imagine that future presentations of decades-old files may actually be more robust than when they were originally archived, let alone conceived. However, anticipating the necessity to modify or convert ETDs to other formats, whether to enhance them or to make them accessible, may be inefficient as well as costly. Recommending software that is mostly likely to persist and educating authors to create easily preservable works will further the cost efficiency for long-term access.

Preservation responsibilities extend beyond those of formal organizational units and should not be left to the end of the creative process. It is a mistake to ignore the role that authors can play in long-term access to their works and the responsibility graduate students can learn that will benefit them in the long run. If universities educate their students about archival issues and practices, authors can create works that are capable of being preserved from the time that they are conceptualized for the long term. ICAP, Informed Creation Aids Preservation,[19] is a philosophy that involves the author in the cycle of information, including responsibilities for enabling preservation. ICAP is a mantra that we can share to promote the belief that preservation responsibilities lie not just in the future with those who will unlock the cool, dry vaults and release an exact copy of the original, not just with the technologists who have the programming skills and computing power, not just with the libraries who have the desire to make information available, but also with the creators of digital works. Digital archiving is one step towards fully integrating ICAP into the life cycle of information management.[20]

ETD PRESERVATION AND THE GRADUATE SCHOOL

The Graduate School's involvement is different from that of Computer Services and the Library's process-oriented foci. ETD preservation is a concern of the Graduate School, in part because ETDs uniquely document the university's student and faculty contributions to research. Therefore, the Graduate School plays an advocacy role in garnering institutional support for, among other things, preservation and long-term access to this evidence of various aspects of master's and doctoral education and research. This marketing role may be similar to the Graduate School's role in establishing an ETD initiative, that is, working with the various stakeholder communities including faculty, students, and staff, along with administrators of academic units, the Library, Computer Services, and Learning Technology.

Intellectual property rights and obligations fall within the purview of the Graduate School, ensuring that the graduate student author's rights are protected. In addition, authors are asked to assure that they have used another's copyrighted work with permission or within fair use. Learning Technology plays a role in disseminating this information and frequently refers authors' copyright questions to the appropriate librarian when legal counsel is not available for this service.

Often there are institutional standards for theses and dissertations. The Graduate School may not be aware that its primary responsibility for creating, maintaining, and revising the document structure has become known as the Document Type Definition (DTD). The Virginia Tech ETD submission software (a.k.a. ETD_db), for example, uses this information to display the front matter in HTML regardless of the work's final presentation format (e.g., PDF). Sometimes collaboration is passive. Learning Technology, on the other hand, should keep abreast of the changes in order to most effectively help students prepare their ETDs. Therefore, the Graduate School must see that instruction is available to authors and that the appropriate software is available in open computer labs.

The Graduate School can control digital document format decisions. This influence may be limited to what software students use for finally formatting (i.e., not creating) their ETDs. Decisions should be based on a coalescing of the needs of the Graduate School as well as other campus units, including

- Technology the Graduate School can afford to maintain
- Software the Graduate School has on the reviewer's/approver's desktop
- Software the subject departments want their students to use to most effectively prepare and/or display their works
- What the Library can provide for current and future ETD users
- What Computer Services can provide for future ETD access

Another role for the Graduate School is reassuring students and faculty that preservation is being addressed responsibly. In addition, the Graduate School is often led by an administrator at the vice presidential level who can help articulate that ETD preservation is important to protect the university's considerable investment in graduate education.

CONCLUSION

Born-digital theses and dissertations have been around for nearly a decade, but this certainly does not mean that all of the questions have been answered or even asked. One of the looming questions is: will future generations have access to today's ETDs? By taking advantage of the expertise and activities in disparate units, policies and practices can be put in place leading to long-term accessibility. The politics of collaboration, however, is perhaps the most challenging aspect of long-term preservation. When coupled with ethical and moral reasoning and separated from the technical questions, libraries are leading the effort to foster extended accessibility.

While libraries have a long tradition of preserving the university's original scholarship produced by its graduate students, libraries are less experienced in fulfilling this critical role in the technology-dependent and computer networked environment. Therefore, libraries seek collaborations with Computer Services where the longer traditions of data storage and wired interactions can be applied to scholarly communications. Learning Technology and the Graduate School are in ideal positions to promote digital preservation by informing graduate students and faculty about ICAP as well as about the importance of standards that will facilitate future availability.

ETDs are a good place to begin to determine the processes and policies that will lead to confidence in digital preservation. Input from various sectors of the university can further refine these issues and lead to the convergence of requirements and expectations.

NOTES

1. Preservation and archiving are terms frequently used interchangeably though they have distinct meanings to professional archivists. Here they are both used to mean the "series of actions that individuals and institutions take to ensure that a given resource will be accessible for use at some unknown time." Abby Smith, "New-Model Scholarship: Headed for Early Obsolescence?" *New-Model Scholarship: How Will It Survive?* (Washington, DC: Council on Library and Information Resources, March 2003), 2.

2. A Computer Services unit provides the university community with information technology and support to complement its teaching, learning, research, and outreach as well as to serve administrative operations.

3. A Learning Technology unit provides the university community with a teaching and learning infrastructure that integrates technology for effectiveness and efficiency of effort including through training activities in the use of emerging technologies that support network-assisted teaching, research, and outreach.

4. <http://scholar.lib.vt.edu/theses/somefacts/>.

5. A dark archive is inaccessible to the public but available for preservation and replacement copies for the accessible database. It also serves as a digital repository during disaster recovery. See California Digital Library glossary at http://www.cdlib.org/inside/diglib/glossary/ and Webopedia at <http://www.webopedia.com/TERM/D/dark_archive.html>.

6. Pavan Nigam in Michael Lewis, *The New New Thing: A Silicon Valley Story.* (New York: Norton, 2000), 113.

7. Kevin M. Guthrie, "Archiving in the Digital Age: There's a Will, But Is There a Way?" *Educause Review*, Nov./Dec. 2001, 58.

8. Edward A. Fox, *Electronic Theses and Dissertations*, 197.

9. Brian Lavoie and Lorcan Dempsy, "Thirteen Ways of Looking at . . . Digital Preservation," *D-Lib Magazine*, July/Aug. 2004, <http://www.dlib.org/dlib/july04/lavoie/07lavoie.htmls>.

10. <http://scholar.lib.vt.edu/theses/data/>.

11. Lavoie and Dempsy, <http://www.dlib.org/dlib/july04/lavoie/07lavoie.htmls>.

12. PID: Personal IDentifier is a case-sensitive alphanumeric string that is assigned to an individual so that s/he can be recognized as a unique member of a specified community of networked users.

13. Corporation for National Research Initiatives, <http://www.handle.net>.

14. Persistent Uniform Resource Locator, <http://purl.oclc.org/>.

15. Thomas H. Teper and Beth Kraemer, "Long-term Retention of Electronic Theses and Dissertations." *College & Research Libraries*, vol. 63, no. 1, Jan. 2002, 70.

16. <http://www.copyright.iupui.edu/digpreserv.html>, Copyright Management Center, Indiana University.

17. <http://www.oclc.org/research/projects/pmwg/> re PREMIS (PREservation Metadata: Implementation Strategies), <http://www.nla.gov.au/preserve/pmeta.html> re Preservation Metadata for Digital Collections, National Library of Australia.

18. *Redundant Array of Independent Disks.*

19. Suzie Allard and Gail McMillan, "Informed Creation Aids Preservation (ICAP)" Initiative (unpublished). Library of Congress NDIIPP grant application, Nov. 2003.

20. Gail McMillan and Nan Seamans. "Digital Library Definition for DLI2" 1996 <http://scholar.lib.vt.edu/DLI2/defineDL.html>.

REFERENCES

Allard, Suzie, and Gail McMillan. "Informed Creation Aids Preservation (ICAP)" Initiative (unpublished). Library of Congress NDIIPP grant application, Nov. 2003.

Copyright Management Center, Indiana University. <http://www.copyright.iupui.edu/digpreserv.html>.

Edward A. Fox et al. *Electronic Theses and Dissertations.* New York: Marcel Dekker, 2004.

Guthrie, Kevin M., "Archiving in the Digital Age: There's a Will, But Is There a Way?" *Educause Review,* Nov./Dec. 2001.

Lavoie, Brian, and Lorcan Dempsy, "Thirteen Ways of Looking at . . . Digital Preservation," *D-Lib Magazine,* July/Aug. 2004 (vol. 10, no. 7/8) <http://www.dlib.org/dlib/july04/lavoie/07lavoie.html>.

Lewis, Michael. *The New New Thing: A Silicon Valley Story.* New York: Norton, 2000.

McMillan, Gail, and Nan Seamans, "Digital Library Definition for DLI2." Blacksburg, VA: Virginia Polytechnic Institute and State University, 1996. <http://scholar.lib.vt.edu/DLI2/defineDL.html>.

Preservation Metadata for Digital Collections. National Library of Australia. <http://www.nla.gov.au/preserve/pmeta.html>.

Smith, Abby. "New-Model Scholarship: Headed for Early Obsolescence?" *New-Model Scholarship: How Will It Survive?* Washington, DC: Council on Library and Information Resources, March 2003.

Teper, Thomas H., and Beth Kraemer, "Long-term Retention of Electronic Theses and Dissertations." *College & Research Libraries,* vol. 63, no. 1 (Jan. 2002): 61-72.

VT ETDs. Digital Library and Archives, University Libraries, Virginia Polytechnic Institute and State University, <http://scholar.lib.vt.edu/theses>.

Cooperative Dimensions
of a Digitization Project

Andrew Adaryukov

SUMMARY. After a brief overview of the digitization activities at Florida Atlantic University Libraries, this article describes one project in detail, concentrating on various types of cooperation it reflects. *[Article copies available for a fee from The Haworth Document Delivery Service: 1-800-HAWORTH. E-mail address: <docdelivery@haworthpress.com> Website: <http://www.HaworthPress.com> © 2004 by The Haworth Press, Inc. All rights reserved.]*

KEYWORDS. Cooperative digitization projects, statewide digital libraries, academic libraries, cultural heritage projects, multipurposing, Florida Atlantic University, PALMM

INTRODUCTION

Cooperation, even looked at narrowly in the context of libraries' digitization activities, is a very broad term that covers a range of possible interactions. This article aims to illustrate some of a wide variety of such interactions as reflected in the work of one library's digitization lab.

Andrew Adaryukov, MLIS, is Librarian, George C. Marshall European Center for Security Studies Research Library, CMR 409 Box 018, APO AE 09053. He was formerly Digitization Librarian, Florida Atlantic University, S. E. Wimberly Library, Boca Raton, FL.

[Haworth co-indexing entry note]: "Cooperative Dimensions of a Digitization Project." Adaryukov, Andrew. Co-published simultaneously in *Resource Sharing & Information Networks* (The Haworth Information Press, an imprint of The Haworth Press, Inc.) Vol. 17, No. 1/2, 2004, pp. 175-185; and: *Libraries Within Their Institutions: Creative Collaborations* (ed: William Miller, and Rita M. Pellen) The Haworth Information Press, an imprint of The Haworth Press, Inc., 2004, pp. 175-185. Single or multiple copies of this article are available for a fee from The Haworth Document Delivery Service [1-800-HAWORTH, 9:00 a.m. - 5:00 p.m. (EST). E-mail address: docdelivery@haworthpress.com].

http://www.haworthpress.com/web/RSIN
© 2004 by The Haworth Press, Inc. All rights reserved.
Digital Object Identifier: 10.1300/J121v17n01_14

The article consists of two parts. First, the reader is presented with a bird's-eye view of the current state of digitization efforts at a library, with an emphasis on participation in a state-wide digitization initiative.

Second, one project is described in detail that illustrates different collaborative aspects of the digitization lab's work. In the case of this project, digitization serves, somewhat unusually, as one of the important driving forces behind development of the physical collection, and it also furnishes examples of cooperation on practically every level–from intra-departmental to international.

DIGITIZATION AT FAU

Part I. Overview of Digitization Initiatives at FAU

Florida Atlantic University Library (FAU) has been involved in digitization efforts for several years through the Department of Special Collections and Archives. It has participated from the beginning in the State University System (SUS) cooperative digital program that, having started in 1998 as a particular digital collection–*Florida Heritage*–evolved within a few years into PALMM: Publication of Archival, Library & Museum Materials. Today PALMM is an umbrella program that encompasses a number of diverse digital collections and allows the Florida Center for Library Automation (FCLA) to provide the participating institutions with common sets of imaging and metadata standards, collection home page design templates, format conversion services, centralized storage space for master images, and Internet server capacity. FAU participates in FCLA's Digital Projects Planning Committee (DPPC) monthly teleconferences during which the digitization project managers address various workaday issues as well as deciding upon the new strategic directions for PALMM.

The bulk of the FAU library contribution to PALMM has been in the *Florida Heritage* collection whose goal, according to the mission statement posted on the collection's homepage, is to digitize "materials broadly representing Florida's history, culture, arts, literature, sciences and social sciences" (http://palmm.fcla.edu/fh/). In addition, the FAU library has been a partner in two other PALMM projects: *Literature for Children* and *Linking Florida's Natural Heritage*.

Today, participation in the PALMM program in general and contribution to *Florida Heritage* in particular constitute what one might call the backbone of digitization activities at the FAU library. *Florida Heritage* is an ongoing project with an established reputation, a relatively stable source of funding, a developed support infrastructure, predictable time-frames, and clear standards. Acceptance of any future collection into PALMM means a level of support that can make a difference in a new idea's feasibility.

In addition, the relatively recent creation of the dedicated position of Digitization Librarian and the purchase of several high-end flatbed scanners, as well as other hardware and software, marked the coming into its own, within the Department of Special Collections and Archives, of the digitization lab that is now charged with identifying and pursuing more digitization opportunities. Below is a brief overview of several exciting long-term projects that are currently in various stages of planning or execution by the lab, in fulfillment of that charge.

Upcoming Projects

The *Judaica Digital Collection* project has been approved by the DPPC for inclusion in PALMM and is being developed in close cooperation with a professor in FAU's Judaic Studies program. Closely related to it is the *Yiddish Curriculum Support* digitization project that anticipates the beginning of Yiddish instruction on the undergraduate level at FAU this coming fall and that would use the items from the Judaica Digital Collection, first of all from its *Children's Literature* category, as raw material for some exciting multimedia technologies. These projects show how the library's digitization efforts can be more closely integrated with the university's teaching activities, thanks to close working together of the digitization lab and scholars from other departments. In addition, the *Yiddish Curriculum Support* project will embody the concept of multipurposing–using the same images in various contexts and applications.

A variety of other digitization projects are in progress. *Historical Geography* is a project being discussed with an Associate Professor of Geography in the Department of Geography and Geology. This professor's expertise is in such areas as remote sensing, cartography, map analysis, and environmental modeling. One of his students has recently finished a trial mini-project of scanning 40 aerial photographs on the library scanners using extra-high resolution of 1,000 dpi.

The *Yizkor Books* project is being discussed with the National Yiddish Book Center (NYBC). Its goal is for the two institutions to complement each other's digitization of these materials. Yizkor books ("Yisker-bikher" or Memorial Books) were written after the Holocaust by survivors to document destroyed Jewish villages and victims' names.

In the *BocaRatoons* project the digitization lab broadened its horizons and assumed a role of reproduction studio for a small departmental press which débuted with a book by a local editorial cartoonist, one of the university's alumni. The negotiations are under way with the author and the DPPC regarding the inclusion of the digitized cartoons into PALMM as a discreet collection.

Cooperation with Local Organizations

Several possibilities exist for joint endeavors with various cultural heritage organizations and historical societies within the South Florida Archivists framework, such as the library's long-standing successful cooperation with the Broward County Historical Commission on the digitization of the Commission's publication *Broward Legacy*. Although the FAU library stopped collecting the physical copy of this magazine in 1991, the Department of Special Collections and Archives receives a new issue as soon as it is published in order to digitize it. Thus the complete run of the magazine is available online as part of PALMM's *Florida Heritage* collection.

The FAU library has been approached by several local religious entities which would like to see their archives digitized and believe that the content of those archives may have wider historical significance and that the library may, therefore, be an appropriate venue for their digitization. At the moment, a volunteer is using one of the digitization lab's scanners to digitize a synagogue scrapbook that we think will be suitable for inclusion in the *Judaica Digital Collection* project.

Also, since its creation, the digitization lab has completed several "one-time quick-response" projects, such as providing digital images for Aaron Kula's *Klezmer Company* concert "Klezmer Does the Blues"; helping a scholar whose collection of rare music and scores is housed in the department prepare his image-rich book on the art of sheet music covers by the 19th century Russian music publisher Belaieff for submission to publishers; doing miscellaneous small jobs for the administration, one of which helped secure a grant of $30,000 for construction of a gazebo on a branch campus; and digitizing, processing, and reproducing the sheet music of Yiddish art songs for performance by two distinguished local cantors as part of the FAU's *Friends of Yiddish* concert series.

Part II. Judaica Music Rescue Project: History of a Cooperative Endeavor

Beginnings

The *Judaica Music Rescue* project is only two years old, but since its inception it has evolved into a very successful endeavor. Its primary goal is to ﹑

collect, preserve, and digitize Jewish music recordings, and to make the collection available to researchers through its online catalog that will include the scanned images of the original disc labels and excerpts of digitally recorded music. Ideally, complete recordings would be available on the Internet, but since this is currently impossible due to copyright restrictions, plans are being developed for installing listening booths at the S. E. Wimberly library and possibly at the other locations.

The collection is treated as consisting of two major parts according to the discs' format: 78 rpm and 33 rpm (LPs). There are also a number of audio tapes, but they are not considered within the scope of the current project. At this point, the priority is given to the 78 rpm recordings, since they are generally much older, more fragile, often in need of intensive cleaning, and irreplaceable. The information below pertains mostly to this part of the collection.

The history of the project is a vivid illustration of various issues of cooperation, both within and outside the libraries. It contains examples of institutional insularity and generous sharing, slow negotiations and unusually fast responses.

Nat Tinanoff, a retired IBM manager, member of the team that created the original PC and, eventually, a driving force behind the project, started his collaboration with the FAU library as a volunteer about five years ago, due to his interest in genealogy. In the beginning he performed a number of regular volunteer tasks, shelving books, and helping with inventories.

Then Tinanoff became interested in the Jewish music recordings collection. At that time, cantor Asher Herman had been working on it for about nine years. The collection originated in the flood of Judaica donations received by the Wimberly Library in the late '80s and early '90s, among which were many audio recordings: 78 rpm and 33 rpm vinyl discs and various sizes of magnetic tapes. Cantor Herman was the most devoted and willing worker, sorting and listing the recordings we had on hand. He was aware of the prohibition on general open access to the discs (scratching, and other damage concerns), and so he began putting some of the discs on audio tapes so that the area cantors could hear the music. Nat Tinanoff questioned the wisdom of, in his words, "transferring materials from an obsolete medium to an obsolete medium," and suggested that the music be digitally recorded.

In the spring of 2002, the collection contained about a thousand discs, 750 of them 78 rpm. Despite Asher Herman's efforts, most of it was still not very well organized and pretty much inaccessible to the public at large. That spring, Asher Herman passed away and the collection faced a real danger of long-term relegation to the back burner, due to fiscal and staff constraints at the library. Nat Tinanoff secured the go-ahead of Dee Cael, head of Special Collections, to start a full-scale preservation and digitization project of historical Jewish music recordings, at that point, still as a volunteer.

Acquisition of the YIVO Database

The first stroke of good luck and a good example of the great value of cooperation between institutions occurred when YIVO (founded as the Yiddish Scientific Institute, *Yidisher visnshaftlekher institut*) gave the database of its recorded music collection, not available to the public through the YIVO web site, to Tinanoff. The database had about 3,000 entries, approximately 700 of which covered recordings in the FAU collection. It was not an easy one-to-one matching, because the database's organization and the information contained within it were not perfect or accurate in every instance. An interesting example: the creators of the YIVO database did not always follow one of the cardinal rules of librarianship, that of the faithful reflection of information contained in the item. Apparently, much information from record labels that were in Hebrew and, especially, in Yiddish was entered in the database not as is, but edited to meet the database creators' ideas of normative usage and spelling.

In a way, this normalization is understandable. Since its inception, one of YIVO's main concerns and areas of expertise has been the codification of the Yiddish language. The most dramatic example of YIVO's labors can be seen in the 1930s Yiddish language reform that was quickly adopted by the literary and scholarly worlds and has since become the standard Yiddish orthography. But discrepancies such as those discovered in their database made necessary a painstaking process of going over and double-checking the information in the database against the information on the labels. This was the only way to make sure that, as an academic library, we would conform to the Library of Congress transliteration standards.

Still, the YIVO database provided an enormous impetus and a great starting point for the project's development. No further opportunities for collaboration with YIVO have yet arisen, but we are looking forward to working together with this venerable institution in the future.

Acquisition of the NYBC's Recordings

By the time the project was taking shape, the FAU library and the National Yiddish Book Center (NYBC) had been close partners for some time, the mutual book exchange between the two institutions measuring in the tens of thousands. Tinanoff thought that the center might also have recordings suitable for the FAU collection and contacted it with an inquiry. The initial response was not very encouraging, as Tinanoff was told that NYBC did have around 4,000 recordings, but was not interested in parting with them. As it turned out, this hesitancy was due to the fact that, at that time, NYBC was doing background research on several institutions around the country involved in audio digitization projects. By the time of Tinanoff's next call, FAU's *Judaica Music Rescue* project emerged, despite its youth, as the forerunner in NYBC's investigation, and this time, Tinanoff was invited to come up to Massachusetts and go through the recordings.

After two days of examining 1,100 discs, Tinanoff found approximately 780 recordings to add to the FAU collection (a 100% increase!), some of which were rare enough not even to be included in the YIVO database. And then one of those things happened that are impossible to predict and that constitute one of the unique rewards and heartaches of somebody working on building an archival collection. Catherine Madsen of NYBC asked Tinanoff whether he had seen the recordings in the corner yet and, when he responded negatively, took him to the storage area in the basement. The place was crowded with recordings. The materials reflecting almost 22 years of collecting effort–an estimate at a glance told Tinanoff that there were at least 2,000 discs there–were stored in a variety of non-archival packaging, including plastic shopping bags and boxes.

NYBC's stated mission is preservation and dissemination of Yiddish in print form. This, along with limited institutional capacity, precluded the organization from providing adequate storage, let alone any kind of access capability, for these unique cultural treasures. Tinanoff offered to provide the packaging and cover the shipping costs to transfer the recordings to FAU, and this offer was accepted. FAU's press release from September 15, 2003 stated that "a unique agreement was reached between the two organizations. FAU's *Judaica Music Rescue* project incorporated the old recordings into its own collection and has agreed to take additional albums presented by the Book Center. In return, the Book Center will receive digitized recordings of the music."

In the end, the total number of recordings turned out to be 4,015, many of which, unfortunately, turned out to be broken beyond repair and had to be discarded. Of the intact ones, Tinanoff was able to add a total of 1,762 new recordings to FAU's collection. Now NYBC has a note on its web site directing potential donors of Jewish music recordings to contact the *Judaica Music Rescue* project at FAU.

As information about the project spreads, more and more people are bringing in their recordings. In 2003, the project received 5,000 items and in the first three months of 2004 almost 1,000 more were donated. All in all, the project currently has 2,650 unique copies of 78 rpm recordings of Jewish music. From the many duplicates, best copies are selected for digitization and long-term preservation, and the rest are available for trade with other cultural organizations. Today, although the FAU collection is not the largest in the world in absolute numbers, it is the largest whose monthly updated database is freely available to the public.

Working with Others Within the University

A very good example of fruitful cooperation between entities within the University came about when the necessity of a functional interactive online database for the collection was brought to the fore by the guidelines of a grant proposal Tinanoff was working on at the time. He visited and talked to the head of the University's IRM department, and gave him a detailed tour of the collection, which enabled IRM to make project support a priority. The database was up on the Web within three weeks, which, as Tinanoff said and as all of us working in the academic environment would probably agree "just doesn't happen."

At this point, the database is searchable by *Artist*, *Title*, *Label*, *Catalog #*, *Genre*, and *Language*. The next update will add more information (type of musical accompaniment, date and place of recording), as well as scanned images of the album labels. Short high-quality audio snippets in MP3 format will be added as an ongoing part of database maintenance and development.

Cooperation with Other Agencies

The *Judaica Music Rescue* project continues to attract outside entities that see entering into cooperation with it as an ideal way to maximize their own resources and further their organizational goals. One such association is with *Save the Music* (an Internet Development Fund Project, a 501c3 corporation). Since it focuses mostly on LPs, while having in its possession a number of 78 rpm discs, a great opportunity exists for recordings exchange. The details of the agreement are being worked out at the moment, while 260 LPs have been sent by FAU to California, home of *Save the Music*, as a demonstration of the extent and scope of FAU's collection.

A chance meeting led to Tinanoff's correspondence with the Jewish Museum of Maryland in Baltimore. It ultimately resulted in the Museum sending FAU its archives of 600 recordings in exchange for digital versions.

Another new partner is the Feher Jewish Music Center of Beth Hatefutsoth, the Museum of the Jewish Diaspora in Tel Aviv, Israel. Discovering the *Judaica Music Rescue* project web site prompted the museum to contact FAU with an offer of collaboration. Tinanoff, in his turn impressed and inspired by the museum's collection and the physical infrastructure it uses to make that collection accessible to the public, countered the offer with a specific suggestion of "sharing the music," bringing the two organizations together in a common virtual space, so that researchers in the Feher Jewish Music Center listening booths would have complete access to FAU's collection database, and vice versa. This agreement is also in the active negotiation phase, and there is definite goodwill and a desire to work together on both sides.

Cooperation with the Community

Community support has been instrumental for the project from its very beginning in the labors of Asher Herman, through the current volunteer efforts. The latest development in this area has been the creation of an advisory board for the project comprising several community leaders who are willing to lend their names, time, and expertise to the project. Of all of the functions of the board, fundraising will be the first priority, which would be of great help to the advancement of the project.

Finally, there are zamlers–collectors within the community. The project's ultimate goal is to have a network of zamlers throughout the country and possibly internationally as well. The zamlers are trained to make an initial judgment on recordings offered by donors in their home area, to use protective packaging techniques and thorough documentation, and to mail donations to the project. The project sends future zamlers a kit that includes proper boxes, packaging materials, labels, business cards, etc. With virtually no publicity, the project has already recruited a number of zamlers who hail from such diverse places as Birmingham, Alabama, Rochester, New York, and Toronto, Canada.

Digitization Workflow and Technical Aspects

Musical recordings contain visual and aural information, and the *Judaica Music Rescue* project is committed to preserving and digitizing both kinds. In the case of 78 rpm discs, the carriers of visual information are the labels. These labels are digitized on a flatbed scanner at 300 DPI by a person dedicated to this specific task. The original high-resolution scans are archived, and scaled down JPEG files are created for online display.

Before audio digitization, discs undergo a thorough cleaning on a special piece of equipment that uses a vacuum to remove dirt from the grooves after the cleaning solution had been manually applied to the disc surface. The sound is recorded using Sony's *Sound Forge* software (version 7.0) as 44,100 Hz, 16 bit mono WAV files. These files are stored as is, and second copies are created. These get processed by *Sound Forge* noise reduction plug-in with a human providing the quality control and are saved as MP3 files optimized for web broadcasting. Several people have been trained to perform these operations.

Because the project has attracted a high number of dedicated volunteers, it has been possible to sustain this labor-intensive system. But stasis is not the goal of the project. New standards in the audio digitization are emerging, new technologies are developed, better equipment becomes available. The project will always strive to identify and use the best means of bringing the music to scholars and the wider community. At the same time, since digital media are not considered an archival format, a high priority is awarded to physical preservation of the recordings.

Judaica Music Rescue Project and PALMM

For some time the *Judaica Music Rescue* project did not quite fit with FAU's activities within the PALMM framework, as DPPC's collective energies had been directed towards building the infrastructure and ensuring high-quality standards for digital collections of text and visual materials. However, other SUS institutions were also working on learning and adopting new digital technologies, while taking stock of the audio and video resources in their collections with an eye towards their eventual digitization.

Recently these trends culminated in the question of audio and video digitization being officially put on the DPPC agenda. The plans are afoot for this summer's annual meeting of the DPPC to be held at Florida State University (FSU), which recently established a state-of-the-art audio and video digitization lab. The sharing of expertise, skills, and ideas that are expected to occur during the meeting will lay the groundwork for a new PALMM category of audio and video materials. Although it seems that the initial focus will be mostly on the spoken word, as in various oral history projects, we at the FAU library are looking forward to sharing our experience of working with audio gained during the *Judaica Music Rescue* project, and we hope to see it eventually incorporated under the PALMM umbrella, which will provide one more access point to the public.

CONCLUSION

More often than not, digitization projects are based on existing collections, wide access to which is deemed beneficial to the scholarly community and general public. One of the remarkable things about the *Judaica Music Rescue* project is that the ultimate goal of digitization and access provided the initial impetus to the traditional activities of collection development and preservation. People and organizations send their recordings to FAU not only, and often not primarily, because they are assured that these cultural treasures will be well cared for and preserved, but because the most salient commitment of the project is to using modern digital technology and the power of the Internet to make these treasures as open and accessible as possible. To quote Catherine Madsen of NYBC, "This project will do for Yiddish music what the Book Center has done for Yiddish literature." Of course, this will only be possible if the project continues its tradition of fruitful cooperation with diverse partners–from those inside the University to those halfway across the world.

Using the Assessment Cycle
as a Tool for Collaboration

Christie Flynn
Debra Gilchrist
Lynn Olson

SUMMARY. Assessment efforts document the academic library's contributions toward student success and institutional outcomes. Use of an Assessment Cycle at Pierce College Library enhances outcomes-based education and facilitates the library's role in the institutional assessment plan. Three examples of the Cycle are used to illustrate its application in instruction, in all library departments, and at the institutional level. Working collaboratively on assessment, both internally within the library and externally with other campus programs and departments, provides for maximum effectiveness and furthers student learning. *[Article copies available for a fee from The Haworth Document Delivery Service: 1-800-HAWORTH. E-mail address: <docdelivery@haworthpress.com> Website: <http://www.HaworthPress.com> © 2004 by The Haworth Press, Inc. All rights reserved.]*

Christie Flynn is a member of the library faculty, Pierce College, 3910 39th Avenue SE, Puyallup, WA 98439 (E-mail: cflynn@pierce.ctc.edu).

Debra Gilchrist is Dean of Libraries and Media Services, Pierce College District, 9401 Farwest Drive SW, Lakewood, WA 98498 (E-mail: dgilchrist@pierce.ctc.edu).

Lynn Olson is a member of the library faculty, Pierce College, Fort Steilacoom, 9401 Farwest Drive SW, Lakewood, WA 98498 (E-mail: lolson@pierce.ctc.edu).

[Haworth co-indexing entry note]: "Using the Assessment Cycle as a Tool for Collaboration." Flynn, Christie, Debra Gilchrist, and Lynn Olson. Co-published simultaneously in *Resource Sharing & Information Networks* (The Haworth Information Press, an imprint of The Haworth Press, Inc.) Vol. 17, No. 1/2, 2004, pp. 187-203; and: *Libraries Within Their Institutions: Creative Collaborations* (ed: William Miller, and Rita M. Pellen) The Haworth Information Press, an imprint of The Haworth Press, Inc., 2004, pp. 187-203. Single or multiple copies of this article are available for a fee from The Haworth Document Delivery Service [1-800-HAWORTH, 9:00 a.m. - 5:00 p.m. (EST). E-mail address: docdelivery@haworthpress.com].

http://www.haworthpress.com/web/RSIN
© 2004 by The Haworth Press, Inc. All rights reserved.
Digital Object Identifier: 10.1300/J121v17n01_15

KEYWORDS. Assessment, outcomes, institutional success, assessment cycle

> Stand in the place where you work
> Now face west
> Think about the place where you live
> Wonder why you haven't before
> If you are confused check with the sun
> Carry a compass to help you along
> Your feet are going to be on the ground
> Your head is there to move you around
>
> –"Stand," REM

Assessment elicits a spectrum of attitudes, opinions, and feelings from academic library faculty, staff, and administrators as we attempt to determine a meaningful approach to this multi-dimensional and sometimes confusing subject. Shaping a philosophy and methodology to guide our work, determining what scope of assessment is appropriate, and deciding what degree of integration is manageable spurs us to engage new territory. Similarly, negotiating different types of partnerships with our discipline-faculty colleagues challenges us in new ways. Through assessment results, librarians can firmly demonstrate the effectiveness of library departmental operation, the impact of library instruction, and the development of information literacy within the institution. They can also more effectively reach out to other campus constituencies.

By its nature, the assessment process lends itself to collaboration. Writing outcomes, developing assessment methods for instruction, services, and facilities, and analyzing assessment results are all partnership activities, calling on our ability to work together across library departments and throughout the institution. For example, the individual librarian's instructional assessments are more relevant when they are considered alongside the assessments of other librarians as well as within the context of reference desk assessments; the impact and use of a library collection is best examined through the lens of acquisitions, technical services, interlibrary loan, collection development, reference, student learning, faculty perspective, and circulation. Outcomes are more powerful when developed with all college constituents lending voice.

Pierce College Library has been on a path to incorporate assessment into our daily lives for the past ten years. Prompted by a college-wide move in this direction, the library has taken a leadership role in the college's effort to develop a culture of assessment. More specifically, the library faculty and staff have committed to embracing their role in that culture and in consciously examining what we contribute and what barriers prevent or impair that contribution. Most important in our progress is determining the library's role in the larger picture of college-wide assessment, and how we attempt to measure our impact on students and their success.

Critical to our college and library success with assessment has been the deliberate use of what we refer to as the Assessment Cycle. This article addresses use of the Assessment Cycle in outcomes-based education, how a library fits into an institution's assessment plan, how the cycle can be applied in instruction and all library departments, and how it enhances institutional collaboration.

PIERCE COLLEGE

Located in Western Washington, Pierce College is a comprehensive community college district that serves nearly 30,000 students annually from 35 sites, including two major campuses. Across the curriculum, all faculty teach and assess five core abilities that have been incorporated into courses (Figure 1).

FIGURE 1. Pierce College Abilities

Printed with permission.

In addition to multiculturalism, responsibility, critical thinking/problem solving, and effective communication, faculty members teach and assess information competency in an ongoing process to improve student learning.

Because the college places such value on student learning, the transition to assessment seemed logical and natural. The entire curriculum has been transitioned into outcomes-centered course outlines based on the core abilities developed by the college. When designing instruction, faculty first ask, "What do we expect our students to be able to do as a result of our teaching?" Curriculum is further defined with a second question: "How will I assess that learning?" These two questions provide the focus for the assessment cycle implemented by Pierce College. Across the district, use of the assessment cycle ensures continuous improvement of both student learning and best teaching practices.

The assessment cycle (Figure 2) launches from the center with the institutional mission, values, and goals as its base. The strategic directions established by the college provide additional framework. The cycle then moves to the outcomes phase located at the top of the circle and proceeds clockwise. Each element in the cycle's progression is explained below.

Outcomes form the initial step of the cycle, clearly stating what we want to achieve based on the mission, values, and strategic directions. Outcomes can be designed on several levels, e.g., college-wide, library-specific, library department, and instructional session. The wider the scope of the outcomes, the

FIGURE 2. Assessment Cycle

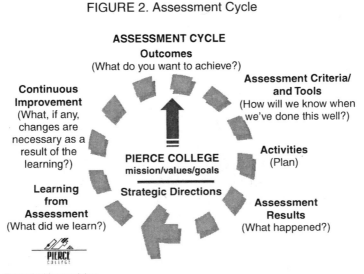

Printed with permision.

more we suggest that they be developed collaboratively. Throughout the library, outcomes for each department establish what we want to achieve in order to contribute to student success. These outcomes, when considered holistically, describe what we want to collectively achieve as a library.

Assessment Criteria and Tools are the more traditional tools of assessment.

Assessment Criteria set the standard by which the assessment results will be evaluated by asking, "How will we know we have done this well? How will we know that we've done a good job?" Criteria can be best described as value judgments, benchmarks, quality standards, behavior standards, or, less formally, what an individual or a department will be happy with. Criteria help us describe what's observable. They help us delineate the picture.

Tools establish the assessment process through design, instruments, and data collection methods. They can be formal or informal. Tools could consist of student focus groups; student surveys; assessments of student learning, including self-assessments; statistics; and informal anecdotal feedback that is systematically documented.

Activities represent the implementation of the tool and can be described as any action that is carried out in pursuit of the assessment goal.

Assessment Results indicate what happened when the tools were administered and the criteria applied. Qualitative assessments can be analyzed for themes, and quantitative results can be logically presented in formats such as graphs or charts.

Learning from Assessment continues the process by analyzing the information/data. Through individual and group reflection, data and seemingly unrelated facts can evolve into evidence and consensus about what is going well. Connections can easily be made between different areas of the college and the library.

Continuous Improvement is perhaps the most critical element of the cycle. Within this phase priorities for change are established, and actions are determined. What changes need to be made as a result of the learning? What successes can be celebrated? With this step, we determine both what we will continue to do and what we will change through improvement of an existing strategy or by implementing a new strategy.

APPLYING THE ASSESSMENT CYCLE
IN A COLLABORATIVE MANNER

Our story is about how the library optimized our commitment to use an assessment cycle in three very specific ways: (1) Library Departmental Assessments, (2) Instructional Assessments, and (3) College-wide Assessments.

Example #1: Increasing Internal Collaboration Through Library Departmental Assessments

No matter how small the library, communication is a challenge. An important piece in overcoming this challenge involves making the implicit explicit. In order to improve internal communication and subsequently internal collaboration, the Pierce College Library entered into a departmental assessment process. The process led to establishing public outcomes, assessments, and criteria for all library departments, and setting up a standard assessment process library-wide. By engaging all library staff and faculty in the process, barriers to communication are diminished. Through departmental outcomes, each department understood what activities and standards comprise the collective work of the library. In our process, interdepartmental teams developed outcomes for each department in an effort to recognize the interdependence and interwoven nature of the library mission.

Rewriting the mission as outcomes provided departments with a direction and starting point. Table 1 provides an example of how a goal statement from the former Pierce College library mission was transitioned into an outcomes statement.

Although the majority of the content in our mission remains the same in the transitioned statements, an outcomes-focused mission statement links directly to student success in a much more dynamic way. Library departments then developed their individual, departmental outcomes guided by the revised mission outcomes. These became the values statements at the center of the assessment cycle.

TABLE 1. Sample Goal and Outcomes Statements

Sample Goal Statements from Library Mission	Sample Outcomes from Library Mission
To provide comprehensive information-competency instruction that is integrated with the curriculum, enabling all users to locate, evaluate, organize and utilize information.	Teach effectively and in partnership with faculty from all disciplines in order to graduate information competent students.
To support the curricular and other information needs of the college by selecting, acquiring, organizing, producing, preserving and circulating a collection of materials in a variety of formats, as well as equipment necessary for their use.	Provide a high-quality, accessible and curricular-focused print and non-print collection of information resources in order to facilitate access to ideas and information by students, faculty and staff.

Outcomes: Writing outcomes enables departments to more clearly establish priorities and forces an examination of the value in each daily activity. It examines the "why" of departmental activities instead of the traditional focus on the "what" or "how." Each department developed an average of 5-8 outcomes, depending on the scope of its work. Each outcome had several performance indicators under each outcome. Sample outcomes and indicators are illustrated in Tables 2, 3, and 4.

Assessment Criteria and Tools: Teams devised multidimensional assessments that measured contributions qualitatively and quantitatively. They not only measured service levels from student perspectives, but also the impact of departmental work on student success. Formal and informal criteria were developed. Implementation of the assessments required coordination with other areas of the college and the library. One result of that coordination was the design of short and easy to deliver surveys to be completed at the time a student engages with a part of the library. Sample Assessments and Criteria also appear in Tables 2-4.

Activities: For the first year of this process, our activities comprised designing the actual outcomes, assessments and criteria, learning to work together to develop a culture of assessment, and designing work plans. A two-day retreat formed the basis of that work. Interdepartmental teams continued working to-

TABLE 2. Sample Departmental Outcomes–Circulation

Outcome *(one of several for the department)*	Maintain the integrity of the library collection in order to ensure materials are available to students, faculty, and staff.
Indicator *(one of several describing this outcome)*	Patrons' hold requests are filled in a timely manner. Students use more and more diverse resources due to shared campus collections.
Assessment	Comment Cards accompany all hold items Faculty Focus Group and Survey Student CCSEQ Survey
Assessment Criteria	80% of students indicate they use a broader range of resources because holds feature is fast and easy to use. 80% of students indicate they can get items quickly and easily from the other campus. 80% of holds were available within 24 hours. 80% of faculty indicate a positive change in student use of a variety of appropriate resources for papers and projects.

TABLE 3. Sample Departmental Outcomes–Reference

Outcome *(one of several for the department)*	Respond appropriately and pedagogically to individuals' reference questions, in order to develop confident, competent, and independent information seekers.
Indicator *(one of several describing this outcome)*	Model and teach appropriate information-competent behaviors and practices.
Assessment	Periodic 1-2 question surveys of students who have met with a reference librarian. Assessments of individual students at the reference desk.
Assessment Criteria	At least 80% of students queried will state that they learned something of value they can apply when researching in the future, and that that learning will positively enable their completion of the current project. Reference assessments indicate 90% level of student learning.

TABLE 4. Sample Departmental Outcomes–Technical Services

Outcome *(one of several for the department)*	Catalog, classify, and assign locations to materials in order to maximize access to the library collection for students, faculty, and staff. To order, receive, and process materials in as efficient, accurate, and cost-effective a manner as possible in order to build and maintain the Pierce College Library collection.
Indicator *(one of several describing the outcome)*	Multiple access points are included.
Assessment	Technical Services librarian checks all cataloging to ensure that author, title, subject, and series headings are correct and complete, and reference staff reports any suspected omissions.
Assessment Criteria	The number of requests per month for additional headings is fewer than one percent of the number of items processed per month.

gether for over a year to develop the outcomes, assessment, and criteria that were eventually adopted. Through workshops, reading, teamwork, and discussions, we attempted to enhance our understanding of the assessment process and increase our knowledge base.

Assessment Results: Assessment data were analyzed and assessments rewritten, refined, and redesigned to be more effective in gathering precise information.

Learning from Assessment: Each department has now completed a set of comprehensive outcomes and has implemented a variety of assessments. Unit staff selected which outcomes to assess based on departmental priorities. Therefore, the initial assessments were around issues and services staff cared about the most. Several discovered that their perceptions were not always supported by the assessment information. This gave more credibility to the process and resulted in additional buy-in. The process itself was the learning.

Continuous Improvement: Continuous Improvement speaks to the very human aspect of the learning process. Experience and internalization allow for the development of the critical tools and elements needed to be successful. Success then leads to the need for additional improvement, starting the assessment cycle anew. We discovered that there's a significant disparity between grasping the assessment concept on an intellectual level and implementing the assessment cycle on a practical level; between believing an activity has a certain kind of impact and being able to see/document that. As we implemented small changes, our thinking was reinforced. Once staff members were invested in the assessment cycle, outcomes became a seamless part of how we work instead of the work itself. Other departments on campus have also written outcomes and assessments, using the library as a model.

Example #2: Instructional Program Application of the Assessment Cycle

Library faculty teach in partnership with discipline faculty through a variety of instructional models:

- 50-minute instruction sessions
- instruction that is integrated into course curriculum and occurs over several hours throughout the quarter
- two-credit and five-credit stand-alone classes that focus on library research
- linked credit classes
- learning communities, where library instruction is embedded into the curriculum of another course.

In collaboration with discipline faculty, library faculty interpret outcomes for each course and create multiple, applicable tools that assess student learning. The assessment cycle in this case would include:

Outcome: Library faculty will teach in partnership with faculty from all disciplines in order to develop students' information competency.

Assessment Tools: The Information Competency Discovery Wheel (Figure 3) is an example of a formal assessment.

This is a Student Self-Assessment (pre/post). This self-assessment tool has students score themselves on a scale and write a reflection based on what they discover about their knowledge. Students take this as a pre-test at the beginning of the quarter and as a post-test at the end of a quarter-long course.

Assessment Criteria: Quantitative: 90% of students show improvement in their scores for 4 of the 7 areas of Information Competency. Qualitative: 70% of students show greater depth of understanding of Information Competency in their language and written discussion (e.g., more detail, identify specific concepts covered in class). Although 70% and 90% seem high, we felt it reasonable since this assessment is generally used in a two-credit class that represents 20 hours of instruction. In an English 101 class, where students only have three hours of library instruction, an improvement of 60% might be more realistic.

FIGURE 3. Discovery Wheel Self-Assessment

Self-Assessment Using a Discovery Wheel

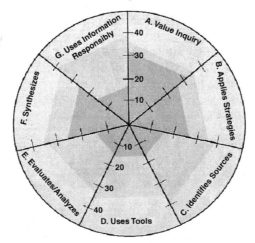

Source: ENGL 114 Library Research Methods Winter, 2003 Pierce College/Christie Flynn. Printed with permission.

Activity: After completing the wheel, the students mark themselves on a 40-point scale. A breakdown of each of the seven outcomes for Information Competency is included. They place themselves on this scale, fill out the blanks, and then mark it on this circle. This gives them a complete picture of themselves as it relates to the entire core ability of Information Competency and their confidence level in executing the outcomes.

Assessment Results: Figure 3 is an example of a completed wheel. The darker shaded area represents the student's pre-self-assessment. This is what the student thought she knew at the beginning of the quarter. The lighter shaded area is where she saw herself in terms of information competency at the end of the quarter. Both the instructor and the student can see that the student, in her eyes, has moved farther along in her knowledge of information competency and her understanding. Additionally, the instructor can see the results of the class as a whole (Figure 4).

The second part of this assessment tool is the students' reflections. The Information Competency Discovery Wheel asks them to reflect on where they placed themselves on the scale and answer questions about that placement. Students are asked to reflect upon their weakest and their strongest areas. Samples of how one student perceived her strengths and weaknesses appear in Table 5.

FIGURE 4. Student Self-Assessment Reports

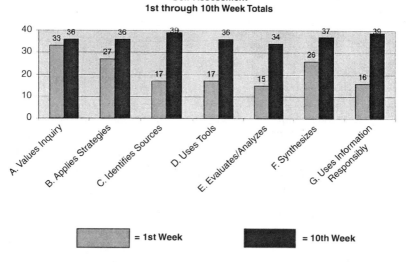

Self-Assessment
1st through 10th Week Totals

= 1st Week   = 10th Week

TABLE 5. Information Competency Wheel–Student Responses

	Week One	Week Ten
Weakest Area	"My weakest area is evaluates/analyzes information; I'm not exposed to computers much. I have been out of school for 30 years and need to relearn how to study."	"Evaluating and Analyzing is still my weakest area. At the beginning of the quarter, I wasn't very confident about my opinion, but I have learned to assess information, to question the bias of articles. I read and check the articles I use for accuracy and authority. I just need to keep practicing."
Strongest Area	"Values inquiry is my strongest area because I like learning new things."	"Values inquiry is still my strongest area because I learned how to do research. I can now pick a topic and do a catalog search to find books, I can find info on the Web in search engines or Web crawlers or I can find journals and magazines in ProQuest."

Learning from Assessment: Quantitatively, both students and instructors can see the student's perception of her own learning. The assessment tool also provides the checks and balances of qualitative data. Pierce College faculty have used this tool and have learned that it is effective in a variety of applications in many different information competency situations.

A surprising bit of learning also came from this assessment. An English instructor used this as a pre/post test for an English 101 class that had received three hours of library instruction during the quarter. His results were considerably different because his classes work with a librarian for a total of three hours. His experience was that at the beginning of the quarter, they marked themselves quite highly in their knowledge of information competency. At the end of the quarter, they gave themselves much lower scores. When he asked the students to talk about their scores, students said that they thought they were information competent at the start of the term, because they didn't really understand how much thinking was involved in information competency and how much more they needed to know. Due to the library instruction and integrated assignments, they eventually recognized the complexity of the research process and that information issues are sometimes difficult to understand. This new perspective caused them to ultimately rank themselves much lower on the scale at the end of the quarter.

Continuous Improvement: The Information Competency Discovery Wheel has turned out to be a valuable assessment tool. Part of the continuous improvement will be to use it with a wider number of students and a variety of learning contexts. After using it, we discovered areas of the tool that could be revised to provide more clarity in the results and a place for students to reflect more fully on their learning. This will not only improve opportunities for stu dents' critical thinking about research and information, but their skills and abilities as well.

Example #3: Application of the Assessment Cycle for Institutional Collaboration

How can the library play a role in the college's effectiveness? At Pierce College information competency is a responsibility of the entire college community, not just the domain of the library. In fact, our strategic plan commits the college to prioritize learning and expects that we will increase the number of faculty, staff, administrators, and students who teach and model Information Competency because it is one of the five core abilities.

Institutional Outcome: Increase the number of faculty, staff, administrators, and students who teach and model the five core abilities.

Assessment Criteria:

- Information Competency will be mapped into 100% of programs in developmental and logical sequences.
- Information Competency will be integrated into syllabi and assignments so that students experience it as blended.
- Librarians will be active team teachers of Information Competency through course-integrated instruction in 100% of departments.
- Faculty value the integration of Information Competency in the curriculum and express how it enhances student performance.

Tools:

- Analysis of Information Competency in syllabi and assignments.
- Work with the office of curriculum development and use formal assessments such as the student survey and other administrative data that the college regularly collects through students' enrollment and courses.
- Faculty surveys.
- Curriculum mapping.

Activities: For some time the librarians had been concerned that the college's definition of information competency was difficult and challenging to assess because the definition was not written in the form of learning outcomes. As a result, the library applied for and received a professional development assessment grant to lead a multidisciplinary committee of both academic and professional/technical faculty that was charged with three tasks: (1) Determining what they valued in the original definition and what they wanted to retain, (2) Sharing what information competency meant within their own disciplines, and (3) Eliciting what Information Competency meant in a two-year college.

At the end of a year, their draft of information competency in outcomes form was presented to the faculty, voted on, and accepted (Figure 5).

The new draft provides additional clarity for our instructors. Faculty can more easily see the outcomes in their courses and how aspects of Information Competency can be incorporated.

Assessment Results: Pierce College course outlines contain a place for faculty to state which component of Information Competency they will be teach-

FIGURE 5. Information Competency Ability at Pierce College

	Values inquiry and information needs in order to engage in lifelong learning.	**Values Inquiry**
	Applies a repertoire of creative and flexible information seeking strategies in order to navigate the unfamiliar, take action, or solve a problem.	**Applies Strategies**
	Identifies appropriate sources in order to access relevant information.	**Identifies Sources**
	Uses technological and organizational tools in order to access and manipulate information.	**Uses Tools**
	Analyzes information in order to evaluate quality, relevance, or perspective.	**Evaluates**
	Synthesizes new information with current understanding and experience in order to create something new, acquire insight, transform values, or expand knowledge base.	**Synthesizes**
	Examines the issues and policies related to information in order to use it responsibly.	**Uses Information Responsibly**

ing or assessing in their classes, clearly indicating how and where information competency is incorporated into the curriculum.

When departmental faculty develop a course outline, they have an opportunity to indicate which specific Information Competency learning outcome they will commit to teach and assess. Librarians can examine any course and know whether or not Information Competency has been integrated into the curriculum. They can also determine which faculty members to approach for collaborative assignment development and team teaching.

Course-Integrated Instruction: Measuring the number of sessions each fall quarter over a period of four years, we learned that integrated course instruction doubled between 1999 and 2000, and then leveled off in 2001 until 2002, still well above our starting point (Figure 6).

We also learned informally through transfer student focus groups that students who had transferred to the University of Washington, Tacoma–one of our main feeder universities–valued and would have liked more library instruction in their courses while at Pierce.

During the same period we measured how many students reported that they had participated in a library instruction session either in the library or as a part of a class. You can see that students reported a 10% growth in participation (Figure 7).

FIGURE 6. Instruction Session Statistics, Fall Quarters

Fall Quarter Sessions

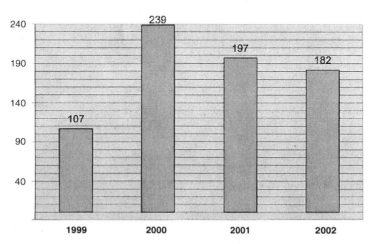

Source: Pierce College Data Express. Printed with permission.

FIGURE 7. Instruction Session Increases, Reported by Students

STUDENT ENGAGEMENT

MEASURE: Participated in a library instruction session either in the library or as part of a class.

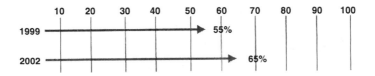

Source: Pierce College Student Survey. Printed with permission.

In 1999, 27 of our 48 academic and professional/technical departments participated in integrated library instruction. In 2002, that number had increased to 42 out of the 48 departments, showing that the library worked with 80% of our departments last year.

Learning from Assessment: Student engagement in library instruction increased at a steady rate, and we learned that our librarians had collaborated with nearly every department on our campuses. This resulted in more faculty buy-in, more effective assessments, and education to more students.

The results of the library instruction increased and leveled off for other reasons as well. In the years after 2000, there was no increase in library staffing, so at this point, we have as much library instruction as we can handle. Because it aids in examining dilemmas such as this in a holistic manner, the assessment cycle becomes not only a process but also a useful tool by clarifying what we value, which then helps determine future action. For example, is it more important that we do instruction and touch every student who walks in the door (but not in a particularly meaningful way) or is it more important that we reach students in an integrated fashion? Based on values expressed as outcomes and our mission, the Assessment Cycle can be repeated with a renewed consciousness of what we do well and what we need to let go of because it won't help us reach our outcomes.

The evidence and data from the assessments provided discussion points for conversations with faculty and administration outside the library about future direction.

Through the Community College Student Experience Questionnaire (CCSEQ) administered in 2001 and 2003, we have learned that students who are with us over time progress in each of the five core abilities. Now we are moving to examine what these abilities might look like at the department or program level (e.g., discipline-specific instruction, use of a capstone, development of a portfolio).

Continuous Improvement: The library's commitment to rewrite information competency into outcomes form was a catalyst for faculty forums that occurred in 2003. During these forums, the Pierce College community revised the other four core abilities and developed rubrics for common assessments throughout Pierce College. For the next assessment cycle, we hope to expand the success that we've had working with students individually and at the classroom level. We can use the assessment cycle to help students map their developments throughout their degree. And finally, we celebrate.

CONCLUSION

The assessment cycle works as a valuable tool for learning and collaborating with students, faculty, library departments, and administration. It directs us to examine what we most value, both internally as a library and externally with the college. More concretely, it helps us identify gaps between the ideals represented as outcomes and actual student performance as measured through assessments. Because of this measurement, we are able to establish a process of continuous improvement based on information rather than perception. Through participation in assessment at the college level, the library is able to help tell the institutional story and demonstrate our direct contribution. Finally, the assessment cycle allows us to examine our results in a holistic manner, which more fully mirrors the role of the library in the life of the college.

Sharing Technology
for a Joint-Use Library

Richard F. Woods

SUMMARY. Building joint-use libraries to foster new types of learning and collaboration is a growing phenomenon that is of great interest to academic library planners around the world. Noteworthy among these efforts, the Dr. Martin Luther King, Jr. Library in San José, California, is a collaboration of a metropolitan university library and a major public library. This article describes the information technology challenges in the design and development of this innovative partnership: (a) selecting a shared library computer system, (b) building a merged web site, (c) designing a new telecommunications network, (d) co-managing IT staff and services, and (e) planning for the new integrated library. *[Article copies available for a fee from The Haworth Document Delivery Service: 1-800-HAWORTH. E-mail address: <docdelivery@haworthpress.com> Website: <http://www.HaworthPress.com> © 2004 by The Haworth Press, Inc. All rights reserved.]*

KEYWORDS. Joint-use libraries, co-managed libraries, information technology, collaboration

Richard F. Woods is Information Technology Director, San José State University Library, One Washington Square, San José, CA 95192-0028 (E-mail: richard.woods@sjsu.edu).

[Haworth co-indexing entry note]: "Sharing Technology for a Joint-Use Library." Woods, Richard F. Co-published simultaneously in *Resource Sharing & Information Networks* (The Haworth Information Press, an imprint of The Haworth Press, Inc.) Vol. 17, No. 1/2, 2004, pp. 205-220; and: *Libraries Within Their Institutions: Creative Collaborations* (ed: William Miller, and Rita M. Pellen) The Haworth Information Press, an imprint of The Haworth Press, Inc., 2004, pp. 205-220. Single or multiple copies of this article are available for a fee from The Haworth Document Delivery Service [1-800-HAWORTH, 9:00 a.m. - 5:00 p.m. (EST). E-mail address: docdelivery@haworthpress.com].

Digital Object Identifier: 10.1300/J121v17n01_16

The *new* Dr. Martin Luther King, Jr. Library opened on August 1, 2003 with two entrances on a common corridor, symbolizing the passage between community and campus. The 475,000 square-foot King Library with ten floors, 4,000 data ports, and 27 wire closets, is a $177.5 M joint-use facility that integrates the services of San José Public Library and San José State University Library. The King Library replaces the main downtown library in San José, a community of just under 1,000,000, and the Clark and Walquist Libraries of San José State University, a metropolitan campus of almost 30,000 students. The collections are open to all and most services are integrated in the facility. There is one circulation desk, one reference desk, one periodicals desk, etc. The King Library is co-managed by the Director of the public library system and the Dean of the university library. Major operating units are merged and co-managed: access services, information technology, reference, and technical services.

When I joined this project in mid-2001, a comprehensive planning effort had been gathering steam for two years. The building plan was set, the never-ending pile driving had ceased, and the infrastructure was starting to emerge. At the center of the project administration was the Core Team, a joint library co-management team, which also coordinated efforts with the San José Redevelopment Agency and city and university administrations. The Core Team established several planning teams, which spawned numerous sub-teams.

This article covers planning and implementation of information technology for this new integrated library, with an emphasis on issues of most interest to anyone planning technology for a joint-use library. Opinions throughout this article represent merely the writer's perspective.

SHARING A LIBRARY INFORMATION AND MANAGEMENT SYSTEM

The best advice is to migrate to the shared library system as early as possible before opening the new building. Avoid adding a huge project on top of moving to a new facility and forming a new co-managed organization.

Key Selection Factors

For the new integrated library, the major objectives of a shared library information and management system were:

- The libraries will support an expanded array of information services serving the public and the university community.

- The system will provide automated services for the 23 branch libraries of the San José Public Library including six new branches, which are in the planning stages.
- The system will also host a separate bibliography database and a reference and referral community information database.
- The libraries will remain separate administratively and the library system must support separate budgets and collection development policies. Each library will handle its own acquisitions. The public library will continue to catalog and shelve its materials using the Dewey Decimal system and the University collections will continue to be cataloged with Library of Congress classification. With the exception of the reference collection, the materials will be shelved separately.
- A single patron record will be used, yet each organization needs to retain some of its own borrowing policies to support its service mission. The system must be able to distinguish between, and provide different options for, services available to a registered borrower as a university-affiliated user of university materials and services available to that same borrower as a member of the public using public library materials, and vice versa.
- Although users of the joint-use library will borrow materials from a single service point, each library retains ownership of its own materials. This means that the system must be able to manage the financial aspects of circulation control and acquisitions separately for each institution. For example, when a public library book is lost and paid for there must be a way to identify that the funds collected should be credited to the public library. End-of-term student financial obligations reported to the University registrar should not include transactions related to their use of public library materials.
- Customer self-service features are crucial in the new system, particularly support for the public library's Express Check, customer self-charging of materials, and the university library's self-service interlibrary loans, offered via the Link+ (INN-Reach) system.

Seven key features were identified as crucial to the success of the shared library system:

- Materials usage and financial reporting
- Implementation planning
- Support for a single customer file
- Experience with complex conversions
- Customer empowerment features
- Support for 3M self-circulation machines
- Compatibility with the Link+ (INN-Reach) interlibrary lending system

The Selection Process

The libraries formed jointly staffed teams to develop functional requirements for the online library system. The Online Systems and Technology (OST) team was established to oversee the selection of the system vendor and plan for implementation, among other things. OST team members were selected carefully to provide balance for each library's viewpoint and to represent major functional expertise. The libraries hired a consultant, Diane Mayo, Information Partners, Inc. to coordinate planning efforts, to create a Request For Proposal (RFP), to review and evaluate vendor proposals, and to assist with implementation. Thirty jointly staffed sub-teams, grouped by function, wrote specific parts of the requirements.

The libraries decided to limit the choices to the two vendors supplying their current library systems. Each library was satisfied with its own system vendor. Neither was interested in changing. The challenge was to select the vendor that could best meet current requirements and provide a platform for future development. The RFP was issued. Vendors provided demonstrations and submitted proposals. Vendor conferences helped to nail down the details.

Evaluating the Options

Neither vendor could supply all features that both libraries enjoyed in their individual library systems. Both libraries had developed programs to improve customer self-service features with the public library promoting self-circulation to 80% of checkouts, including media, and the university library focusing on the customer-initiated LINK+ (INN-Reach) interlibrary lending system to supply critical research materials for students and faculty. Either vendor would have to develop additional functionality for its system to meet the customer self-service requirements of the library that was not using its system.

The OST team determined that the selected system would also be better than the other option at meeting the needs of the two libraries in the areas of:

- Multi-language support, especially Chinese, Japanese, and Korean
- Online catalog features, notably language interfaces for Spanish and Chinese readers and a special catalog for children, and embedded customer self-service features
- Enhanced online catalog features that include linking to related materials and simultaneous broadcast searching of local and Internet resources
- Electronic reserves and Reserve Book Room administration
- Electronic mail notification to customers

- Serials check-in and management
- E-commerce

Implementing the System

If I could choose anything to do over again, I would have insisted that the libraries have an on-site, full-time project manager to implement the new shared library system. While a consultant was hired to assist with the project from beginning to end, an on-site project manager was not hired or reassigned from within current staff. Library staff that might have been good candidates could not be considered because of the demands of their regular assignments. Simply, there wasn't anyone that could be spared. The libraries discussed the prospects for hiring an implementation manager on contract. The fiscal climate was not good for adding a new consultant but the service might be included within a system purchase. We approached the selected vendor to provide an on-site project manager from amongst its staff or associates. Even though the vendor was located within the same metropolitan area, it couldn't come up with anyone. This wasn't a service that this vendor had provided in the past. I would have worked harder with the system vendor to emphasize the importance of an on-site project manager to the quality of a successful implementation. A project manager would have relieved a great deal of stress and strain on the team leaders, who were already consumed with their other duties.

To carry out the implementation of the new library information system, a jointly staffed, co-leader sub-team was formed to:

- develop detailed implementation plans
- determine system parameters
- manage data conversion tasks
- coordinate staff training
- assign limited-term task force groups

The OST Team would monitor the work of the Library Information System Implementation sub-team. Implementation-related issues that would be determined by the OST Team, rather than the sub-team, included issues related to policy, issues which required contract changes, any additional costs, changes to the general implementation calendar, and any sub-team decisions that could not be approved by all sub-team members.

The acquisition of the shared library system included a number of modules and features that would be new to both libraries. However, there was not enough time or energy available to consider implementing new features so the primary goal for implementation of the shared library system would be to turn on all functionality required to replicate the customer services that were available in the prior system(s). Additional features would be scheduled for implementation following the opening of the new library. Anticipating a library opening in August 2003, the implementation schedule kicked off in July 2002.

While it could be considered a system upgrade for one of the library partners, the migration to the shared library system was comparable to a migration to a system from a different vendor, even for the library which had used the same vendor for the previous system. The major savings was in training and basic system structure knowledge. All records had to be loaded and indexed, all tables had to be reconfigured, the entire location lexicon was significantly modified, and a new public access catalog interface was developed. The library partners went back and forth on whether acquisitions would be performed as one library on the system or as two libraries.

One of the consequences of combining libraries is a much bigger library with much more traffic. This is the result of adding the modest circulation of a university library to one of the busiest public libraries in the country. The shared King Library is now so active all of the time that we encountered problems that may not be so obvious in a smaller, lower-use library. Implementation of system features such as holds management, self-circulation, telephone notification and renewal, and e-mail notices have been more problematic in this setting. Symptoms may show in smaller settings and be cured by work-around procedures but the high level of business done by a joint-use library turns those work-around situations into huge disasters.

BUILDING A MERGED WEB SITE

There is no clean and easy way to merge the web sites of two libraries into one (three web sites, if you consider that part of the fundraising web site was migrated to the new merged web site). The new web site, at a minimum, had to replicate services available on both of the individual library web sites. Introduction of new content was considered only for very high priority projects. Much of the existing content was posted in a new context to complement the new integrated library concept.

The first truly co-managed staff work team, other than planning teams, was created to build the new web site using in-house staff. The team members from each library had complementary skills and, with a little help in graphics from graduate student assistants, the new web team was well-rounded. However, the members of the team worked in different library buildings, several blocks apart. At first, casual weekly meetings were not serving well to move the project forward. Next, we tried to improve communications among team members by creating a group workspace and scheduling weekly work sessions. As it turned out, setting a formal structure for the weekly meetings with a rotating meeting chair and posting meeting notes helped more than anything else to form an effective team.

Evaluation and Study

A third party was brought in to review each library's web site, to develop design guidelines, to perform a heuristic evaluation of a working prototype, and to conduct a usability study, which helped to bring two web teams with different design experience together. First, the consultants reviewed each library's web site and learned about the project. Then, design guidelines were developed with the merged web team, which set the new web site development work in motion. A heuristic evaluation of a working prototype focused on the ease of finding content within the web site, intuitiveness of navigation, and overall design of the prototype web site. Of the recommendations from the heuristic evaluation, three stood out that pertained to the joint-use library:

- The collective identity of the University and the City of San José was not apparent. A new identity was needed for the new entity combining San José Public Library System (with all of its branch libraries) and San José State University Library. The web site called for a broader identity than that of the shared King Library. The constant banner that resides in a permanent space on the site and that can be seen from all pages was changed from the King Library name to "SJLibrary.org" with a tag line reflecting the collaborative effort, "A collaboration of San José Public Libraries and San José State University Library."
- The rotating City/University logos were an indicator of the collaboration but were not very noticeable.
- The lists of university library databases were so extensive that many public library users might have trouble finding the best database for the topic of their search.

A usability study based on one-on-one interviews was conducted to gain a thorough understanding of users' ease of finding information and specific content within the web site, intuitiveness of navigation, and reactions to overall design. Among the findings, beyond confirming that the new web site was better than the old web sites, two stood out as pertaining to the joint-use library:

- The "Collective Identity" of the site was clear to the majority of users.
- Many users were not familiar with the term Link+ (direct ILL system), and/or did not understand how it differed from Interlibrary Loan (both appearing on the "Requests from Other Libraries" page).

Features of the New Web Site

This new web site tries to strike a balance between town and gown and, especially, to emphasize those areas where public and academic library services converge. The home page strikes the opening balance with quick links to branch locations as well as to interlibrary lending. Across the page from quick links is a promotions area for the frequent public library events. The major site divisions in the banner are Services, Research, Paths To Learning, and About Us. Special gateway links are provided on the home page for SJSU students and faculty, Kids, Teens, and Adults & Seniors.

The Services page provides quick links to Best Books, Literacy Services, Youth Services, as well as Course Reserves, Distance Learning and Faculty Services. The promotional area features Readers' Advisory, and Homework Help alongside Library Instructions and Information Competence, and Getting Help With Research. The Research pages provide quick links to resources for specific academic majors, the SJSU electronic journals list, eBooks, and web site guides and search engines. Paths To Learning pages are a gateway to special resources for Kids, Teens, Multicultural interests, SJSU Students & Faculty, SJSU Distance Learners, Business Community, and Adults & Seniors. The About Us page is designed to highlight the unique partnership as well as provide common information on employment, events, exhibits, history, locations, vision, and parent organizations.

Other Web Team Applications

An early web project was the development of a policy and procedures database that would benefit any two organizations planning to provide a jointly managed service. The policy and procedures database was designed with a public viewing mode and a staff-only mode. As every policy has to be recast in light of the integrated library, over 200 new policies were created during the planning process. Having a database instead of a binder of policies has been a substantial improvement.

During the planning process, a joint library staff intranet web site was developed alongside staff web sites for both libraries. Early on in the planning, it was understood that a new merged staff intranet would be built. Later on in the planning, it was determined that a new merged staff web site was too big of a project and would have to be postponed until the public web site was built. At this time, the web team is using a shared facility to store commonly held content for the two staff intranet web sites.

DESIGNING A JOINT TELECOMMUNICATIONS NETWORK

Installing a new telecommunications network should be the most straightforward part of the IT challenges for the new integrated library. After all, one expert consulting firm had laid out the cabling infrastructure, network operations center, and wiring closets and another consulting firm was taking charge of the network design and equipment installation. It may also be seen as the most risky for the library IT unit since nearly total support for the telecommunications network would fall on the shoulders of library IT staff while the library information system had substantial vendor support.

Joining the Networks

Networking for both libraries represented a major connection with their parent organizations, the city and the university, and that's where many of the twists and turns started. Locating the shared King Library on the edge of the campus enabled a closer technology linkage to university resources. But, for the public library, the move resulted in the installation of a highly secure, VPN connection for the public library staff to access the city's network resources. Because of the security requirements of the VPN connection, support for public library staff computers can be provided only by IT staff that work for the city. Most university computing has evolved to a secure web-based environment and it is not necessary to have a VPN linkage to the campus computer center.

The university has a very high-capacity broadband Internet connection, which the shared King Library uses as its primary access to the Internet. Marking an issue with strong opinions held by the partnering libraries, the public library insisted on an alternate Internet connection that would maintain Internet access for its branch libraries and limited access for King Library in case there were disruptions with the university's Internet connection. A major effect of deciding to have dual Internet service providers was a more complex network environment based on a load balancing system at the apex of the network.

Operating System

The libraries, with the aid of consultants, decided that the best operating system base for the libraries' wide-area network would be Windows 2000, utilizing Active Directory network management. While the university took an active interest in supplying technology resources, there was no direct influence exerted regarding network management. The city mandated a Windows NT operating system environment for all of its departments. However, the city was planning a migration to Windows 2000 and Active Directory for the entire city government enterprise in conjunction with the building of a new city hall when, all of a sudden, the city IT department realized that the library could be the first city department to implement Active Directory, and with an "untrusted" partner, the university library. After many long discussions and alternative design explorations, an analysis was presented to the city's IT Planning Board. The university had to take a strong stance supporting the technological independence of the shared King Library.

E-Mail

One particularly thorny dilemma when forming a co-managed, joint-use library revolves around electronic mail, distribution list services, and contact directories. In this case, the university library staff had not adopted a standard e-mail client/server, although there was a push to standardize the campus on Lotus Notes. The city had a Microsoft Outlook Exchange enterprise application and the public library ran its own Exchange server. Further complicating the situation, when the city realized that the public library's e-mail server might be supported by a merged IT unit composed of university and city staff, the city decided that the e-mail server and administration must be returned to city administration and made accessible to library staff only through a secure VPN connection.

At this time, the university library staff use IBM Lotus Notes administered by the university and the public library staff use Microsoft Outlook Exchange administered by the city. When one wants to send an e-mail notification to library staff, the message must be sent to two lists. A more integrated approach is desired by all and, one hopes that it will be an approach that does not lose the seamless connections for e-mail and contact information to parent organizations that exist now.

Telephones

Another particularly thorny dilemma revolved around the selection and administration of a telephone system. The city provided telephone service to the public library and the university provided telephone service to the university library. Neither library wanted telephone service to be fragmented like e-mail, so it was decided that the shared King Library would have an independent telephone switch. The dilemma appeared as we tried to decide whether to out-source support for the telephone system, specifically whether to contract with the university to maintain the telephone system. The city did not express any interest in providing support services for the telephone system. Neither IT unit had responsibility for telephone service and only one staff member had experience in supporting a telephone system. While the decision to contract support to the university was based on cost studies, there was a certain amount of reluctance for the city library to fall too much under the influence of the university and to create a dependence on the university.

Downloading Software

The public library practice of streamlining IT support by not allowing software to be downloaded by library staff came up square against the university library's academic mission. However, the overall concern over staffing resources highlighted a need for efficiency in the use of IT staff that outweighed the need for academic librarians to have an unfettered ability to download software. A policy was proposed to insist that software downloads to staff computers would have to be performed by IT staff. Special computers, isolated from the staff network, would be stationed around the library to download software and try out new programs. If the new piece of software product proved to be useful, then IT staff would evaluate the software and perform the download and installation on the staff member's computer. While the debate at the policy hearings was passionate, the hearings were not well-attended. When the decision to approve the downloading policy became well-known, it was not many weeks before the academic librarians presented a much stronger and well-illustrated defense and were able to overturn the downloading policy. In the end, the Core Team decided that downloading software on staff computers would be allowed until IT could demonstrate that the policy causes an extreme hardship due to increased workload.

Wireless Network

When the shared King Library was being planned, wireless networks were in their infancy. The new joint-use library was not wired for wireless networking. Either data cabling or electrical circuits or both will need to be installed for 802.11 type of wireless networking in the building. However, when the day approaches that we can afford to install support for a wireless network, we will have the dilemma of how to support wireless networking for both campus and city. Neither city nor campus have well-established wireless networks, but both are in the process. This is just a harbinger of networking challenges to come in the shared King Library.

MERGING AND CO-MANAGING IT STAFF AND SERVICES

To merge IT staff from two different employers, represented by two different unions, into one coherent and effective staff unit is no small challenge. Up front, it was stated that the organizational structure would be transitional and staff should expect evolution over time. To learn more about each other, a period of time was allocated for staff from each library to work in the shadow of staff from the other library. Joint staff meetings were held to review technical planning, determine development and implementation schedules, and discuss merged unit organizational structure.

Co-Managed Library Units

The libraries enlisted the help of a consultant, Sheila D. Creth, Progressive Solutions, to plan the new co-management organizational structure. Three models for the IT unit were evaluated. A new organizational structure was planned with two unit heads, one from each library, to co-manage all of the merged staff units including the IT unit. Lead responsibility for day-to-day operation of specific functions was assigned to each unit head. Assignment of specific functions to unit heads was designed to recognize expertise, service priorities, and workload, as well as to represent a balance of responsibilities between the unit heads.

To maintain lines of authority within the two library organizations, staff in the new IT unit would be assigned to work a primary assignment under the unit head of their employer, who would be responsible for their performance evaluation. Most staff would also be expected to work a secondary assignment under a team leader from the other library. The team leader and unit co-head for the other library would be asked for verbal input as part of the performance evaluation process.

Integrated IT Staff Teams

The team structure of the IT unit was set out as illustrated in Figure 1.

A team leader is responsible for the work of the team and participates as a working team member. Specific responsibilities include:

- assigning tasks and directing the work of team members
- setting work schedules for team members

- participating in performance evaluation of team members
- hiring and supervising student assistants and pages assigned to team
- acting as primary liaison to other library units and staff

Unit Co-Heads are responsible for the work of the IT unit. Specific responsibilities include:

- assigning teams and team leaders
- directing the work of team leaders
- evaluating staff performance
- representing the unit to management and library staff

The practice of web administration and development evolved over time for both library partners. For the university library, web support started in IT and then moved to become part of collection management and, as the new King Library was taking shape, web staff were moved back into IT. For the public library, web support started in IT and then moved to Reference. The merged web team consists of public library staff from a Web Services team that is part of the Reference unit, and university library staff from a Web Technology team that is part of the IT unit. The merged web team is co-managed by the public library co-head of the Reference unit and the university library co-head of the IT unit.

FIGURE 1. IT Unit Teams

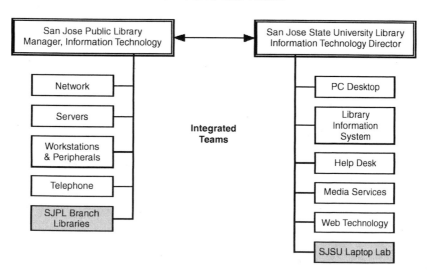

Merge Before the Move?

As with the shared library system, we might have merged the two IT units prior to moving into the new library building to lessen the amount of change required at the same time as moving into a new building and implementing a new integrated library service. In many ways, the development of the co-managed unit with integrated staff teams is the biggest challenge of this joint-use library venture.

However, we didn't merge the IT units prior to the move to the new joint-use building. We didn't seriously examine the possibility, and I'm not convinced that it would work anyway. The amount of knowledge transfer and training that would have been necessary to merge the units and form new teams and continue to support daily operations in both libraries might have been too much to do. I expect that it will take some time to settle on the best co-management structure. So it goes with the transitory nature of an evolving organization.

IT PARTNERS FOR THE NEW INTEGRATED LIBRARY

As any successful IT manager will tell you, the first IT partners to enlist are those that reside in-house. The university had only a web advisory group and the public library had an informal group left over from the recent implementation of a new library information system. As the libraries moved from planning to implementation and operations for the shared King Library, the management and advisory structure was changing.

Internal Planning Teams

The Core Team was reconfigured as the King Management Team and a Strategic IT (SIT) Group was formed to monitor IT implementation for the shared King Library, to monitor ongoing IT operations, and to approve new IT projects and directions. The SIT Group is comprised of university library Dean and IT Director, the public library Assistant Director and IT Manager, and the Library Project Manager. As noted earlier, a Library Information System Implementation sub-team was formed and, as the OST planning team disbanded, the SIT Group took over monitoring implementation of the shared library system.

To pursue the new shared web site development and implementation, the Core Team formed two groups: (1) a Web Implementation Group to develop overall web site plan and design, content, and templates, to set priorities, and to formulate and revise policy in communication with the Web Advisory Group and (2) a Web Advisory Group to provide feedback to the Web Implementation Group for evaluating user/customer needs (including in-house needs), to advise on policy development, and to serve as a liaison to the rest of the library system. In hindsight, it would have been very helpful to have had a formal liaison between the Library Information System Implementation Team and the Web Implementation Group for the development of the online catalog.

External Advisors

A Technology Advisory Committee (TAC) was formed to bring advice from outside the library to assist with IT planning and implementation. The libraries were able to reach out to the rich array of technology companies in the Silicon Valley and beyond to bring in expertise. The TAC members were lured by the prospect of working on a major downtown redevelopment project and of providing service to both the city and university in a unique collaboration. The TAC was especially helpful by taking an in-depth review of network design, network security, and media technology, and assisting with plans for a High Technology Showcase in the shared King Library. TAC members were also invaluable in pursuing donations and funding opportunities with their companies, and some TAC members provided invaluable individual pro bono consulting advice.

A High Technology Showcase area in the shared King Library was planned as a collaborative creation of the business community, the library, and the university to provide students, faculty, library employees, and community members a view into new and upcoming information technology. Also, the showcase would provide a venue from which firms can receive product feedback from academia and the general public, a local, high visibility location where feedback from a wide variety of users can be obtained. Vendors will be encouraged to provide interactive displays of products applicable to library and information services, which are newly released, or about to come onto the market. In-service workshops would be planned for the library staff, so they can answer questions from library users as well as enlarge their own understanding of what information technological possibilities exist.

CONCLUSION

Our experience in building a joint-use library has been successful for many reasons. Those reasons most related to information technology in joint-use libraries are:

- Participatory planning and management structures
- Dedication of key staff to pursue a successful outcome even if they didn't agree with the choice to form a joint-use library or to change the library information system
- Use of third party consultants to sort through sticky issues and provide a big-picture perspective
- A sincere effort by both parties to understand the perspective of the other party and the effect on network design and systems requirements
- Taking the opportunity to create a more integrated approach for IT in the new organization.

Forming a joint-use library is a big enough project that as much merging as possible should be done prior to the move. Things that we might have done better, or more of, before moving into the new shared library, even if not done perfectly and completely:

- Orient parent organizations to IT issues early on and keep them aware but don't let them control the planning process
- Install and test any major changes to the network connections to parent organization before the move
- Obtain a full-time project manager to implement the new library information system for two to three years
- Migrate to the new library system with a plan for global location code changes as the two former library collections are integrated in the new shared library
- Merge IT operations and support responsibilities to gain the efficiency needed to support a larger, more complex enterprise without additional staff.

Index

Page numbers followed by n indicate notes.

BOOK ORDER FORM!

Order a copy of this book with this form or online at:
http://www.haworthpress.com/store/product.asp?sku=5585

Libraries Within Their Institutions
Creative Collaborations

_____ in softbound at $ ISBN-13: 978-0-7890-2720-7. ISBN-10: 0-7890-2720-8.
_____ in hardbound at $ ISBN-13: 978-0-7890-2719-1. ISBN-10: 0-7890-2719-4

COST OF BOOKS _____

POSTAGE & HANDLING _____
US: $4.00 for first book & $1.50
for each additional book
Outside US: $5.00 for first book
& $2.00 for each additional book.

SUBTOTAL _____
In Canada: add 7% GST._____

STATE TAX _____
CA, IL, IN, MN, NJ, NY, OH, PA & SD residents
please add appropriate local sales tax.

FINAL TOTAL _____
If paying in Canadian funds, convert
using the current exchange rate,
UNESCO coupons welcome.

❏ **BILL ME LATER:**
Bill-me option is good on US/Canada/
Mexico orders only; not good to jobbers.
wholesalers, or subscription agencies.

❏ **Signature** _____

❏ **Payment Enclosed: $** _____

❏ **PLEASE CHARGE TO MY CREDIT CARD:**
❏ Visa ❏ MasterCard ❏ AmEx ❏ Discover
❏ Diner's Club ❏ Eurocard ❏ JCB

Account #_____

Exp Date _____

Signature _____
(Prices in US dollars and subject to change without notice.)

PLEASE PRINT ALL INFORMATION OR ATTACH YOUR BUSINESS CARD

Name

Address

City   State/Province   Zip/Postal Code

Country

Tel   Fax

E-Mail

May we use your e-mail address for confirmations and other types of information? ❏Yes ❏No We appreciate receiving
your e-mail address. Haworth would like to e-mail special discount offers to you, as a preferred customer.
We will never share, rent, or exchange your e-mail address. We regard such actions as an invasion of your privacy.

Order from your **local bookstore** or directly from
The Haworth Press, Inc. 10 Alice Street, Binghamton, New York 13904-1580 • USA
Call our toll-free number (1-800-429-6784) / Outside US/Canada: (607) 722-5857
Fax: 1-800-895-0582 / Outside US/Canada: (607) 771-0012
E-mail your order to us: orders@haworthpress.com

For orders outside US and Canada, you may wish to order through your local
sales representative, distributor, or bookseller.
For information, see http://haworthpress.com/distributors

(Discounts are available for individual orders in US and Canada only, not booksellers/distributors.)

Please photocopy this form for your personal use.
www.HaworthPress.com

BOF05